W9-BON-834

SHAKER STYLE

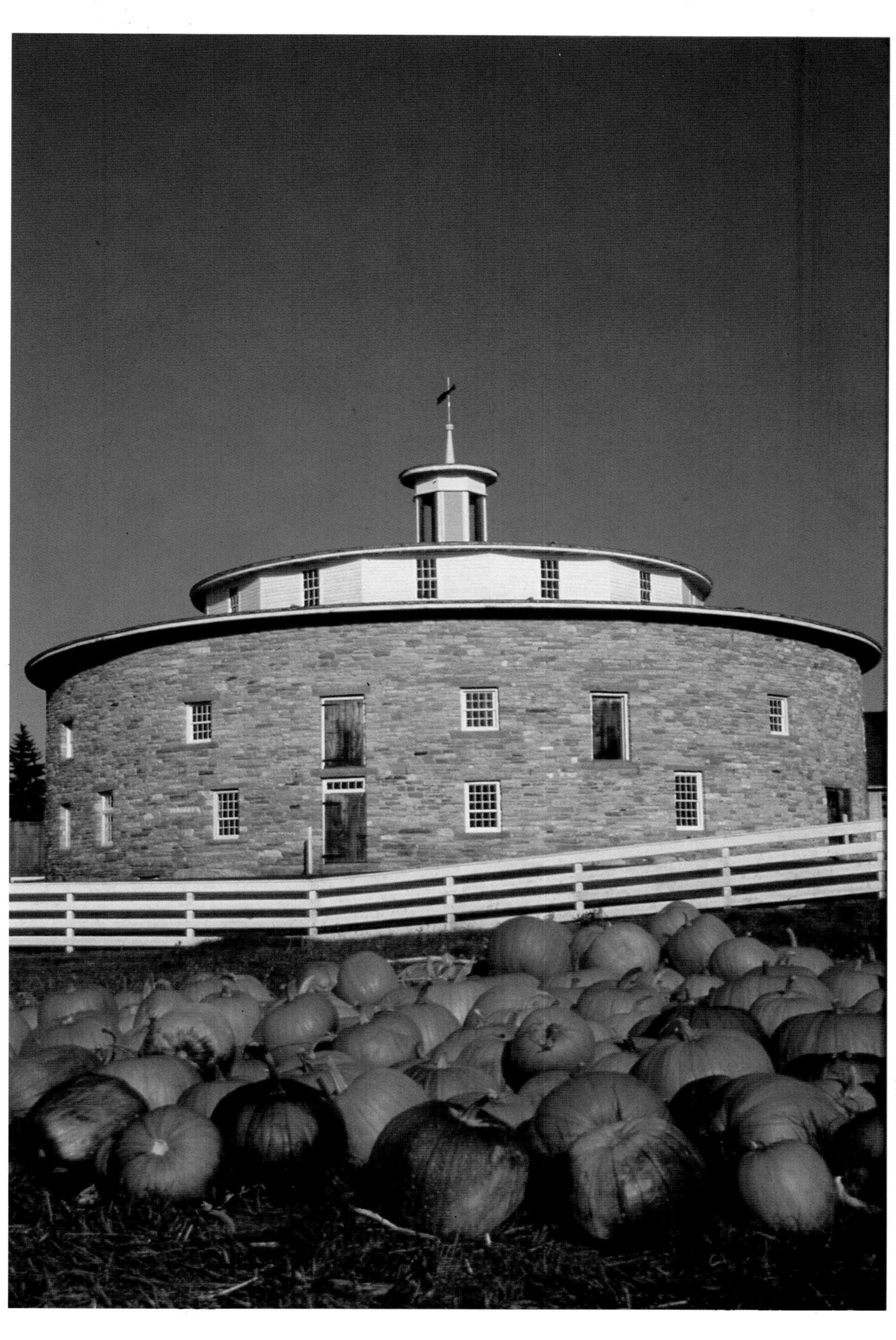

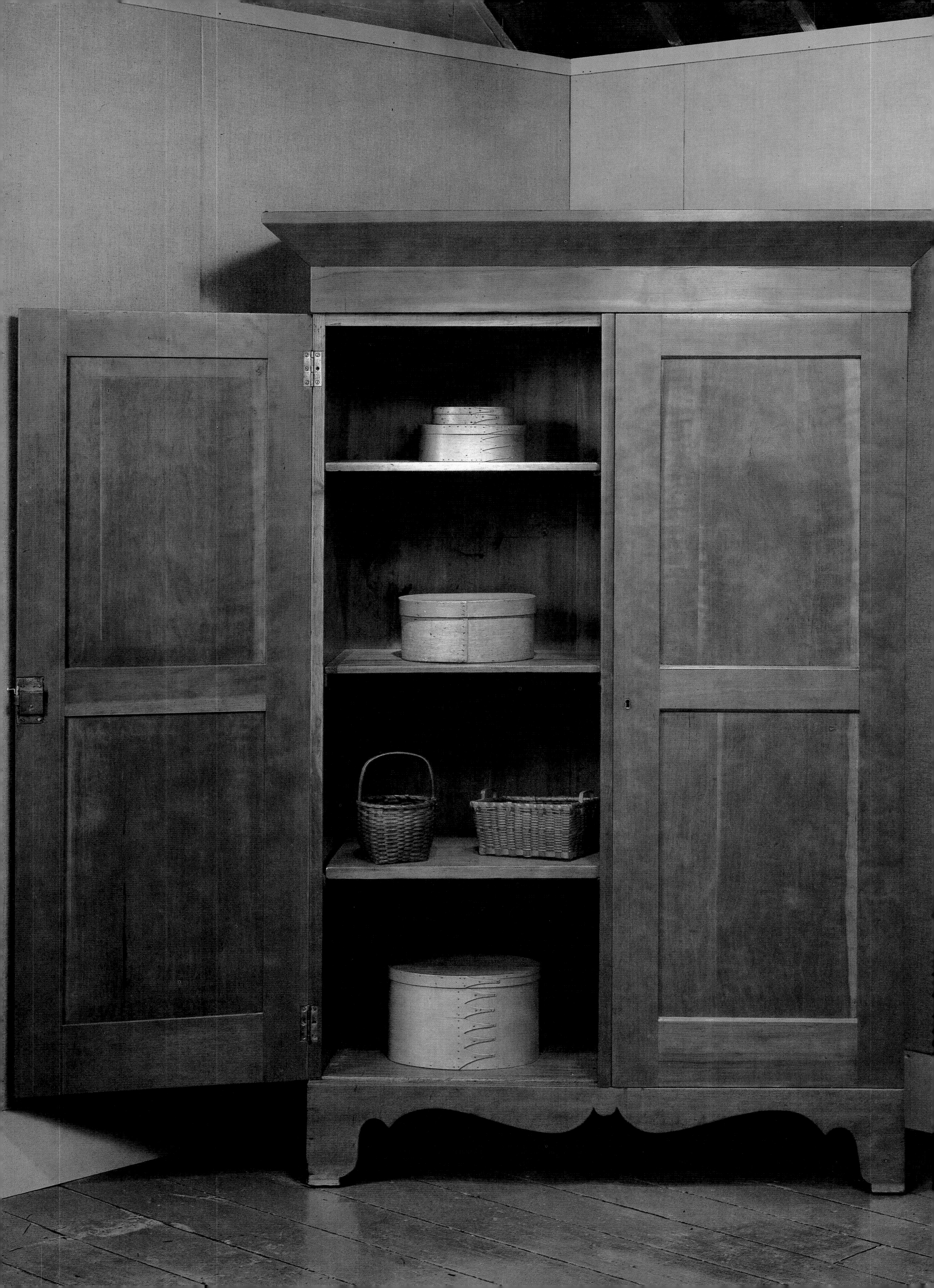

SHAKER STYLE

JOHN S. BOWMAN

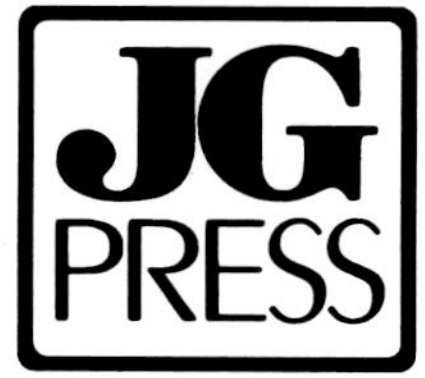

Published by World Publications Group, Inc.
455 Somerset Avenue
North Dighton, MA 02764
www.wrldpub.com

ISBN 1-57215-381-4

Printed and bound in China by Leefung-Asco Printers Trading Ltd

PAGE 1: **Round Stone Barn, 1826**
Hancock Shaker Village, Pittsfield, MA
Photo by Elizabeth Fitzsimmons

PAGE 2: **Cupboard housing Shaker boxes and baskets, from the Shaker community of Pleasant Hill, KY**
The Shaker Museum and Library, Old Chatham, NY
Photo by Paul Rocheleau

PAGE 5: **Group of Shaker side chairs, c. 1830, Canterbury, NH**
Private Collection
Photo by Paul Rocheleau

CONTENTS

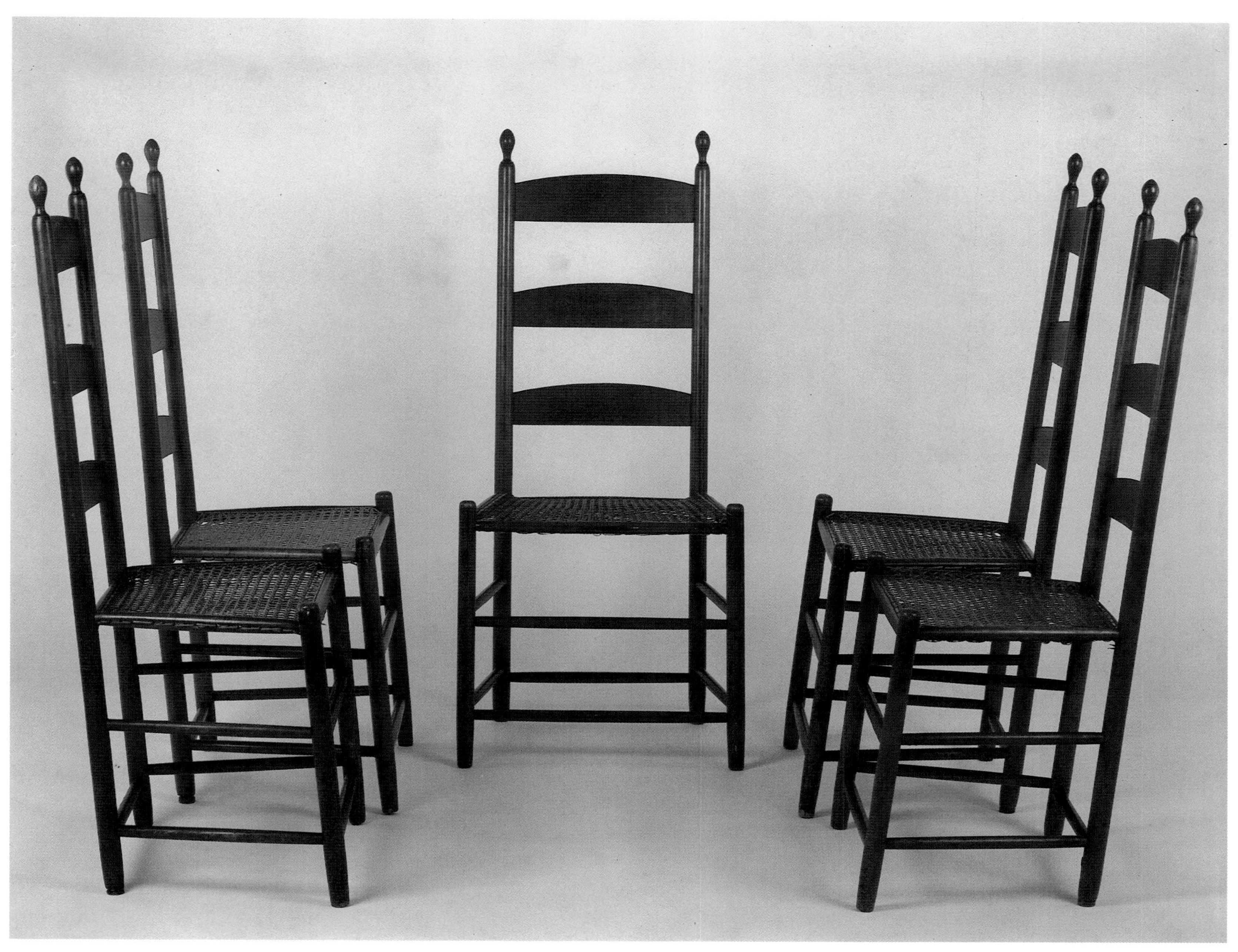

INTRODUCTION

The group known today as the Shakers formally called itself the United Society of Believers in the First and Second Appearance of Christ. Although clearly organized around a Christian-religious core, it also had a strong utopian-communal component. During their peak years – approximately 1830 to 1860 – the Shakers numbered some 6,000 members living principally in 19 communities from Maine to Kentucky. The origins of the Shakers, however, were far removed from that archetypal American realm.

The exact beginnings of the Shakers remain somewhat obscure but lie somewhere in the 1760s in and around Manchester, England. Manchester, in northwest England, was then emerging as one of the first manufacturing towns of the Industrial Revolution. For many decades there had also been emerging in England a number of Christian sects that have been characterized as "pietists" or "enthusiasts," whose adherents relied on a personal experience of God and expressed themselves with an overt emotionalism, often accompanied by "trembling" due to their seizure by the spirit of God. Among the best known of these was the Society of Friends, founded by George Fox around 1650; because of their reputation for "trembling" during devotional services, they were popularly called "Quakers." What is less known is that they were also occasionally called "Shakers."

By the late 1760s, James and Jane Wardley, a couple in Bolton, near Manchester, were leading a small group of such religious enthusiasts. Although they shared many elements with the Quakers, they also differed in several respects from the Quakers of their time. The Wardley group believed they were "the only true religion," condemning all others. They depended on a personal "vision," met frequently for their informal services, discussed Biblical texts, and emphasized the "future" – meaning the end of the world.

Especially in this last-named belief, they appear to have been heavily influenced by another religious sect, known in England in the 1700s as the French Prophets. These were French members of a radical Protestant sect called the Camisards; persecuted in France, some of them had fled to England early in the eighteenth century. In England, these French Prophets and their English converts engaged in ecstatic, dance-like "agitations." They added another dimension that would also emerge in the Shakers: women were accorded a special place because they were believed to be more prone to be "inspired."

The Wardley group soon became known as "Shakers" because they conducted their services with markedly overt physical motions and ended their meetings with singing and dancing. Although the explanation for this activity was that they were "seized" by the Holy Spirit, there was also a social aspect to it – a sense of community for people who felt they had little to gain from the British establishment and the Industrial Revolution. All these early Shakers seem to have been relatively poor and working-class.

Among their adherents was a young woman, Ann Lee, born in 1742 (some say in 1736). She had little formal education and probably worked in one of the small textile factories in Manchester. In 1762 she married a blacksmith, Abraham Standerin, signing the registry only with her mark; during the next years she evidently lost the four babies she bore. Perhaps because of her sufferings over this, she began to meet with the Wardley group of Shakers, but it is also true that other members of her family became Shakers. Whatever her motives, Ann Lee seems to have become extremely active, even fanatical in her devotion to the Shakers. She was arrested and jailed on several occasions as a result of confrontations with the authorities. This

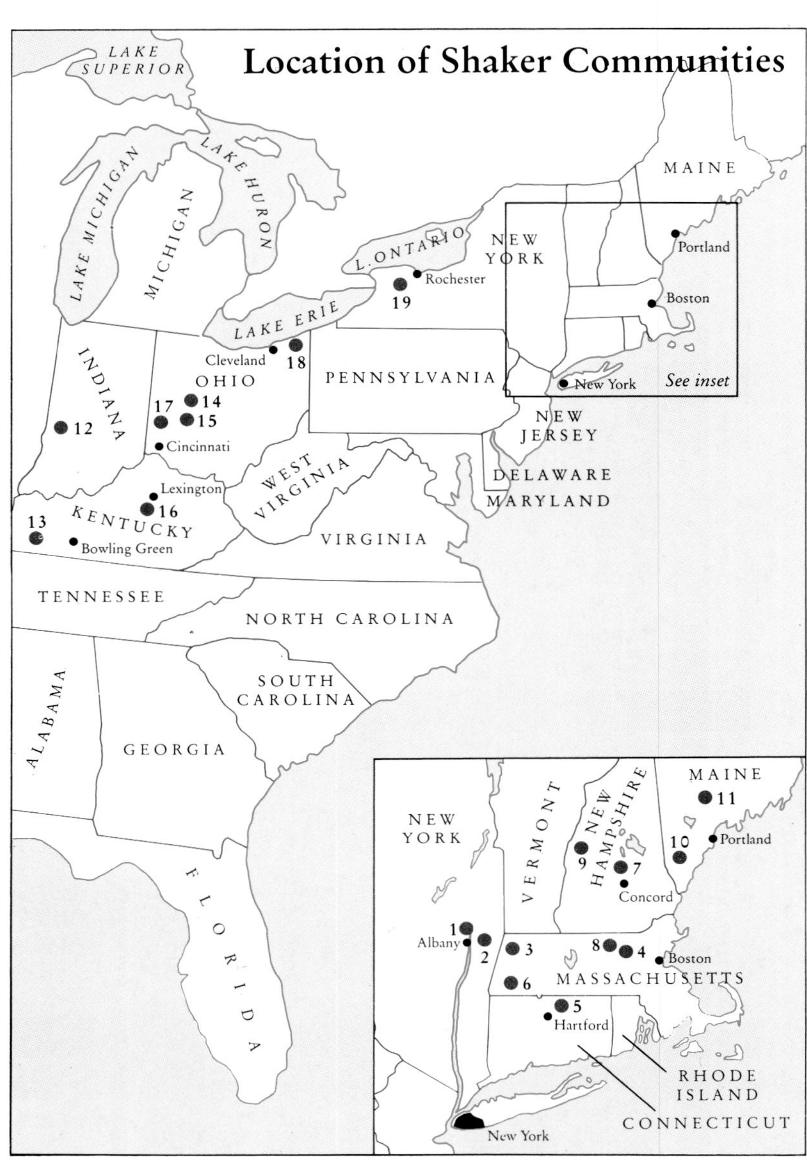

(Photo Courtesy Hancock Shaker Village, Pittsfield, MA)

1. Watervliet, NY 1787-1938
2. Mount Lebanon, NY 1787-1947
3. Hancock, MA 1790-1960
4. Harvard, MA 1791-1919
5. Enfield, CT 1792-1917
6. Tyringham, MA 1792-1875
7. Canterbury, NH 1792-1992
8. Shirley, MA 1793-1909
9. Enfield, NH 1793-1918
10. Alfred, ME 1793-1931
11. Sabbathday Lake, ME 1793-active
12. West Union (Busro), IN 1810-1827
13. South Union, KY 1811-1922
14. Watervliet, OH 1813-1900
15. Union Villiage, OH 1812-1910
16. Pleasant Hill, KY 1814-1910
17. Whitewater, OH 1824-1907
18. North Union, OH 1826-1889
19. Groveland, NY 1836-1892 (Formerly Sodus Bay, NY 1826-1836)

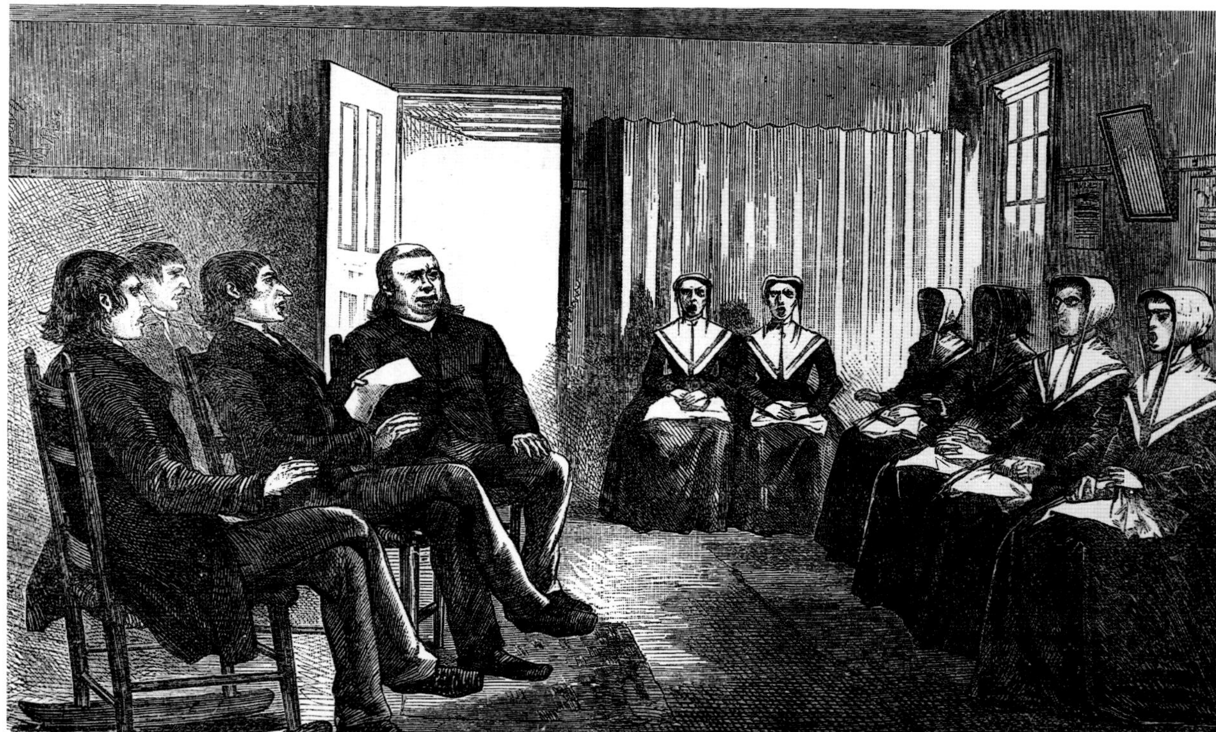

Right: An engraving of a group of Shakers at a singing meeting in Niskeyuna, New York, the original Shaker village, in 1885. (The Bettmann Archive, New York, NY)

Below: Shakers were characterized by their manner of worship which included singing, dancing, shaking and whirling. Some whirled so quickly that they fell prostrate on the floor. They believed these activities displayed the "gifts" of the Holy Spirit. (Hancock Shaker Village, Pittsfield, MA)

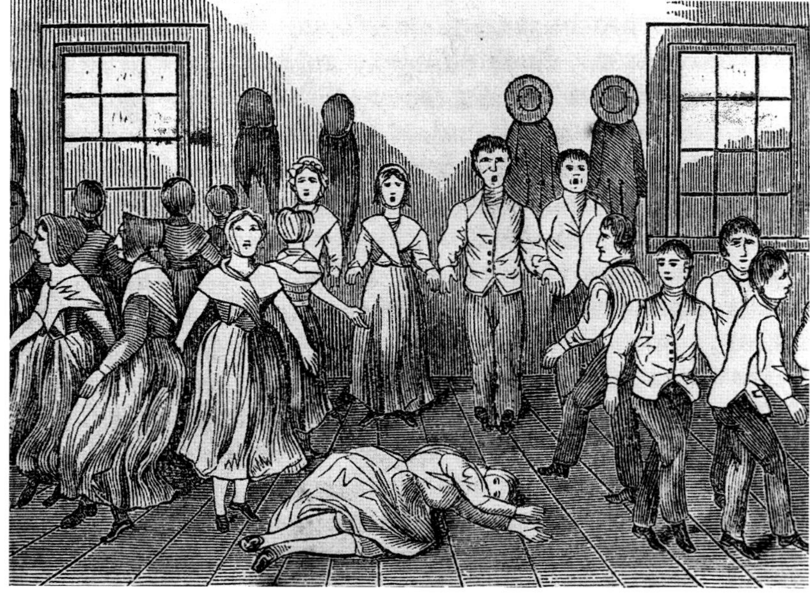

conflict resulted partly from the established community's dislike for such unconventional religious behavior. The Shakers also brought it upon themselves by openly attacking the established Anglican Church, and even interrupting church services.

Although nothing is known for sure about their motives, it is assumed that it was these troubles that in 1774 led Ann Lee, her husband, and a few other Shakers from Manchester to emigrate to America. Later Shaker traditions would fix the date of her arrival as August 6, 1774, in the port of New York City; in fact, there are no records of this. The first actual record of this group of Shakers dates from 1779 when they are being taxed for land near Troy, New York, in a district known as Niskeyuna. By this time Ann Lee and the original small group of Shakers had been joined by several other Shakers from England. By 1780, Ann Lee, her younger brother William, and James Whittaker appeared to be emerging as the leaders of this American branch of the Shakers.

These are the bare facts of the origins of the Shakers in America. Many years later the Shakers would set down in writing a spiritual version of these years that promoted Ann Lee to the forefront of the sect. As Mother Ann she was made the central figure of a story that involved sufferings, miracles and revelations, much like the stories told of early Christian saints. Both the historical truth and the official spiritual version agree, however, that the founders and early members of the sect were poor and working-class; that Ann Lee was illiterate; and that she separated from her husband and endorsed a life of celibacy. Eventually these factors would help to shape what is distinctive about Shaker style.

The first Shakers in America seemed content to practice their faith at Niskeyuna in isolation, although early reports of their "religious exercises" already singled out their "dancing in extravagant postures." Two events disturbed this isolation. One was the American War of Independence. Because of their recent links to England and also because their religion called for non-cooperation with civil authorities such as the military, and even an outright rejection of war for secular ends, the Shakers at Niskeyuna found themselves under suspicion of being supporters of the British. Several of them were arrested, among them Ann Lee, who spent some five months in jail in late 1780.

Simultaneously, another and even more influential event was occurring: a religious revival of an evangelical nature in the region not far from Niskeyuna. The "New Light" movement was centered to the southeast, in New Lebanon, New York, and just over the border in Massachusetts at Pittsfield and Hancock. When members of the New Lebanon and Pittsfield churches visited the Shakers at Niskeyuna in 1780, they were so taken by that sect's beliefs and practices that they were soon proclaiming it to embody the authentic "spirit, kingdom and work" of God. As word of the Shakers began to spread, the Niskeyuna sect began to attract increasing numbers of visitors and converts. This soon led to the next and most dramatic phase in the growth of the Shakers.

In May 1781, Ann Lee, her brother William, and James Whittaker and several other Shakers set out on a missionary journey that occupied them until September 1783. They spent most of this time in western and central Massachusetts, but they also went down into eastern Connecticut and up along the edge of eastern Massachusetts. They spent anywhere from a few days to several months in the towns and villages they visited. Sometimes they preached in public gatherings, but most of their time was spent "counseling" on an individual basis. Gradually they enlisted a small but devoted band of converts. On several occasions, people in the local communities were so incensed by the Shakers' teachings that they physically attacked the missionaries and drove them out of town.

By the time they arrived back at Niskeyuna in September 1783, the foundations for the Shakers' version of "Christ's kingdom on earth" had been laid. There was, however, no immediate change in the actions of the Shakers. The converts – and by now there were hundreds in those communities visited by Ann Lee and her companions – were left to pursue their new faith as best they could. Because at this time there were still no written Shaker texts, they depended on a strictly oral tradition consisting of individual sermons, personal testimonies, and private counselings.

This absence of the written or printed word would have two far-reaching impacts on the Shakers: It would allow considerable latitude to later Shakers when they came to set down the official history and dogma, and it would allow these later writings to attribute the dominant role in the founding of the sect to Ann Lee. Thus several of the most famous sayings attributed to Ann Lee were not in fact ever written down until 1816 (although some were supposedly reported by individuals who had known her). Such sayings as, "Do all your work as though you had a thousand years to live, and as you would if you knew you must die tomorrow," and "Hands to work and hearts to God," express the essence of Shakerism, but it is not clear whether Ann Lee ever actually said them.

Ann Lee had died in 1784, only a year after returning from her missionary journey and two months after the death of her brother William. Although she was certainly honored as one of the most important of the founders of the Shakers in America, she was not treated at that time as the "Mother Ann" she would become in later Shaker theology. Indeed, it would be 1808 before she would be singled out in a Shaker text, and 1845 before the newly established Millennial Laws placed her just below Jesus Christ in the Shaker hierarchy.

After her death, her fellow missionary James Whittaker took

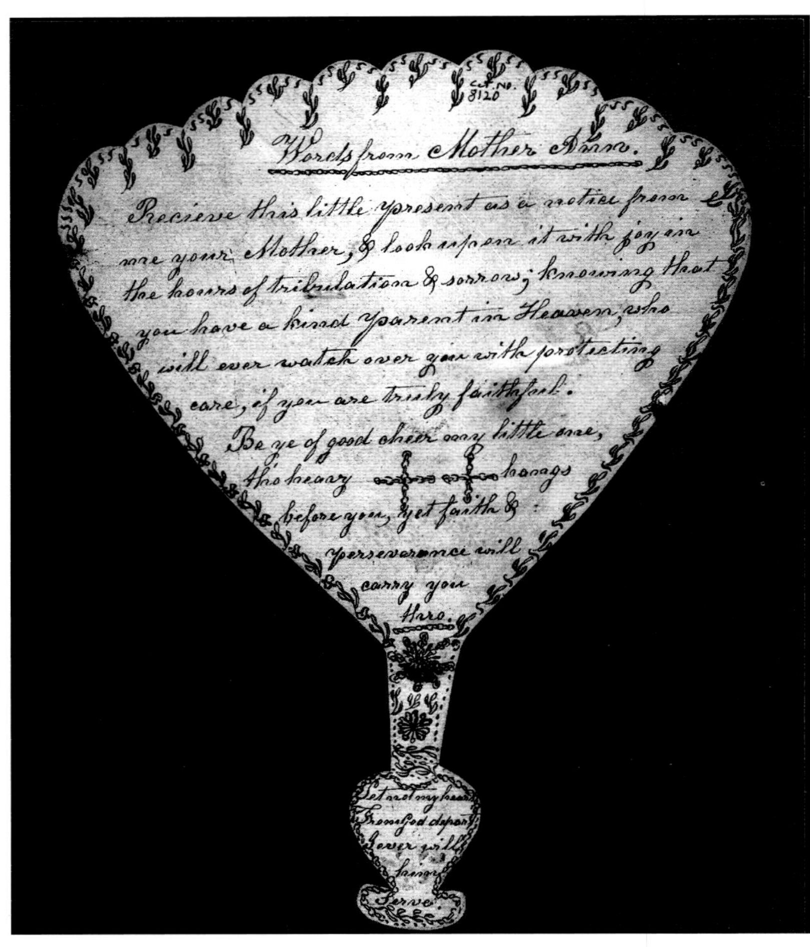

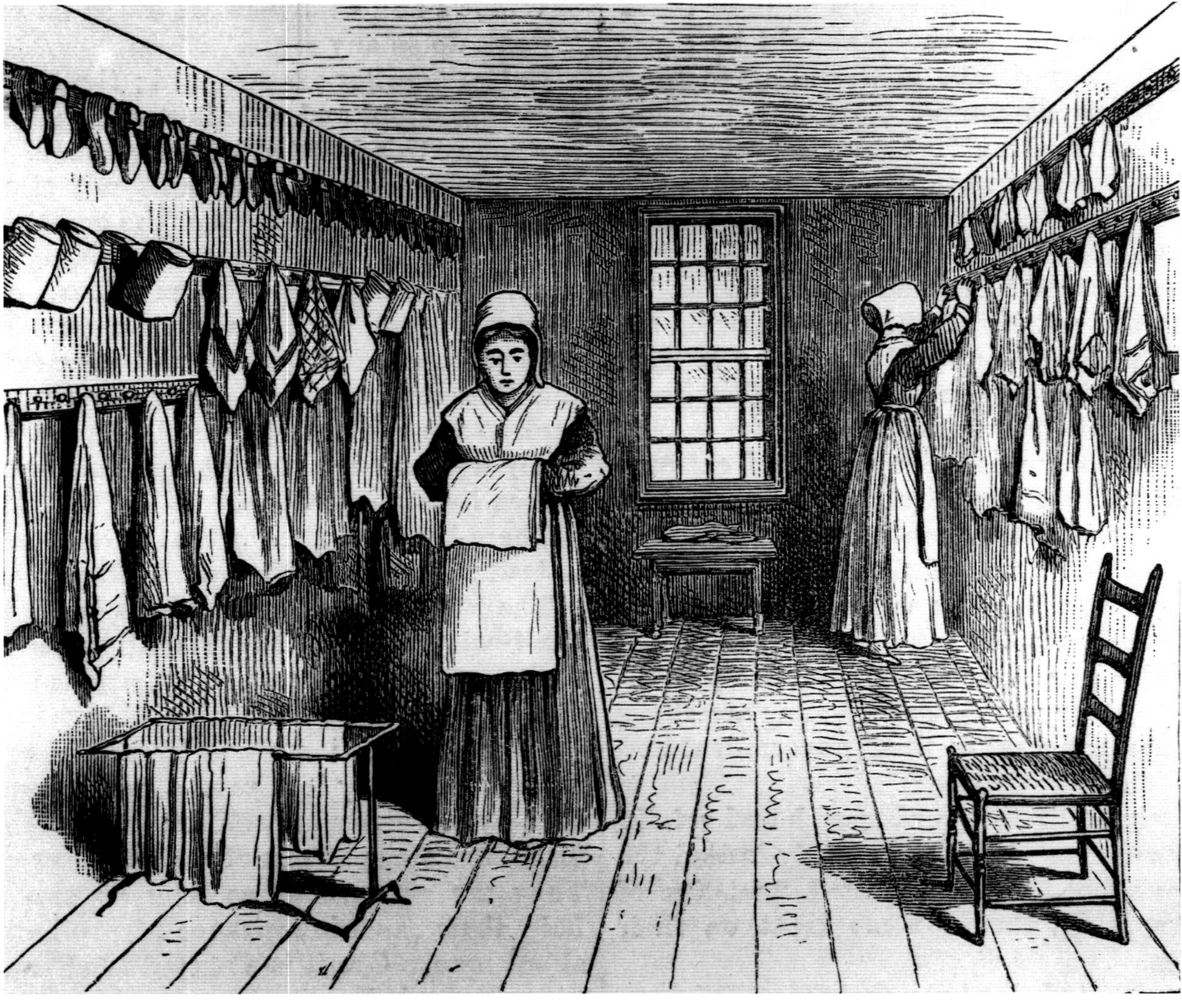

Above: This inspirational drawing in the shape of a fan has words from Mother Ann that helped to remind Shakers of their duties and the precepts behind their religion. (The Shaker Museum and Library, Old Chatham, NY)

Left: An engraving of the girls' clothes room in the Shaker community of Niskeyuna, New York, in 1885. Note the peg rails, which provided convenient storage. Simplicity, cleanliness, functionality and order were the religious principles behind Shaker design. (The Bettmann Archive, New York, NY)

Opposite above: A typical Shaker religious activity was a processional dance. This meeting is at the fountain stone site at New Lebanon where one Shaker was summoned by an angel and wrote down "the sentences of the Eternal God and Creator" in the Shaker book, the Sacred and Divine Roll. (Hancock Shaker Village, Pittsfield, MA)

Opposite below: This is the earliest surviving photograph of a Shaker meeting. It was taken at the Sabbathday Lake, Maine, community on September 20, 1885. (Collection of the United Society of Shakers, Sabbathday Lake, ME)

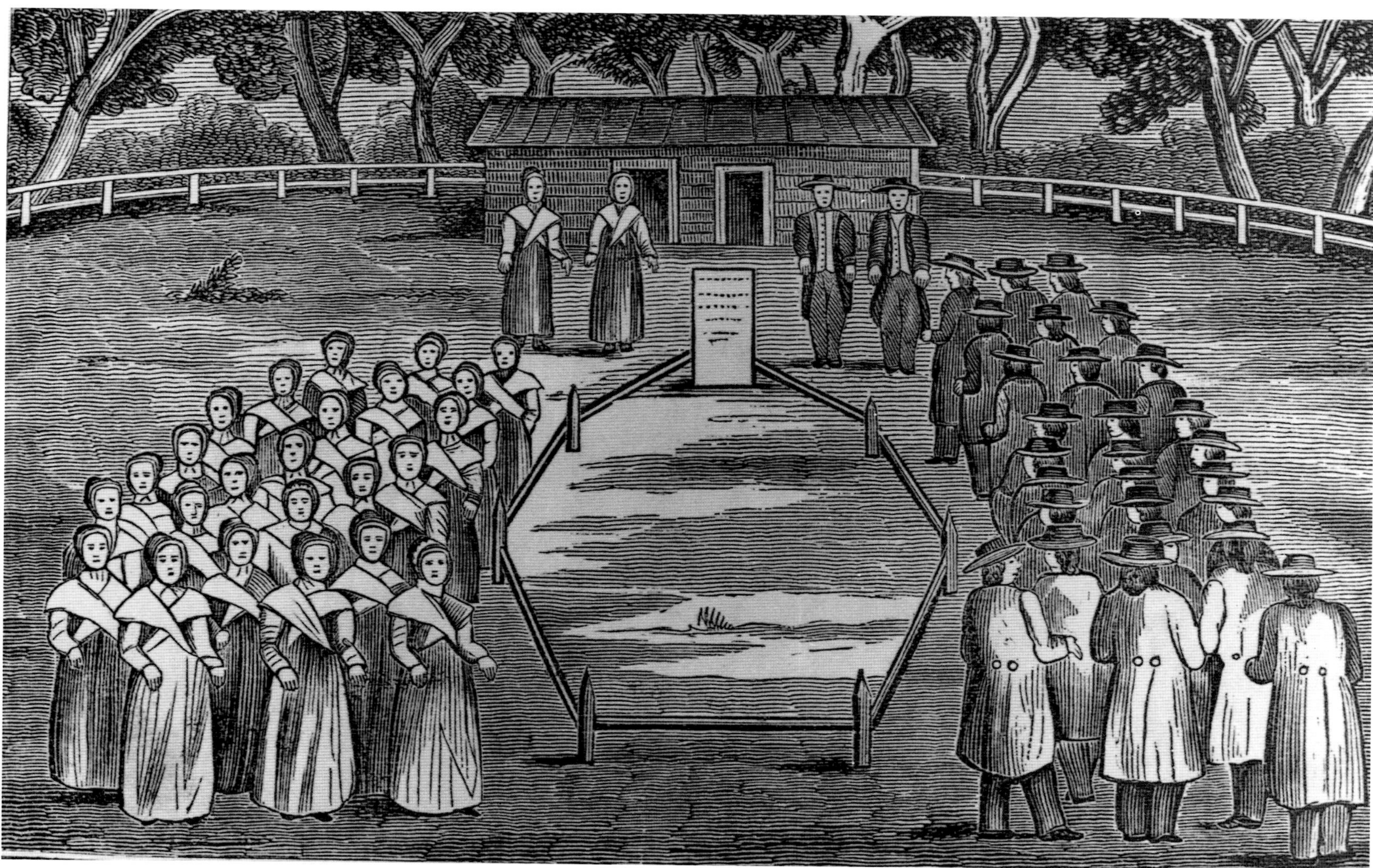

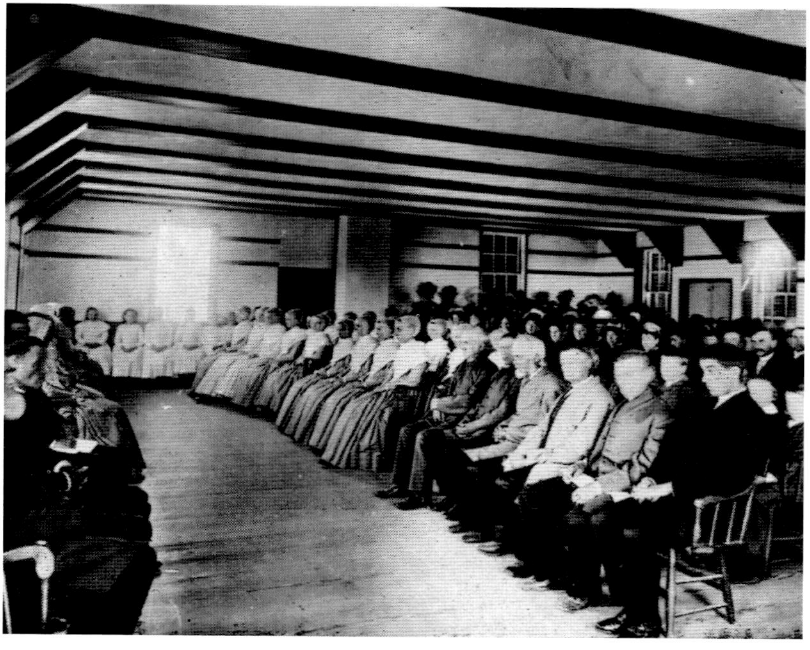

over as head of the Niskeyuna community. More importantly, he immediately set about to encourage Shaker families to come together in more concentrated communities. This would allow them not only to combine their financial and other resources but also to concentrate their lives on the Shaker way. It was Whittaker, too, who strongly reinforced the need for complete withdrawal from the world, for severe self-denial, and for total celibacy. Shaker celibacy would later be attributed to Ann Lee and her own inability to bear children, but in fact there is no written record of her position on this matter. Whittaker died in 1787 before he could accomplish much else, but he did evidently influence the construction of the first Shaker meetinghouse, at New Lebanon, New York, in October 1785.

Within six years of Whittaker's death, ten of the major Shaker communities began to come together in a more organized fashion – constructing numerous buildings, pooling economic resources, and sharing in labor. In addition to New Lebanon, these first communities included Hancock, Harvard, Tyringham and Shirley in Massachusetts, Enfield in Connecticut, Alfred and Sabbathday Lake in Maine, and Canterbury and Enfield in New Hampshire. This came about in part because isolated Shakers continued to find themselves attacked by certain elements of their communities. It also reflected a major change within the Shaker sect itself, one that was greatly influenced by Joseph Meacham, one of the earliest converts from New Lebanon, New York.

With Whittaker's death, Meacham emerged not only as the head of the New Lebanon Shakers but also as the proponent of a new approach to Shakerism. Ann Lee and the other early leaders of the Shakers depended on charismatic leadership – that is, they depended on a special divine gift or grace, granted to them as individuals. Meacham was a man of great faith, even one who claimed to receive direct revelations from God. The new aspect he introduced, however, came from the fact that he was a more practical man of the world, completely literate, and possessing organizational instincts and abilities. He turned the New Lebanon community into the model for other Shaker communities, not just in the style of buildings but also in the internal structure of the administration.

For instance, he appears to have devised a hierarchical system of "courts" or families that were to operate each Shaker community. The most important was the inner court of elders and eldresses, whose spiritual authority would take precedence over any temporal concerns. It was Meacham, too, who appears to have formalized the strict separation of the sexes, not just in living quarters but in their chores and daily contacts. As the Shakers

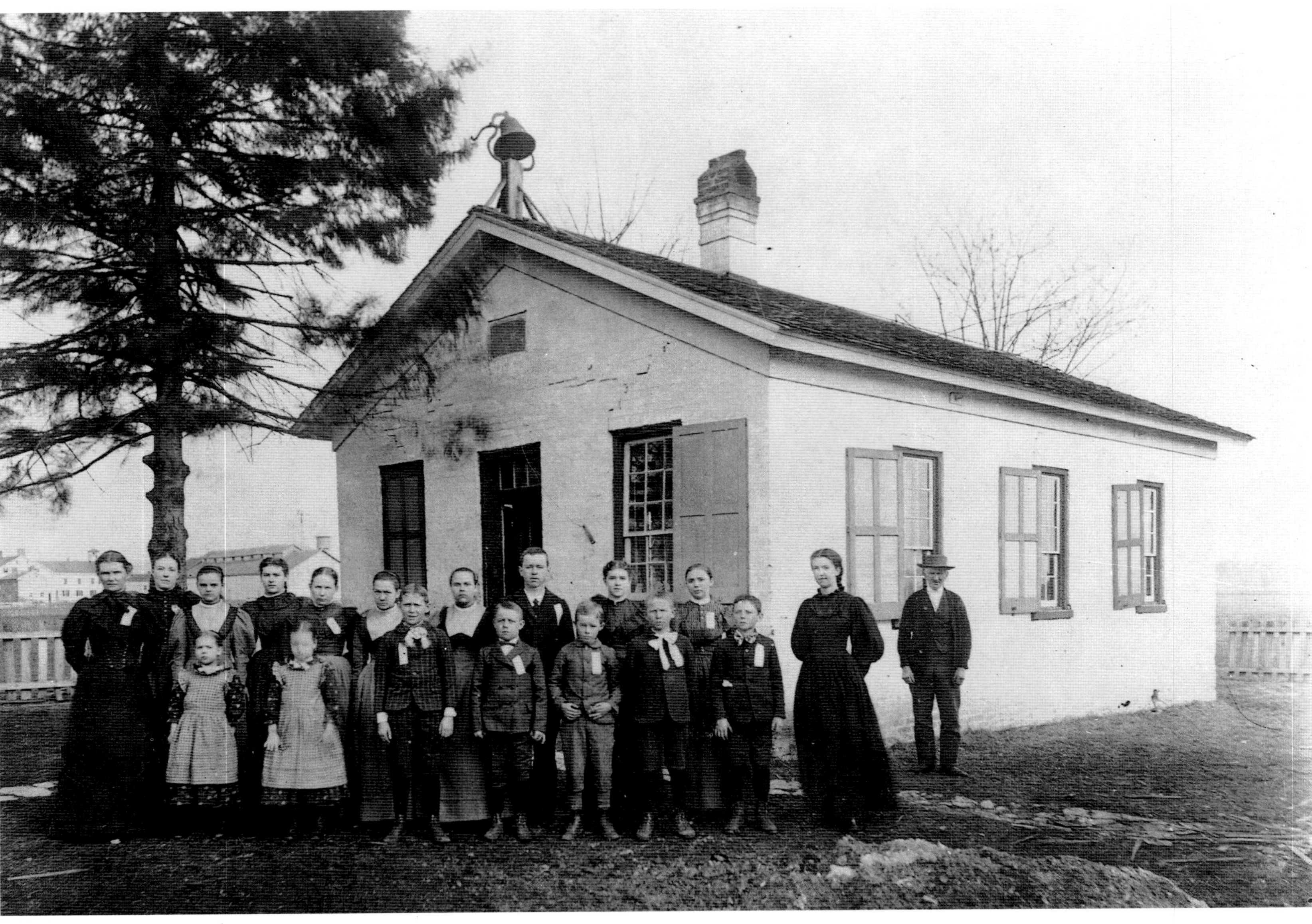

gathered in their various communities during the early 1790s, they tended to replicate all these structures of the New Lebanon community. Through it all, above all, they preserved and passed on their distinctive church services with the emphasis on the dancing and singing, the marches and processions, and the "whirlings" and "seizures" that attested to their personal experience of God.

Meacham died in 1796, but there was no loss in the dynamics of the New Lebanon community or in the Shaker movement, largely due to the emergence of a remarkable woman – Lucy Wright. From western Massachusetts, she had evidently been an early convert to Shakerism; according to tradition, she had joined Ann Lee at Niskeyuna and nursed her through her final illness. By tradition, too, she had been invited by Meacham to become the leading eldress at New Lebanon. After his death, she quickly assumed a leadership role and began to open up the somewhat ingrown sect. She authorized a number of published texts that began both to codify the Shakers' history and theology and also to make them better known to the outside world. She also instigated a new phase of missionary activity to gain new converts throughout New England and eastern New York.

She also authorized Shaker missionaries to go to the Ohio River Valley. On January 1, 1805, a group of four male Shakers from New Lebanon set off for the West; traveling through parts of Ohio and Kentucky, they soon were gaining converts. More Shakers from the East, women as well as men, soon appeared and within a few years a number of Shaker communities were established in Ohio, Kentucky, and Indiana – both the buildings and the organizations reflecting their Eastern sources.

By the time of Mother Lucy's death in 1821, the Shakers had accomplished a most remarkable feat. In less than 50 years in America, without great material resources but with primarily their own faith and energy, they had established a network of at least 17 communities. There were estimated to be some 4,000 members resident in these communities, with still other scattered converts (many of whom would soon enter communities). The Shakers were now on the verge of carrying out one of the most successful of the many utopian-communitarian social experiments that occurred in the United States during the mid-nineteenth century.

The classic phase of the Shaker communities – the activities and material culture that are now regarded as their distinctive signifiers – was between 1825 and 1875. Inevitably, as with any institution that carries on decade after decade, there were changes and problems. At the same time, when measured against the rest of American society during those years, the Shakers did enjoy a certain unity.

Because of the emphasis the first generation of Shakers placed on the one-on-one transmission of the faith and their refusal to commit much to writing, there was a lack of uniformity among the early "gatherings." During the 1790s, different communities would draw up covenants that dealt with their temporal or secular arrangements – how to handle property, finances, lines of authority, and such; some articles in these covenants also dealt with such details as the hours of rising, division of labor, modes of dress, and construction projects. These covenants varied from community to community until Lucy Wright at New Lebanon gave her approval to drawing up a uniform code.

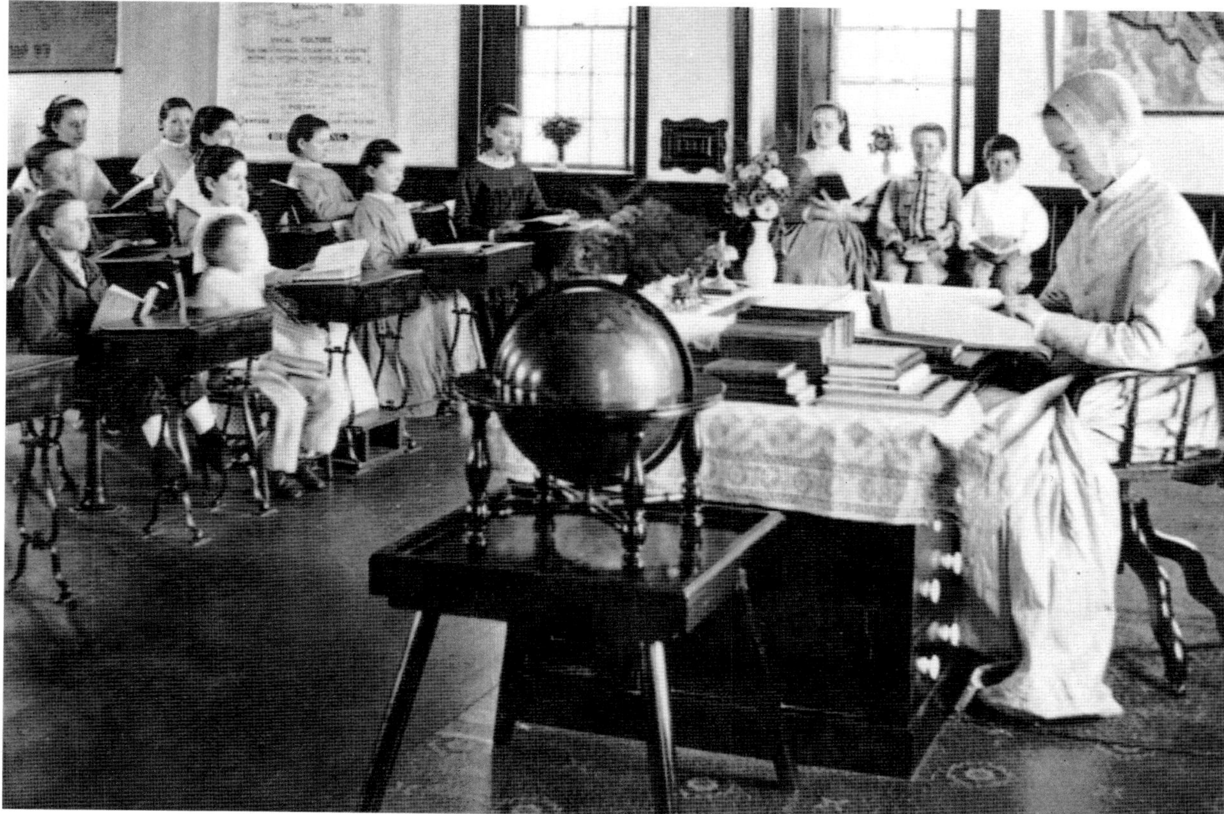

Opposite: Shaker communities started to spring up in Ohio and Kentucky after the missionary trips of Lucy Wright and others in the early 1800s. This photo depicts the students and teachers at the Center Family School at the community in Whitewater, Ohio. (The Shaker Museum and Library, Old Chatham, NY)

Right above: The Shaker schoolroom with teacher and pupils in Canterbury, New Hampshire, c. 1880s. More than other communities, the Canterbury Shakers had a particular interest in education and spent a significant amount on books and school supplies. (The Shaker Museum and Library, Old Chatham, NY)

Right below: The meetinghouse at Mount Lebanon has an arched roof and wide open meeting room that is more than 78 feet long and 63 feet wide with a 25-foot ceiling. It was large enough to accommodate the Shaker dance worship and it served as a model for other community meetinghouses. (The Bettmann Archive, New York, NY)

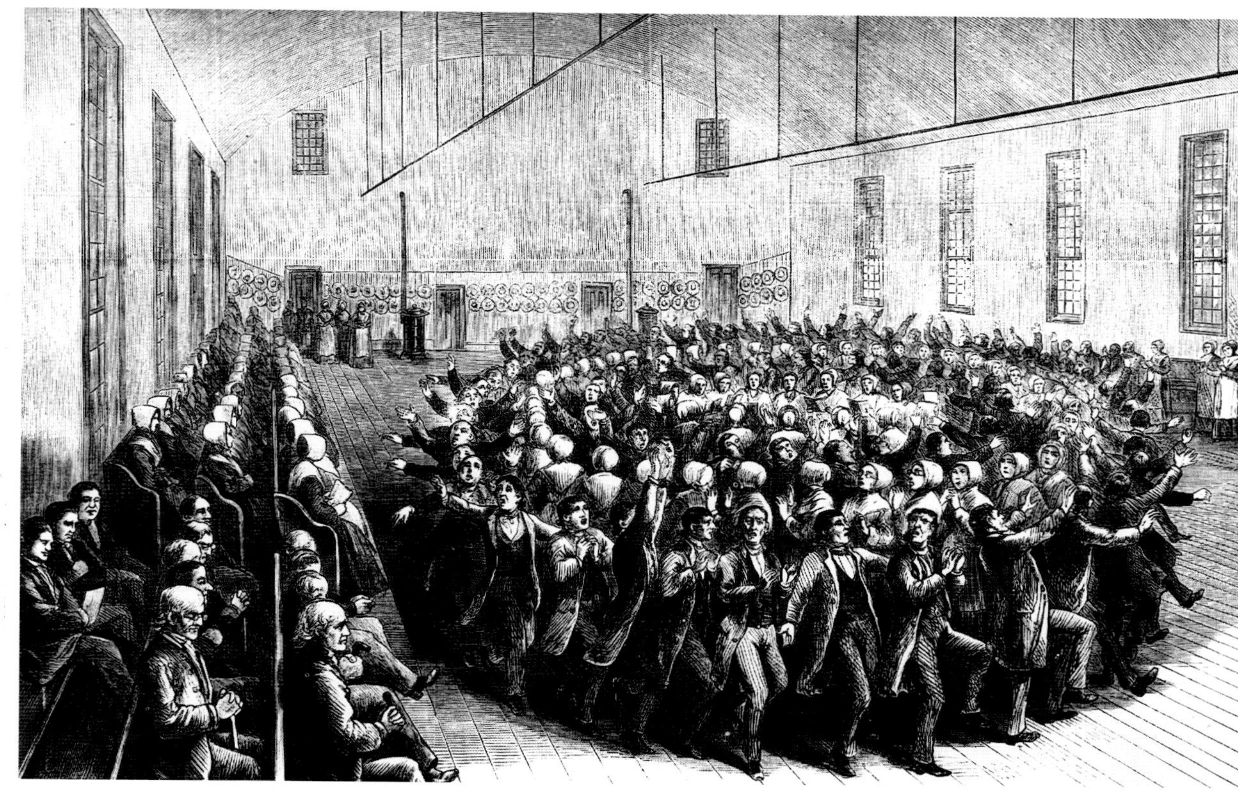

Below: One of the few interactions between men and women was at the meetinghouse, but there was still a strict separation of the sexes in the dance worship. Shakers were taught to step together using precise movements as shown in this engraving of the Mount Lebanon community. Note the peg rails around the room which hold hats and bonnets. (Library of Congress, Washington, DC)

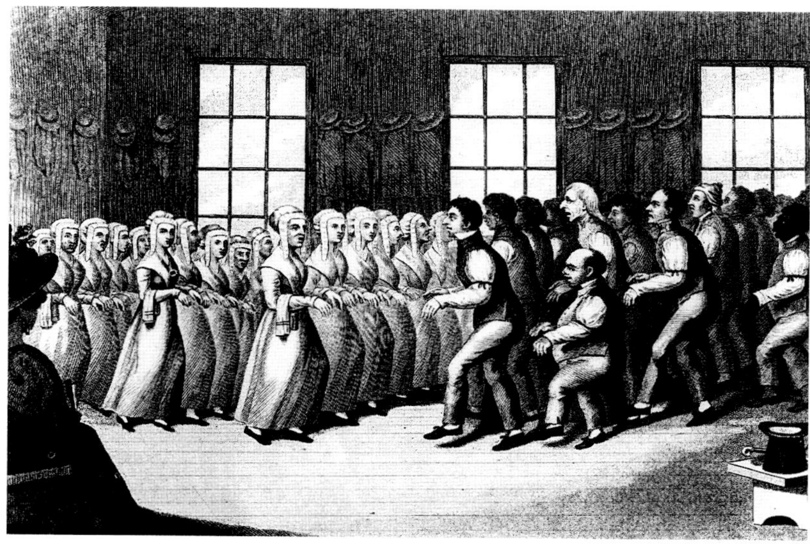

Lucy Wright died only six months before the Millennial Laws were published in 1821. This document has been called "the first systematic codification of regulations within Shakerism." These laws dealt with everything from how to confess one's sins to dining etiquette, from the ban on contact between the sexes to fire safety regulations. These Millennial Laws were never accepted in their entirety by all of the scattered Shaker communities from Maine to Kentucky. The western communities in particular often went their own way, and even the strictest observers periodically modified these laws. But they did provide the matrix for this classic phase of Shakerism because the laws outlined specific ways for maintaining their society and served to further separate Shakers from the outside world that they regarded as extremely decadent and "polluted."

The prime element that separated Shakers from the rest of

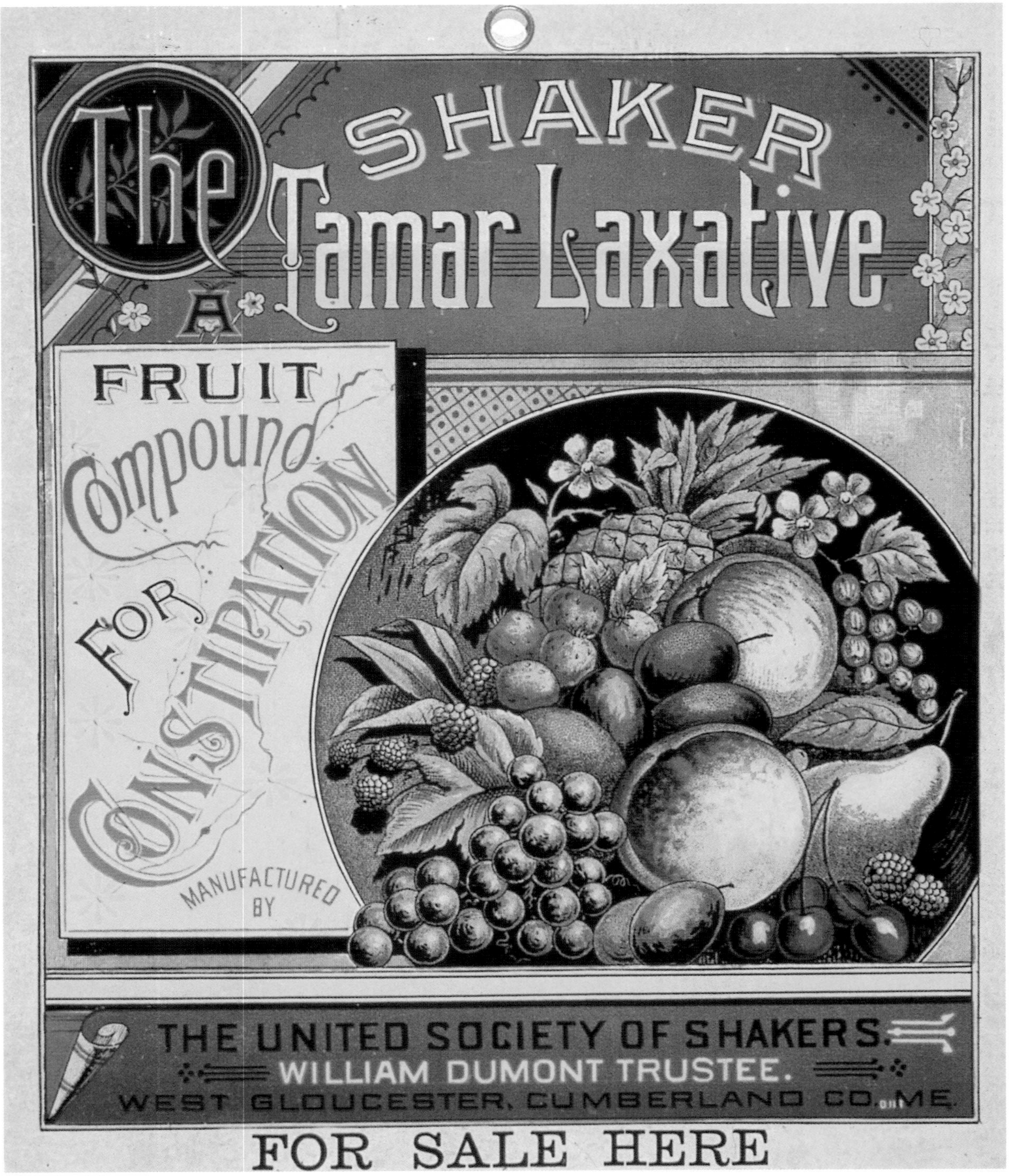

Left: Traveling Shaker salesmen made rounds selling the Shaker products which provided income to help support the communal family. Their religious beliefs instilled a pride in their work which was valued by outsiders in their high-quality products. (Photo courtesy Hancock Shaker Village, Pittsfield, MA)

Below: A peace convention at the Mount Lebanon meetinghouse in 1905. In an effort to recruit new believers, the Shakers started to sponsor lectures for the public, who attended in large numbers but did not convert to Shakerism. (The Shaker Museum and Library, Old Chatham, NY)

Opposite left: Shakers believed in efficiency and invented many labor-saving devices which they would sell to the outside word. This is an ad for the Maine Mower invented at the Sabbathday Lake, Maine, community. The words "durability, perfection, and beauty of execution" are all precepts of the Shaker beliefs. (Collection of the United Society of Shakers, Sabbathday Lake, ME)

Opposite right: An example of another practical product produced by the Shakers to market were their seed packets. The income from these products would help to pay for the items that the Shakers could not produce themselves. (Hancock Shaker Village, Pittsfield, MA)

American society was their decision to live in a community that called for the joint ownership of all land and property. Shakers had to relinquish possession of their former lands and homes and either assign them to the community (if they lived nearby) or sell them and bring their financial assets into the community. If an individual chose at some time to break with the Shakers – and many did over the decades, for a variety of reasons – it often led to disputes (and legal suits) over which parts of this property should revert to the original donor.

By and large, though, this communal property system worked, and communities expanded into thousands of acres, with numerous communal buildings. Some of the converts had been fairly prosperous in the outside world, but most were of modest means. Most, too, lacked much formal education – although as the decades passed, some of the converts did come from slightly more advanced educational backgrounds. The men were by and large farmers, craftsmen, and tradesmen; the women were adept in the many skills that women of that era possessed – cooking, sewing, farm chores. Within a community, work was fairly strictly divided between the sexes, although men and women were regarded as equals.

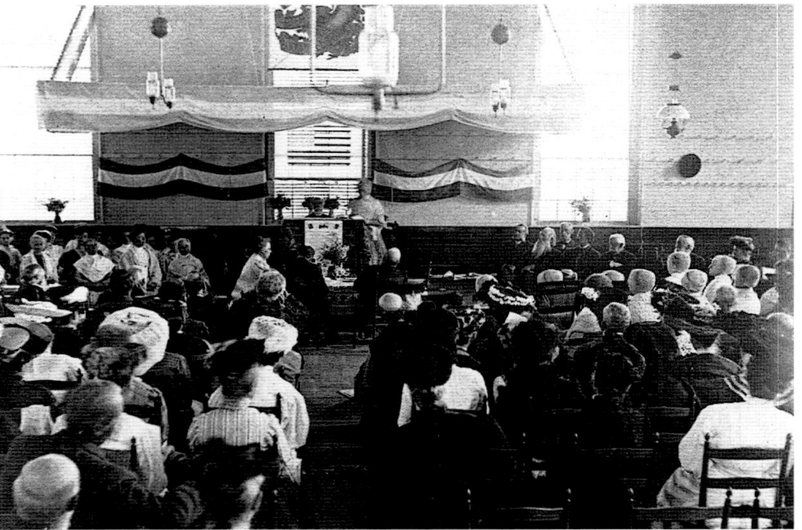

From the earliest gatherings into Shaker villages in the 1790s, shared labor was at the basis of communal life. Manual labor was valued by their religion as well as by the tradition out of which the sect grew, with the result that everyone was expected to work at some task. The goal was for each Shaker village to be self-suf-

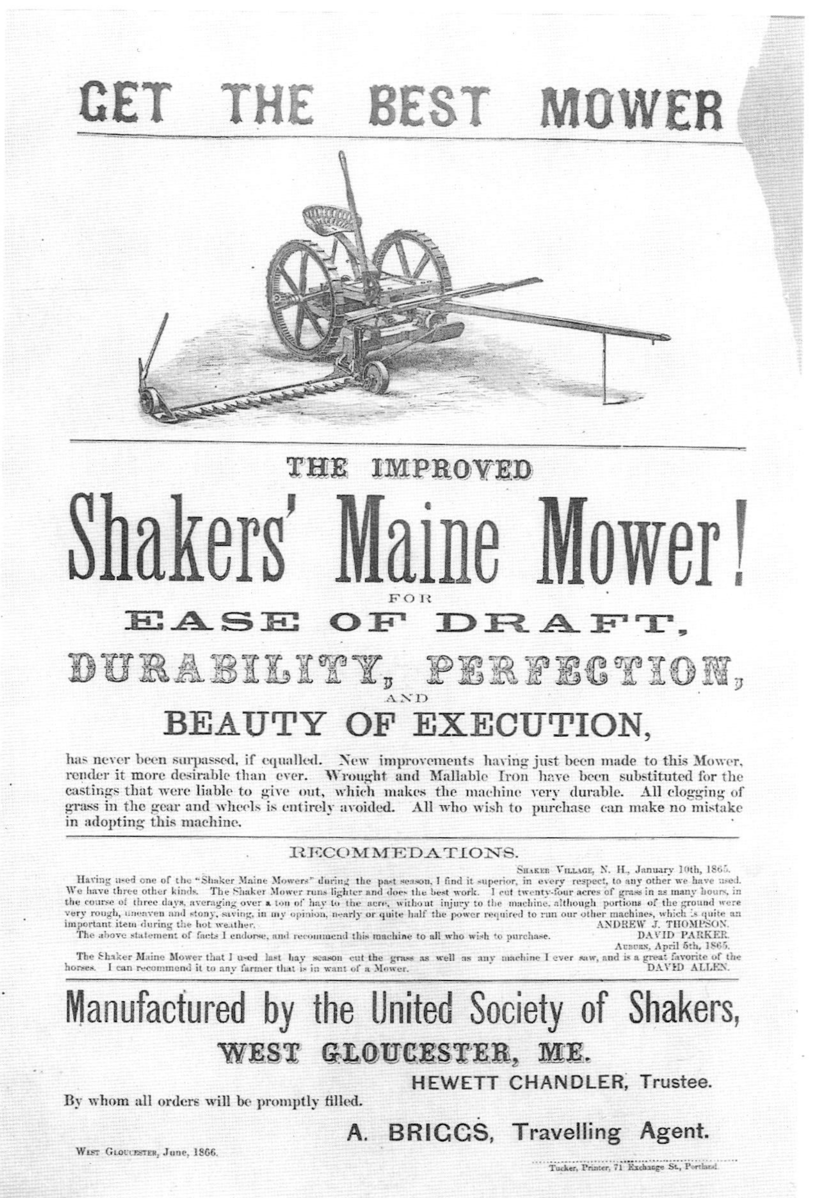

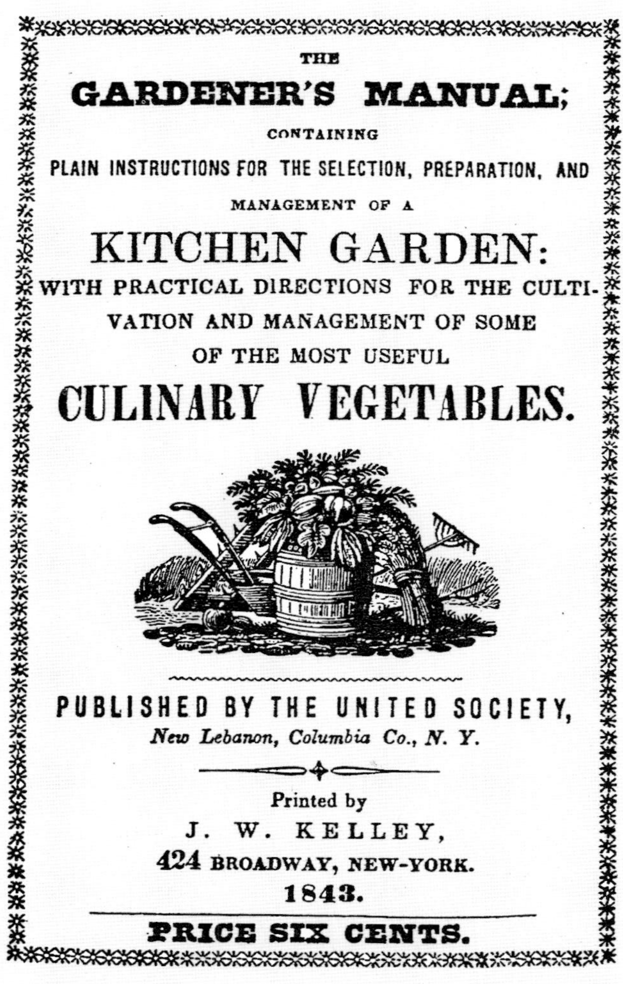

THE
GARDENER'S MANUAL;
CONTAINING
PLAIN INSTRUCTIONS FOR THE SELECTION, PREPARATION, AND
MANAGEMENT OF A
KITCHEN GARDEN:
WITH PRACTICAL DIRECTIONS FOR THE CULTIVATION AND MANAGEMENT OF SOME
OF THE MOST USEFUL
CULINARY VEGETABLES.

PUBLISHED BY THE UNITED SOCIETY,
New Lebanon, Columbia Co., N. Y.

Printed by
J. W. KELLEY,
424 BROADWAY, NEW-YORK.
1843.

PRICE SIX CENTS.

ficient – to isolate itself from the demands and desires of the world around it. And in the early years, as long as Shakers sought only the basics of survival, this worked fairly well.

Yet even from the beginning there were needs that the Shakers could not meet – various provisions, hardware, and other supplies that were best bought. As early as the 1790s the Shakers began to sell such products as seeds and herbs to pay for these materials. During the first half of the nineteenth century, the seed and herb trade became the major source of income for the Shaker villages, especially in the Northeast; the villages in the West tended to rely more on the breeding and sales of cattle. Shaker seed agents, all of whom were male, traveled throughout much of the region east of the Mississippi selling seeds that had been carefully packed in their respective villages. Herbs, barks, roots and liquid extracts were also a source of income for some Shaker villages. Again, although men and women were regarded as equals, the division of labor was strict so that men cultivated the crops and women dried and packaged the seeds and herbs.

The Shaker blacksmiths who eventually came to service the outside community were all male. And men staffed the many mills for grinding grain and sawing wood that soon became the hallmark of Shaker villages. By 1850, a few Shaker communities were even involved in textile mills. Most of the products sold by the Shakers, however, were handcrafted items made by women. Originally they were made only to satisfy the needs of each community. Gradually they were sold to visitors, and eventually many were made in quantity for markets outside. These included such products as brooms and brushes, buckets and churns, yarn and cloth, shoes and leather goods, and knitwear and bonnets. The product for which Shakers would become best known in our own times is their furniture – chairs, tables, chests and such pieces – and baskets. As with the other items, these were originally made only for their own use; only gradually did they come to be produced in large quantities for sale to non-Shakers.

In addition to linking the Shaker villages to the larger American economy, this work had another effect on the Shakers: they became interested in producing labor-saving devices. They often introduced modifications and improvements to existing devices, and sometimes invented new devices or gadgets, and they were admired by many contemporaries for their generosity in making these new devices available to all. It was no coincidence, then, that a young man named Gail Borden went to the Shaker village of New Lebanon, New York, in 1853 to experiment with one of their new "vacuum pans"; from his work came the process to produce what he called "condensed milk," which in turn led to the creation of the Borden Company.

The utilitarian objects the Shakers produced have since become the most tangible examples of Shaker style. But it must be emphasized that the Shakers themselves did not set out to produce objects that would be "stylish." They simply did what they felt was necessary to make objects that fulfilled a function. They had no aesthetic theories, no artistic goals. Indeed, from the outset, they were opposed to any superfluousness in their material world. That is why there are no Shaker works of art in the fields of painting or sculpture: the Shakers were opposed to decorations. The visionary scenes produced during the Era of Manifestations, a period of intense spiritualistic activity that lasted from 1837 to the early 1850s, may be considered an exception, but even these were not conceived with any conscious desire to be artistic.

The only other notable exception might be the hymns that the Shakers were encouraged to compose - both words and music, sometimes written with decorative elements. This form of creativity was allowed because music remained at the core of the Shaker sacred services – the dancing and chanting that, from their earliest days in England, had distinguished the Shakers. Yet even when composing hymns, the Shakers' goal remained what was at the basis of all their accomplishments and what was expressed in their best-known hymn:

'Tis the gift to be simple,
'Tis the gift to be free;
'Tis the gift to come down
Where we ought to be.

After 1875, the Shaker communities began to decline. Individual Shakers had been worrying for some years about the decline of the "religious element" within their communities. They were also aware of their declining numbers – down from the peak of some 6,000 to about only 2,500. In the early 1870s, various Shakers had begun to take steps to build up their membership: they inaugurated a new missionary program that included public lectures as far away as London; they began a publication that was aimed at non-Shakers; they also began to respond openly to attacks on them. But none of this "outreach" gained any significant number of converts.

From the earliest days of the Shakers, as word spread of their insistence on celibacy, the outside world made much of this aspect of their beliefs. Whether it explains the fact that women almost always outnumbered men is a matter for speculation. To the true believers, it did not seem to be the most important part of their faith. However, not all members were able to hold to such an ideal, and for every story of a couple's broken engagement or marriage – when one decided to join the Shakers while

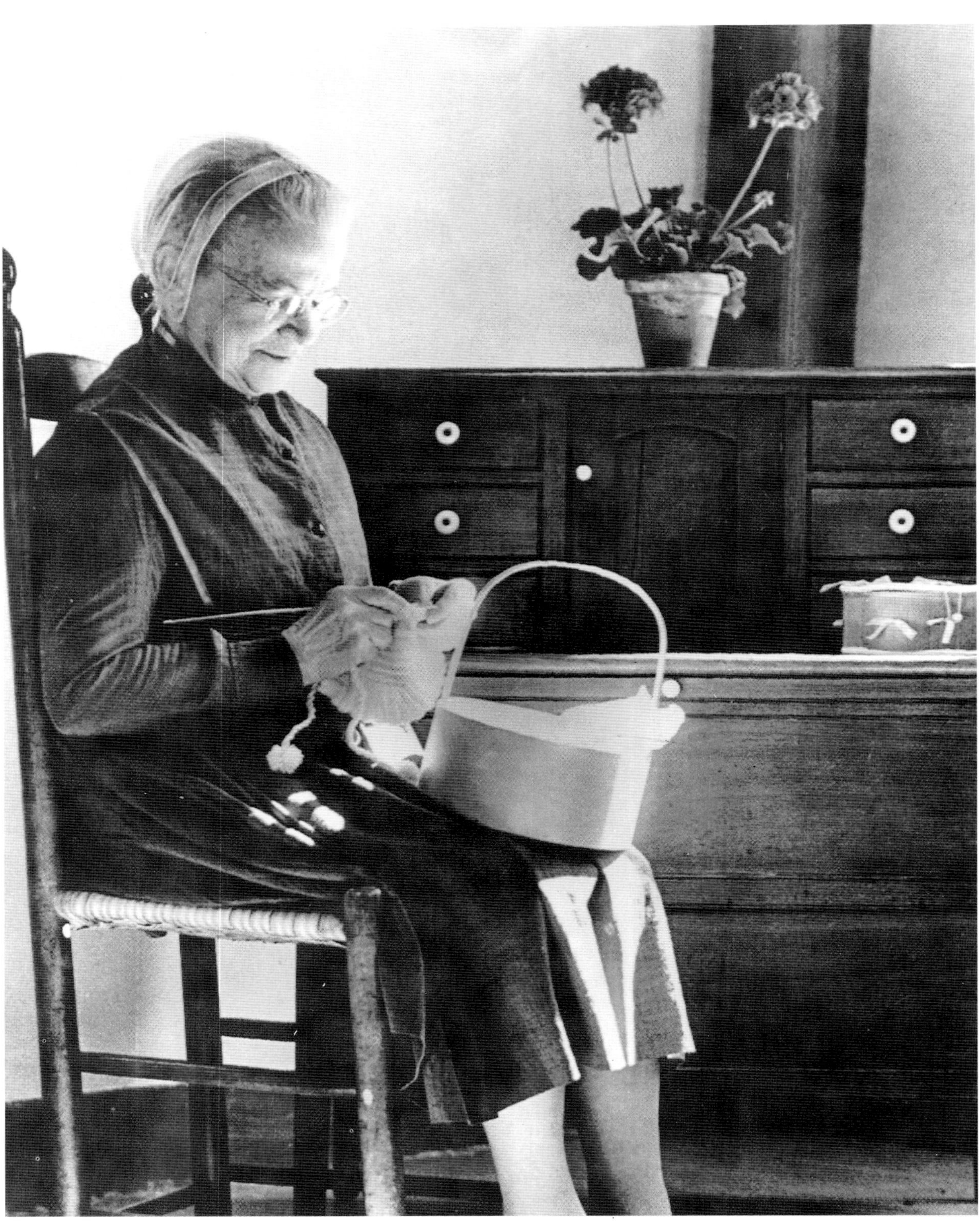

Left: Eldress Gertrude Soule in 1978 was the one of the last three surviving Shakers in the village in Canterbury, New Hampshire. She is shown working at her needlework in the "Sisters' Shop." Her handwork was sold to tourists in the village gift shop. (The Bettmann Archive, New York, NY)

Opposite above: A detail from the plan by Henry Clay Blinn of the Church Family Gardens for the Shaker community at Canterbury, 1848. (Canterbury Shaker Village, Canterbury, NH)

Opposite below: The book of the Holy Laws of Zion is on display at the Shaker Village in Canterbury, New Hampshire. Theology and divine revelations formed the spiritual basis of the deeds and daily routines of the Shakers. (Canterbury Shaker Village, Canterbury, NH, Photo by Todd Buchanan)

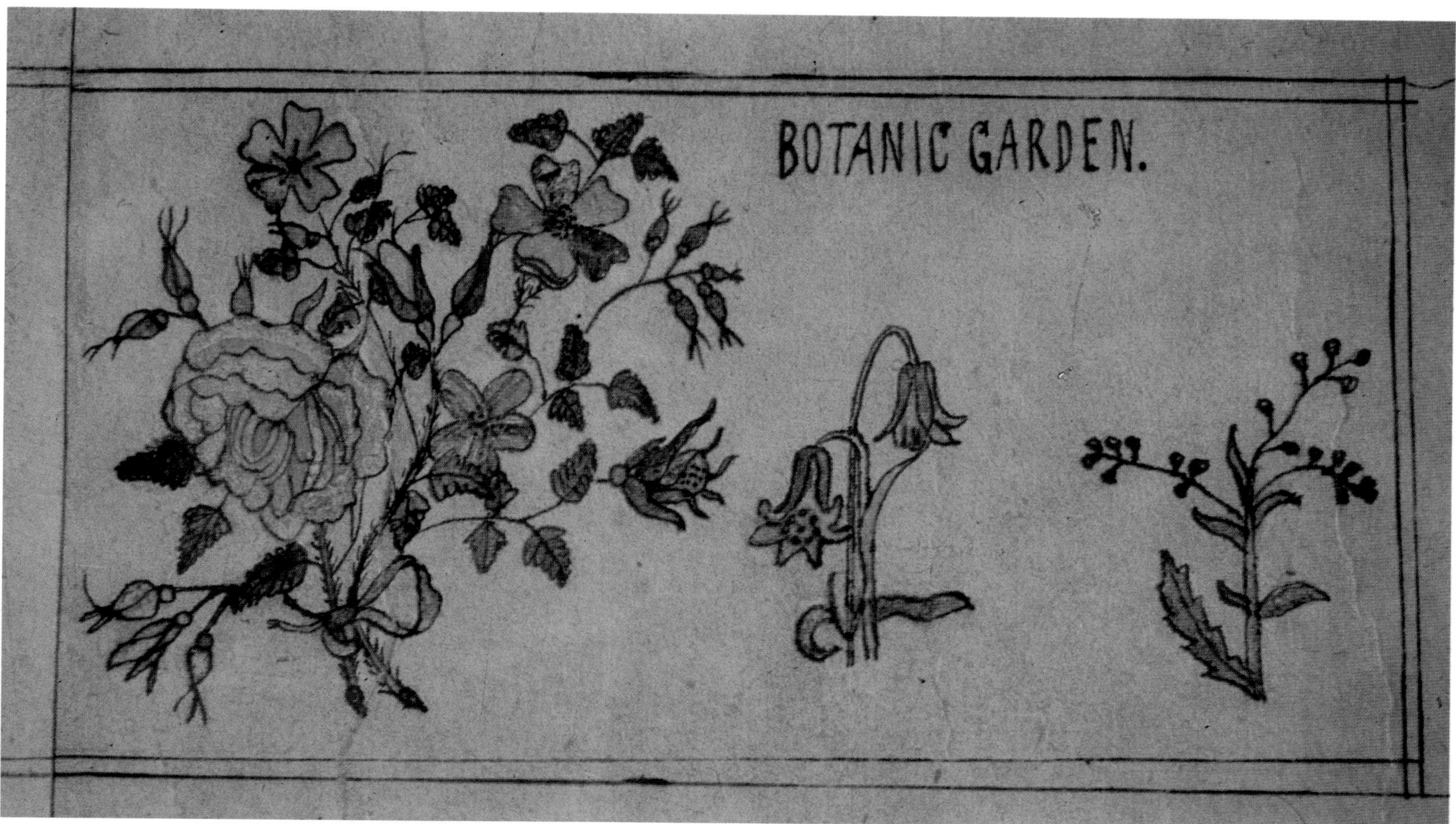

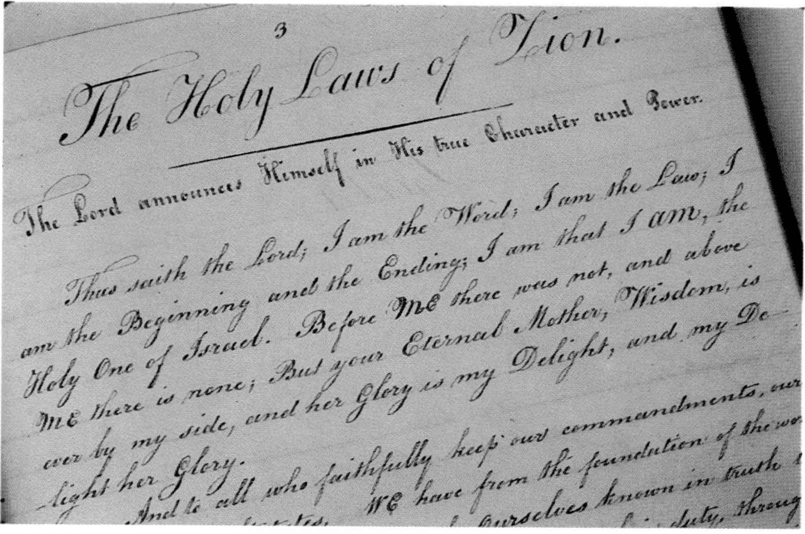

3

The Holy Laws of Zion.

The Lord announces Himself in His true Character and Power.

Thus saith the Lord; I am the Word, I am the Law; I am the Beginning and the Ending; I am that I am, the Holy One of Israel. Before ME there was not, and above ME there is none; But your Eternal Mother, Wisdom, is ever by my side, and her Glory is my Delight, and my Delight her Glory.

And to all who faithfully keep our commandments, our ... WE have from the foundation of the wo... ourselves known in truth ... duty, throug...

the other would not – there is a story of a couple who left a community when their affections became too strong.

Many husbands and wives converted together to Shakerism, and once they joined a community they had to live apart from one another. When they brought their young children into the community with them – as many did – the children were raised apart by special caretakers and teachers, although inevitably parents kept a special eye out for their offspring. Many of the children were orphans or abandoned children, and the Shakers were quite happy to take them in since they could not otherwise have their own and this was one way of perpetuating their communities.

As for the claim that the requirement of celibacy doomed the Shakers from the beginning – that is, unable to procreate, they must die out – the opposite point has also been made: that this was the strength of their society, for it guaranteed only true believers, people dedicated solely to maintaining the Shaker way of life. What gradually wore down the Shaker communities in the years after 1875, according to this interpretation, was not a lack of children in their communities, but the changes in adult society around them.

In one sense, it was the very success of the Shakers that eventually led to their decline. As their villages sprang up in more far-reaching locales – eventually even in Florida and Georgia – they lost a sense of unity. As they prospered economically, they made increased contacts with the world outside. As they attracted more and diverse people, they lost their homogeneousness. By the late nineteenth century, some Shakers saw no reason to withdraw completely from the world and they began to adopt such new inventions as the telephone and automobile. Others saw the possibilities of passing on their Shaker message to the world at large – in particular striving to bring about peace in the world. It was a noble goal, but it served to break down the barriers between the Shakers and that world.

One by one, the Shaker villages declined in numbers and shut down. In 1938, the original community of Niskeyuna – long since renamed Watervliet, New York – closed. By 1947, there were only four functioning Shaker villages – the principal one at Mount Lebanon, New York; Hancock, Massachusetts; Canterbury, New Hampshire; and Sabbathday Lake, Maine. In October of 1947, the few Shakers at New Lebanon moved to Hancock Village, which in turn closed as a Shaker community in 1960. Eventually the last survivors of the Canterbury community died out; now only the Sabbathday Lake, Maine, community survives, thanks to the arrival in recent years of new converts.

The Shaker experiment has effectively ended. Compared to the other great nineteenth-century religious community, the Mormons, the Shakers had failed. Yet in some ways, the Shakers do live on. They have inspired numerous artists, writers and craftspeople, as well as many thoughtful theologians, philosophers and people seeking a worthwhile way of life. The elements that make up Shaker style – the goals of purity, simplicity, health, work and usefulness; the message of concentration, caring, peace and respect – need never go out of fashion.

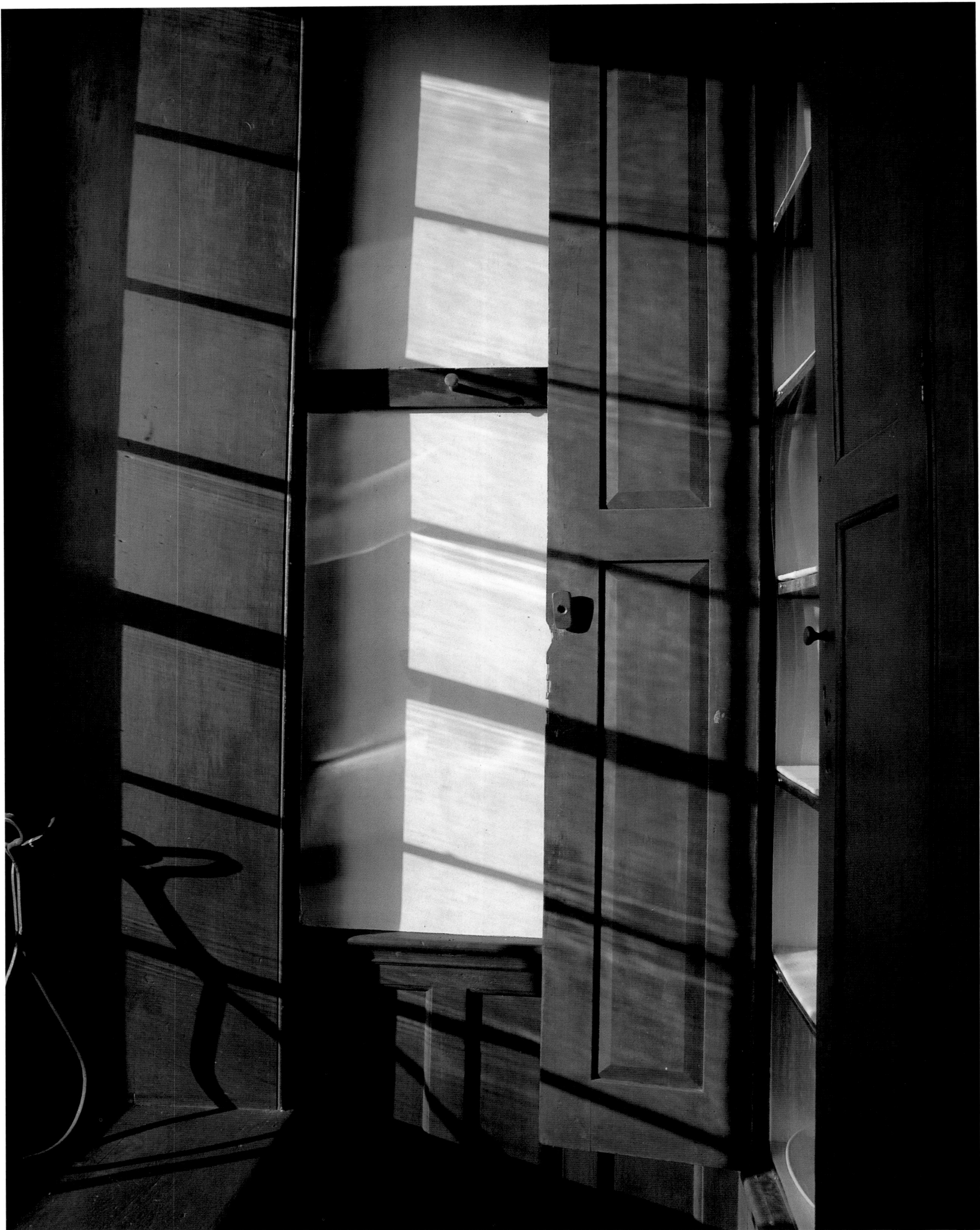

CHAPTER I

STRUCTURES FOR ETERNITY

A walk through any Shaker village would reveal to the visitor a wealth of information about the Shaker people as a whole. Although there was never an official plan for these villages, they tended to have a certain uniformity in their layout and in the individual structures, and both directly reflected the activities and goals of the Shakers. Although Shaker buildings in general were much like those in the world around them, they differed in a number of details that were dictated by the Shakers' unique religious and social practices.

Because they were a communal society, their villages lacked both the concentration and the spread that accompanied typical villages of their time. A typical nineteenth-century American village would have a core of structures – residential, commercial, civic, religious – and farms on the outskirts. The Shakers instead built their structures along a few roads, parallel and perpendicular, with their common fields stretching out behind them. Since everyone lived and worked in relatively few buildings, there was not the organic and sometimes haphazard growth that occurred in a typical non-Shaker village of the time. As new people joined a Shaker community, they went to live in what were essentially dormitories and reported for work in one of the communal worksites. There were no private commercial enterprises – clothing stores, taverns, and such – and certainly no other churches. When a new structure was needed, it was assigned a particular locale depending on its function. When a community split into "families," their residences were set aside in distinct "substations" along the road.

The main building of a Shaker village was the meetinghouse, since religion was the focus of the people's lives and they spent a fair amount of each week in their services. Although there would eventually be considerable diversity as the Shakers spread westward, the meetinghouses of the early villages tended to look similar, mainly because ten of them were designed and built between 1785 and 1794 by Moses Johnson, a Shaker based in the Enfield, New Hampshire, community. The Johnson-designed structures were distinguished by their gambrel roofs and the main floor with its large open space required by the Shakers whose services centered around group dancing, processions, circling and such. Another distinctive feature of the Shaker meetinghouses were the two sets of separate entrances for males and females: those at the ends for the clergy, or leaders, and those on the long side for the rest of the community.

The dwelling houses were also distinctively Shaker in style. From the outside these two- to six-storied buildings often looked rather uninviting. Inside, though, they provided cozy if spare domestic quarters, the separate sections divided by corridors and linked by often elegant staircases. Like the meetinghouses, the dwelling houses had separate entrances for the two sexes, separate staircases, and thus often separate interior doorways into common areas. Males and females were expected to spend most of their time in their separate sections; they slept in small "retiring rooms," with beds for at least four. Each dormitory had a family or common room where the sexes might gather for serious conversation. They also ate together in a common dining room, with males and females at separate tables.

Two other features of the dwelling houses reflect the distinctive Shaker way of life: the many built-in cabinets, cupboards, and chests of drawers, and the wallboards with pegs. Both are responses to the Shakers' desire for neatness and modesty – nothing should be left lying about to gather dust or to attract the eye – but there was also the shortage of space: Chairs as well as clothing were thus hung on the wallboards. The saying, "Everything in its place and a place for everything," if not of Shaker origin, might well be.

The rest of the structures in a village were not that distinctive in appearance, at least on first viewing. There was usually a building called the Office, where the trustees who oversaw the administrative and financial operations lived. This was also the building where outsiders and visitors were expected to go to make contact with the Shakers. Some of these Offices eventually accommodated little stores where the village's products and handicrafts were sold to the public.

In the immediate area of the primary structures were the various shops, barns, sheds, mills, warehouses, livestock pens, and other buildings required for daily living and economic activities. In all of these a fairly strict separation of the sexes was observed: women went to the laundry, men to the smithy, women worked in the herbarium, men in the woodworking shop.

Since cultivation of crops and raising of animals remained at the base of their communities' survival, barns were often among the largest and most ambitious structures. The most intriguing of the many Shaker barns was the circular stone structure at Hancock Village, Massachusetts, originally built in 1826. With several unusual features such as the octagonal framework that supports the roof and cupola while providing an air shaft for ventilating the hay, this Shaker structure attracts thousands of visitors annually.

The neatness in the layout and individual structures of the Shaker villages reflected both the strict communal enterprise and the Shakers' disdain for anything superfluous. The uniformity of the villages is perhaps overemphasized in the various nineteenth-century village views made by Shakers themselves, now recognized as a distinct genre of American folk art. In their earliest versions they were little more than ink-drawn surveyors' maps and diagrams; by the 1830s they were becoming quite elegant views that used colored inks and watercolors to identify the various buildings. (Traditionally only the meetinghouse was to be painted white.) Although the Shakers were not supposed to indulge in artistic expression, such men as Charles Priest, Joshua Bussell or Henry Blinn seem to have taken a special delight in their work. Certainly the Shakers' buildings and their architectural elements continue to excite admiration in our own time.

Kitchen storage corner, Centre Family Dwelling, 1824-34
Shaker Village of Pleasant Hill, KY
Photo by James Archambeault

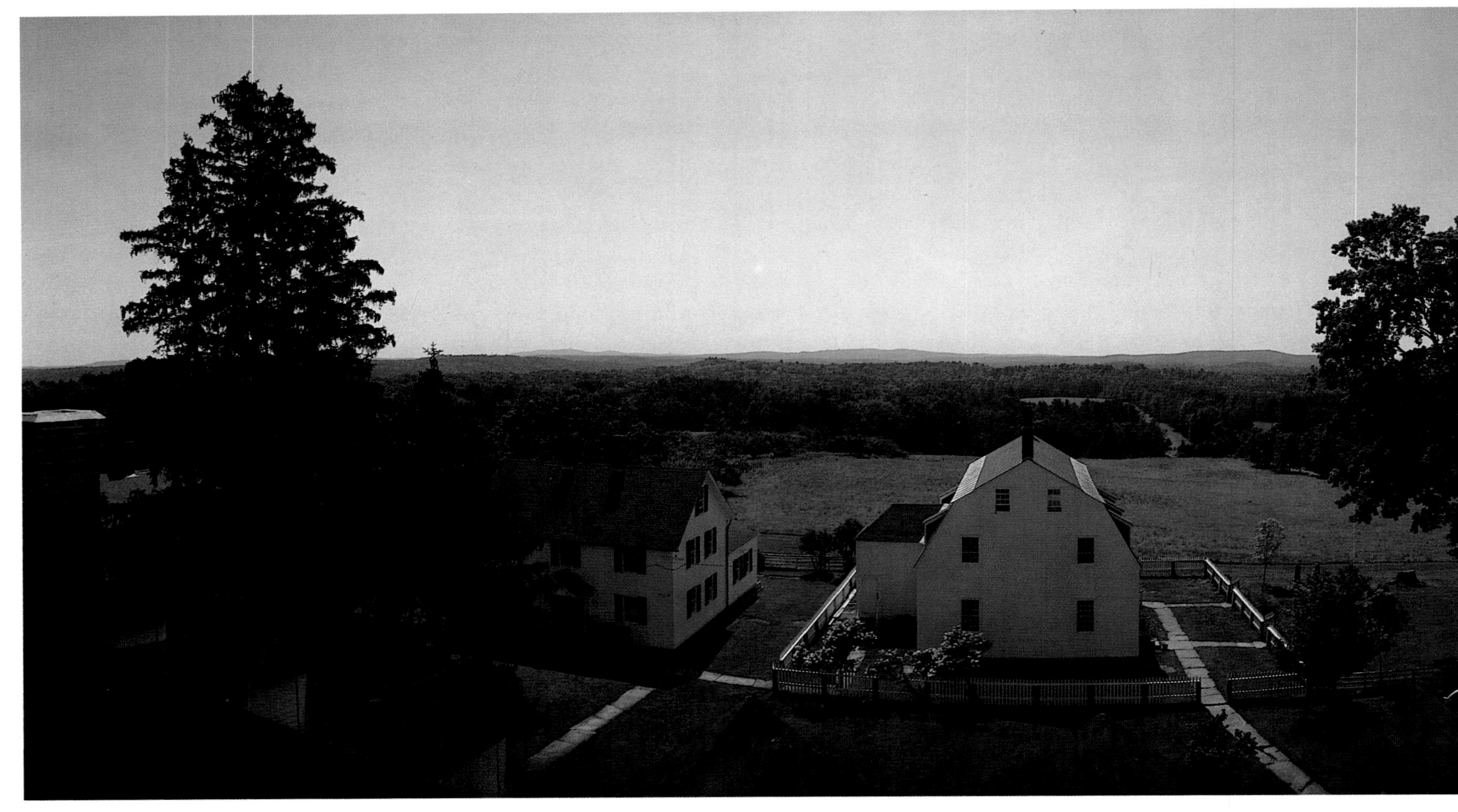

ABOVE:
Panorama, south view, featuring Meetinghouse, 1792
Canterbury Shaker Village, Canterbury, NH
Photo by Todd Buchanan

ABOVE RIGHT:
Shaker Community at Canterbury, NH
Plan by Henry C. Blinn, 1848
Canterbury Shaker Village, Canterbury, NH

RIGHT:
"East View of the Brick House, Church Family, Hancock," c. 1870-75
Hancock Shaker Village, Pittsfield, MA

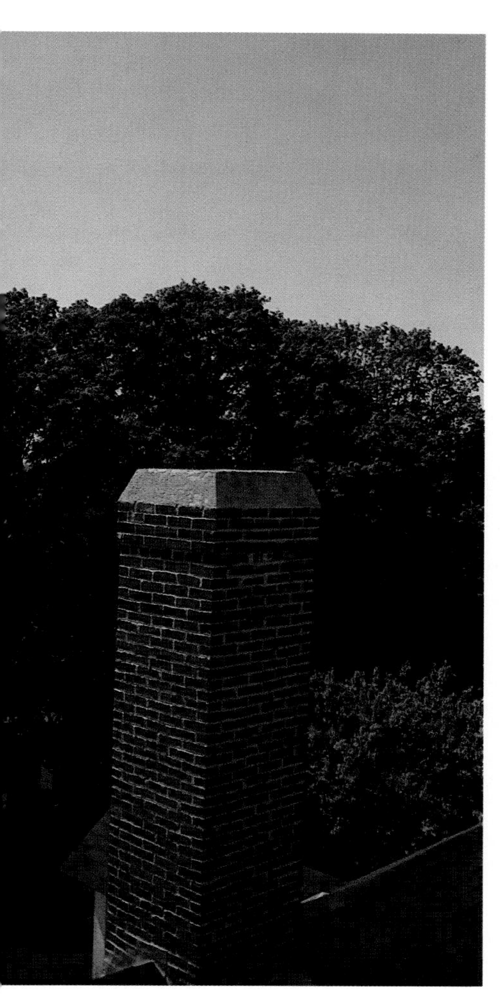

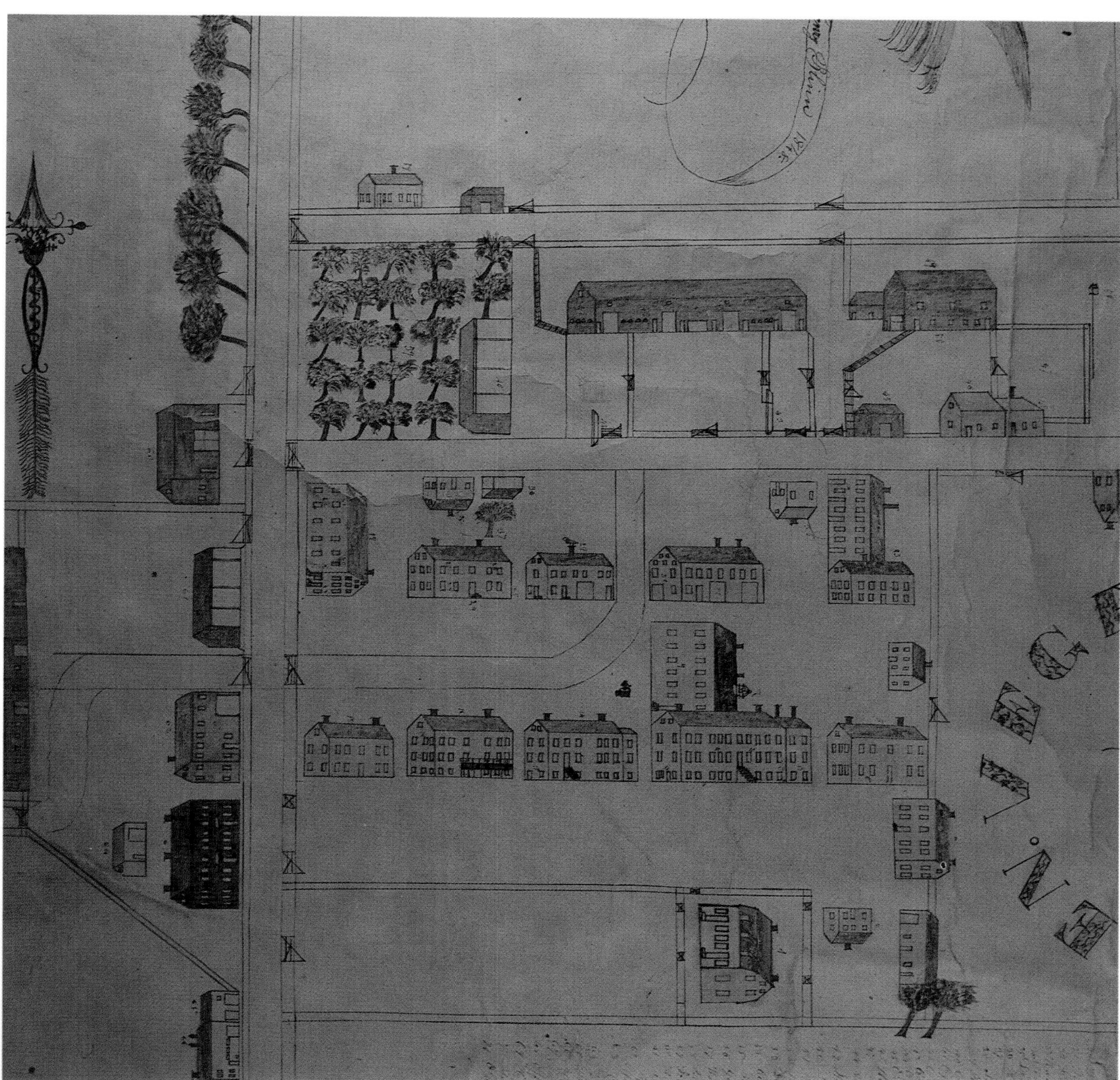

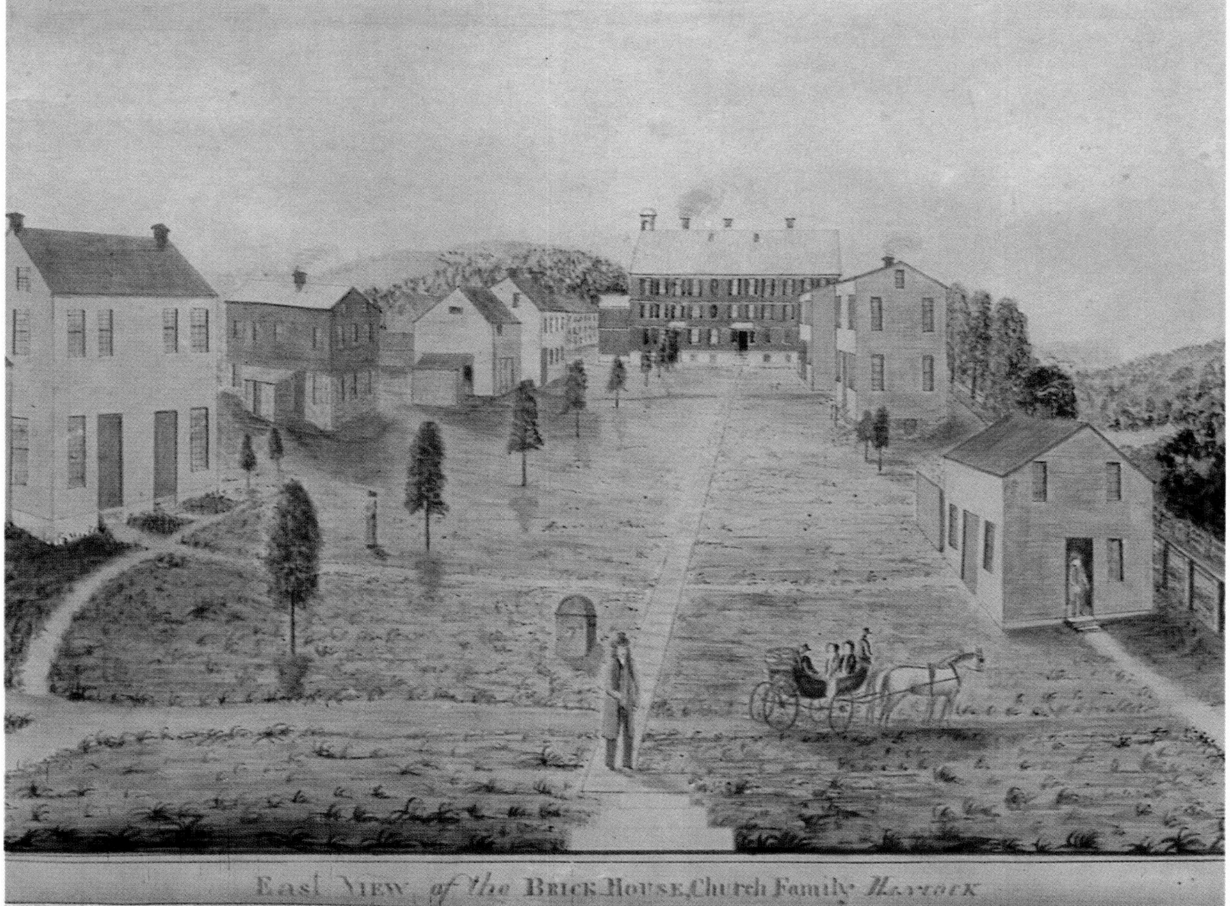
East View of the Brick House, Church Family

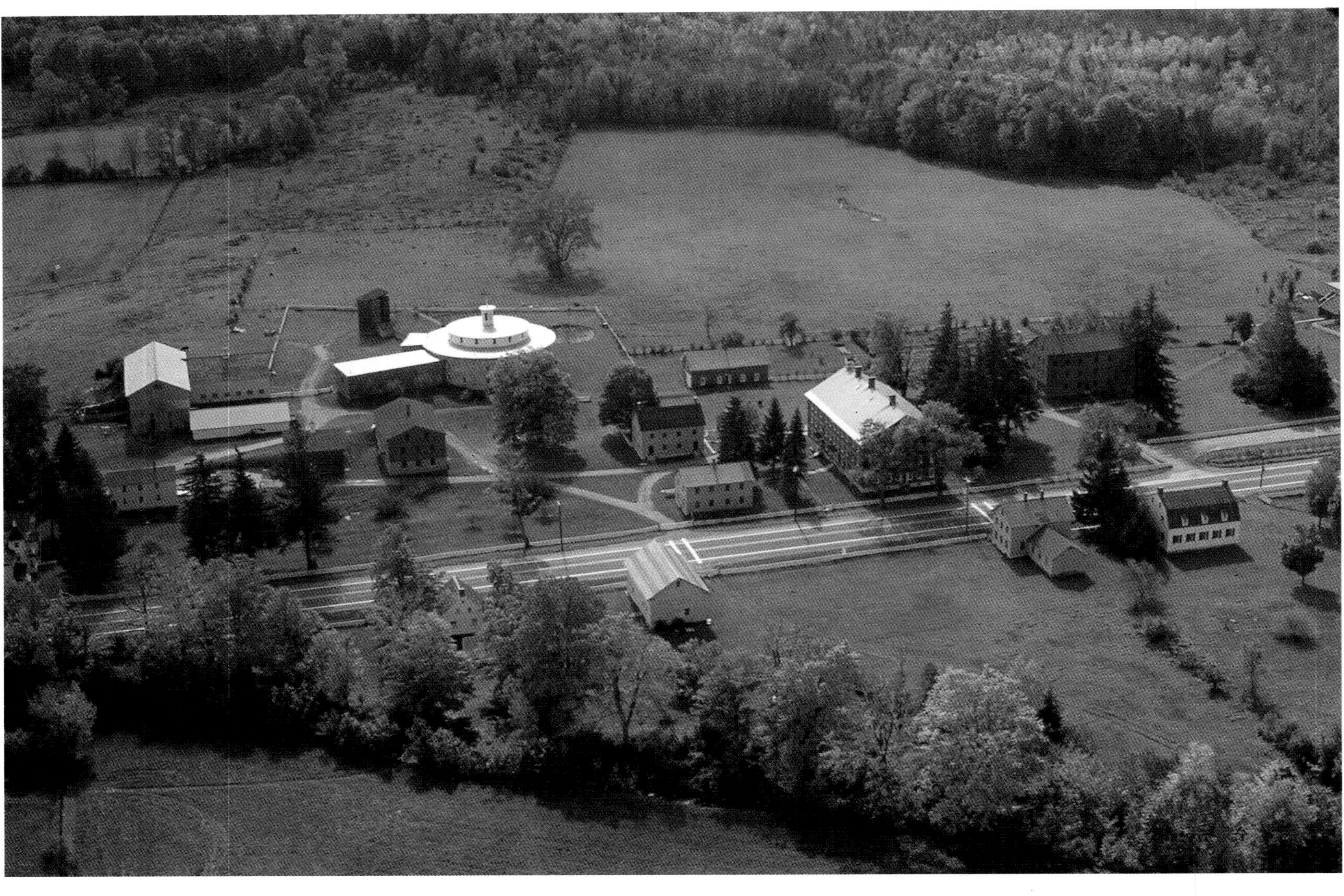

ABOVE:
Aerial view of Hancock Shaker Village, Pittsfield, MA

RIGHT:
View of Shaker Village, Pleasant Hill, KY
Photo by James Archambeault

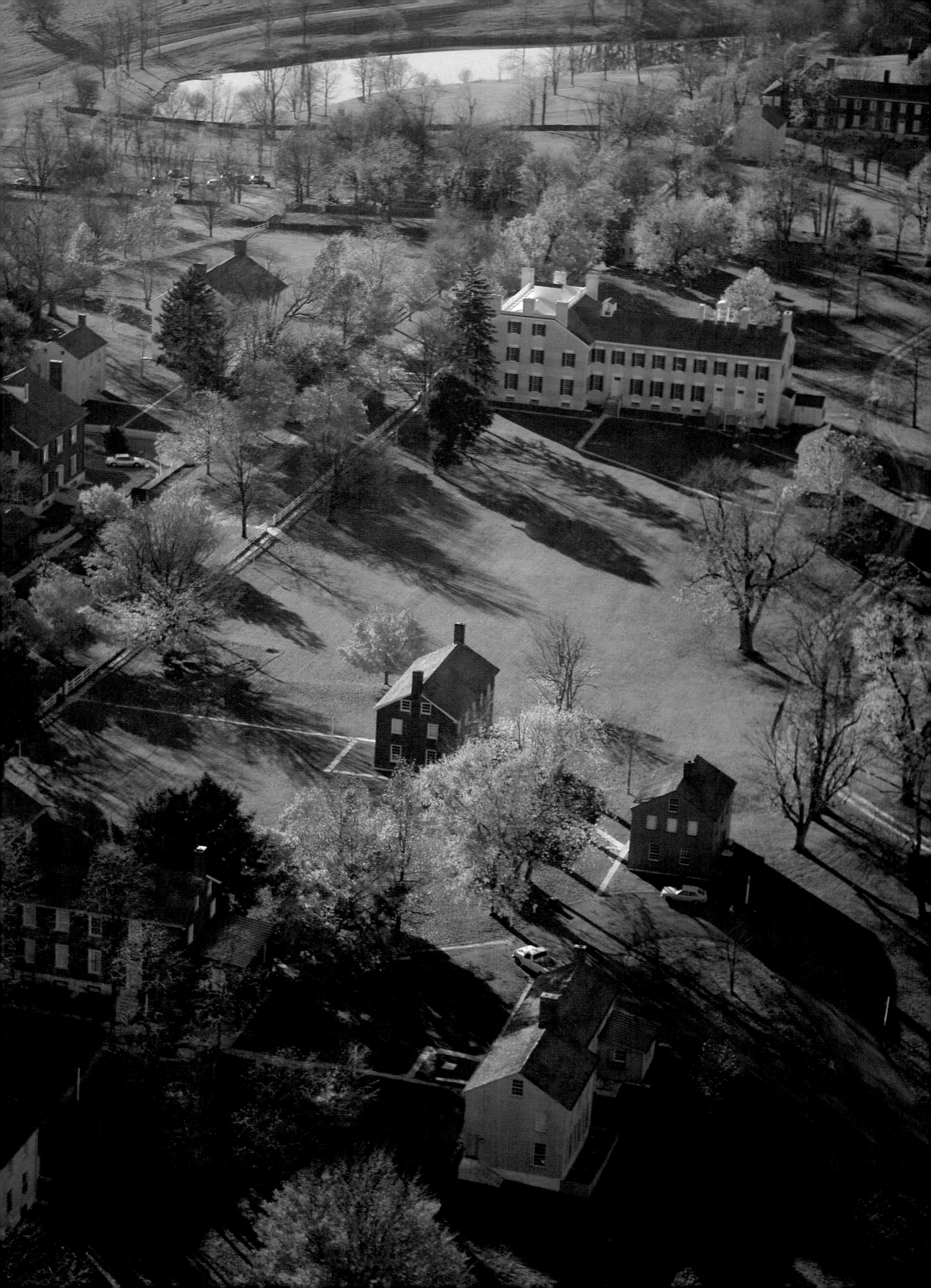

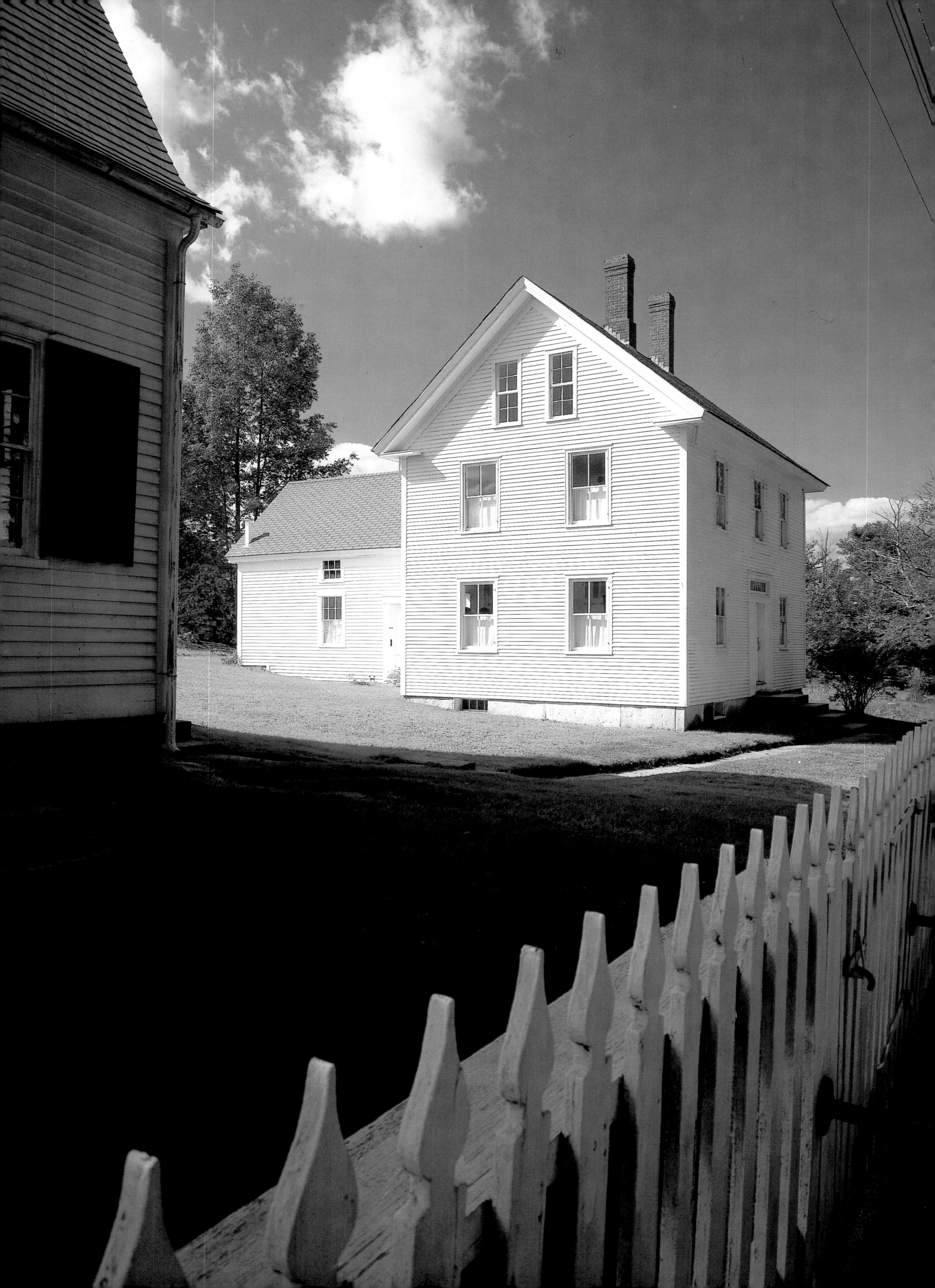

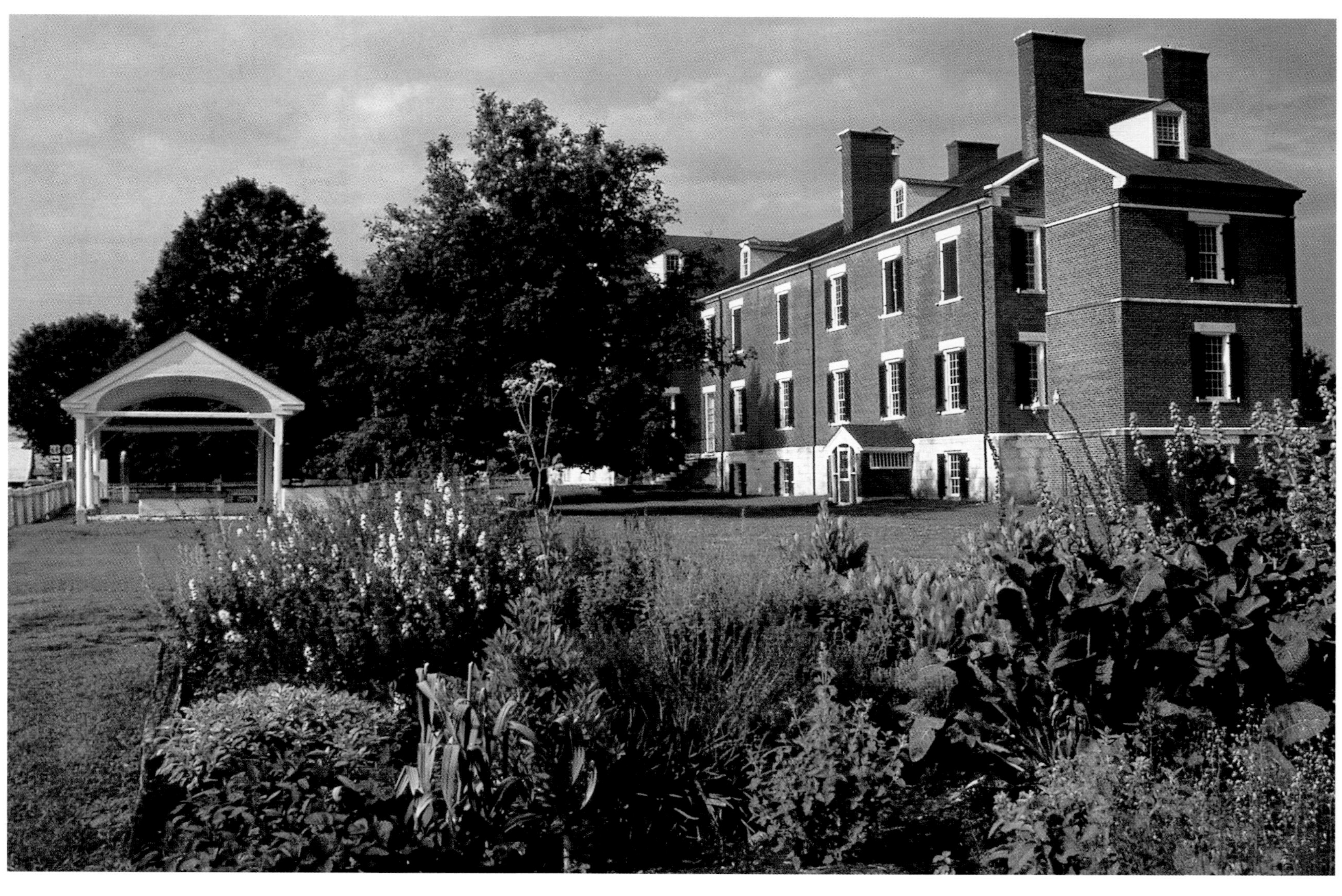

LEFT:
The Meetinghouse, 1794, and Ministry's Shop, 1839
Sabbathday Lake, ME
Photo by Brian Vanden Brink

ABOVE:
Centre Family Dwelling, 1824, and well house
from herb garden, South Union, KY
Photo courtesy Shakertown at South Union, KY

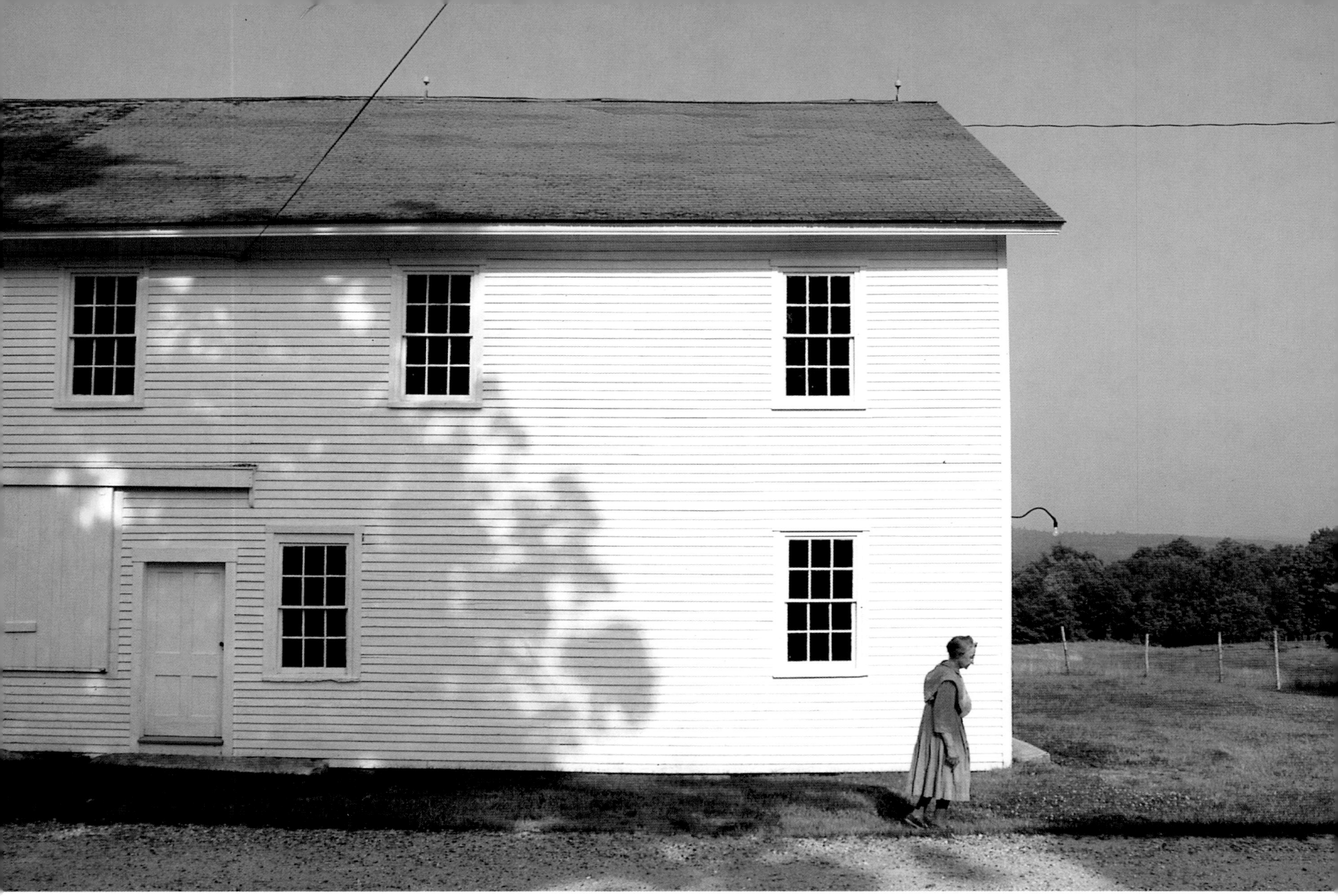

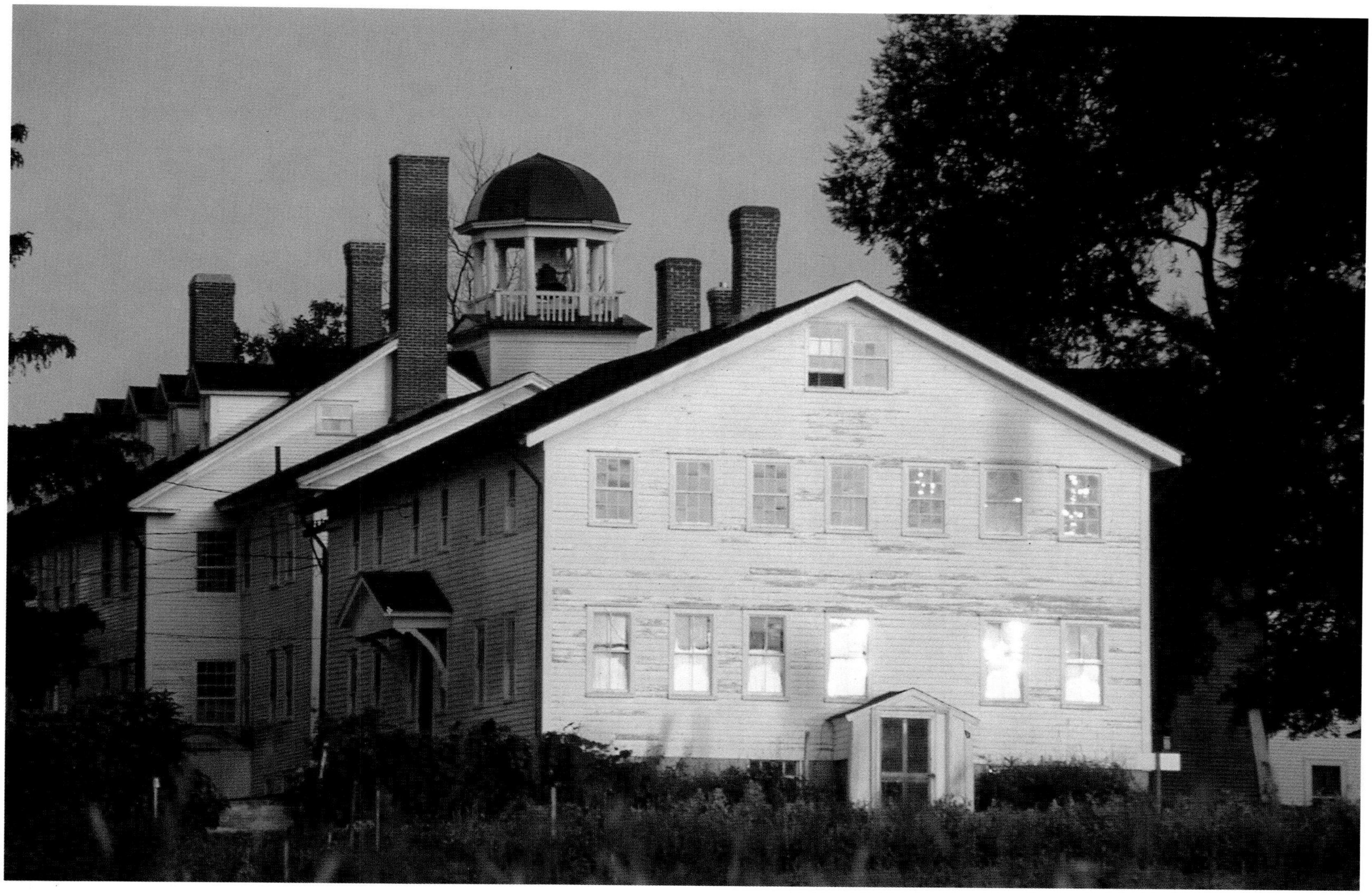

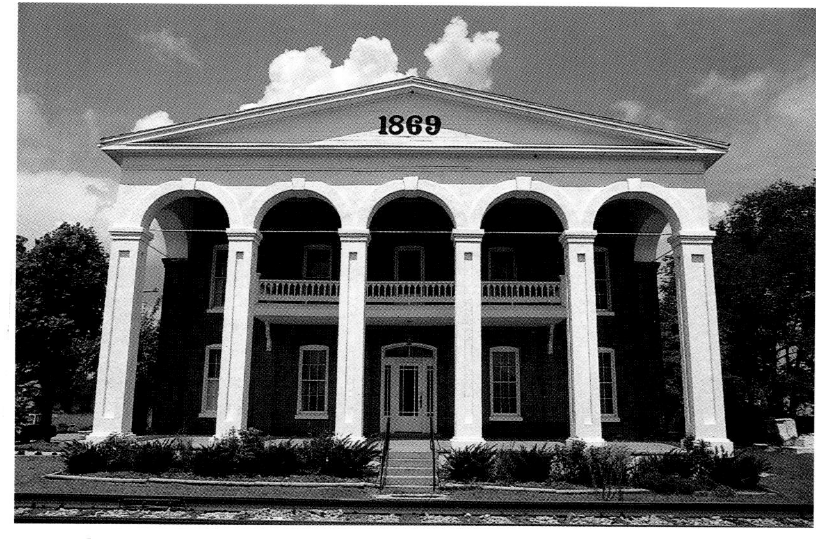

LEFT BOTH:
Scenes from Sabbathday Lake, ME, the only existing family of Shakers
Photos by Brian Vanden Brink

TOP:
Sisters' Shop and Laundry, 1816
Canterbury Shaker Village, Canterbury, NH
Photo by Todd Buchanan

ABOVE:
South Union's Shaker Tavern, built for commercial use, 1869
Photo courtesy Shakertown at South Union, KY

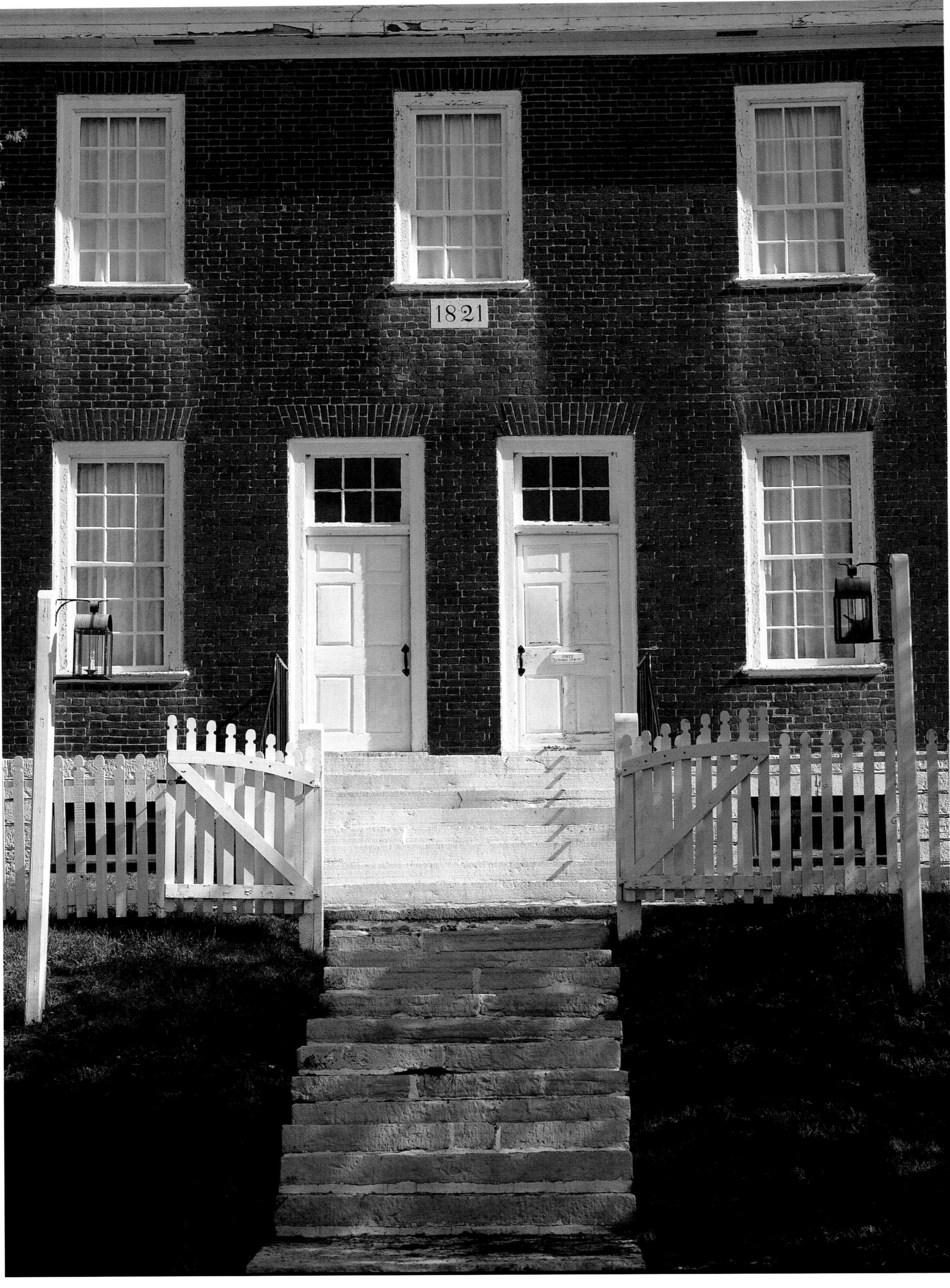
1821

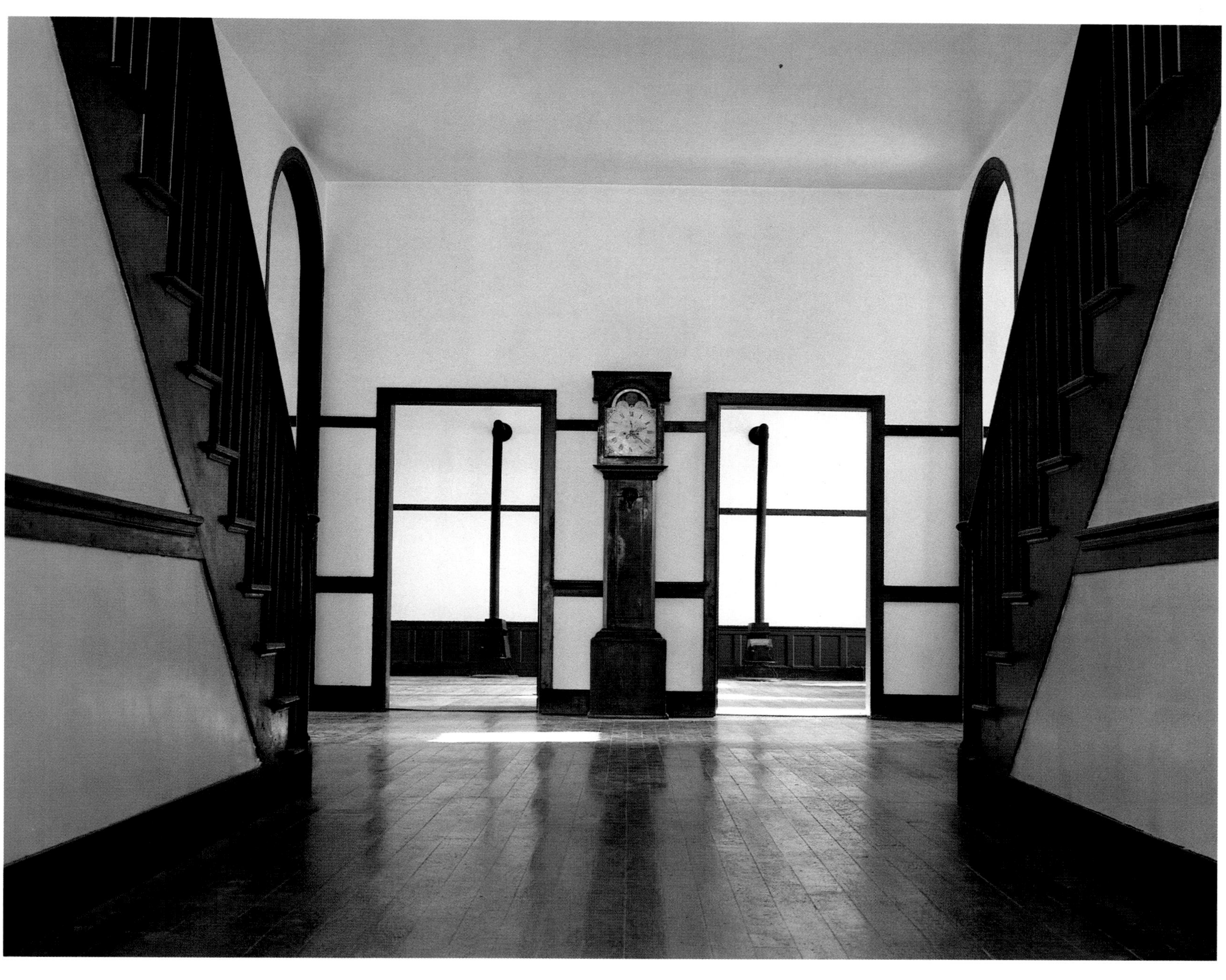

LEFT:
Pleasant Hill's West Family Dwelling, 1821-22
Pleasant Hill, KY
Photo by James Archambeault

ABOVE:
Centre Family Dwelling, 1824-34
Pleasant Hill, KY
Separate doorways illustrate the separation of the sexes
Photo by James Archambeault

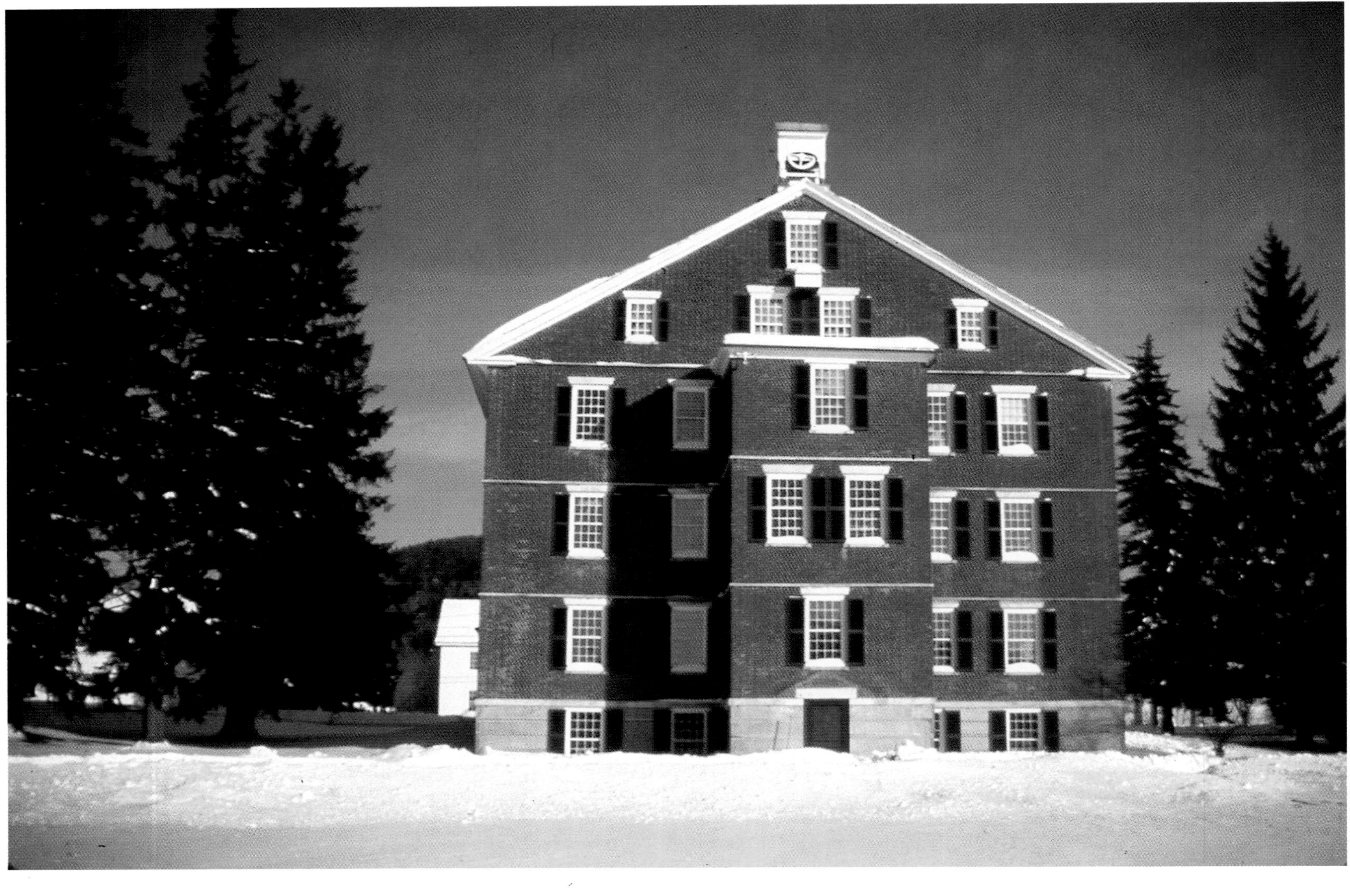

Brick Dwelling, Church Family, 1830
Hancock Shaker Village, Pittsfield, MA
Photo by Elizabeth Fitzsimmons

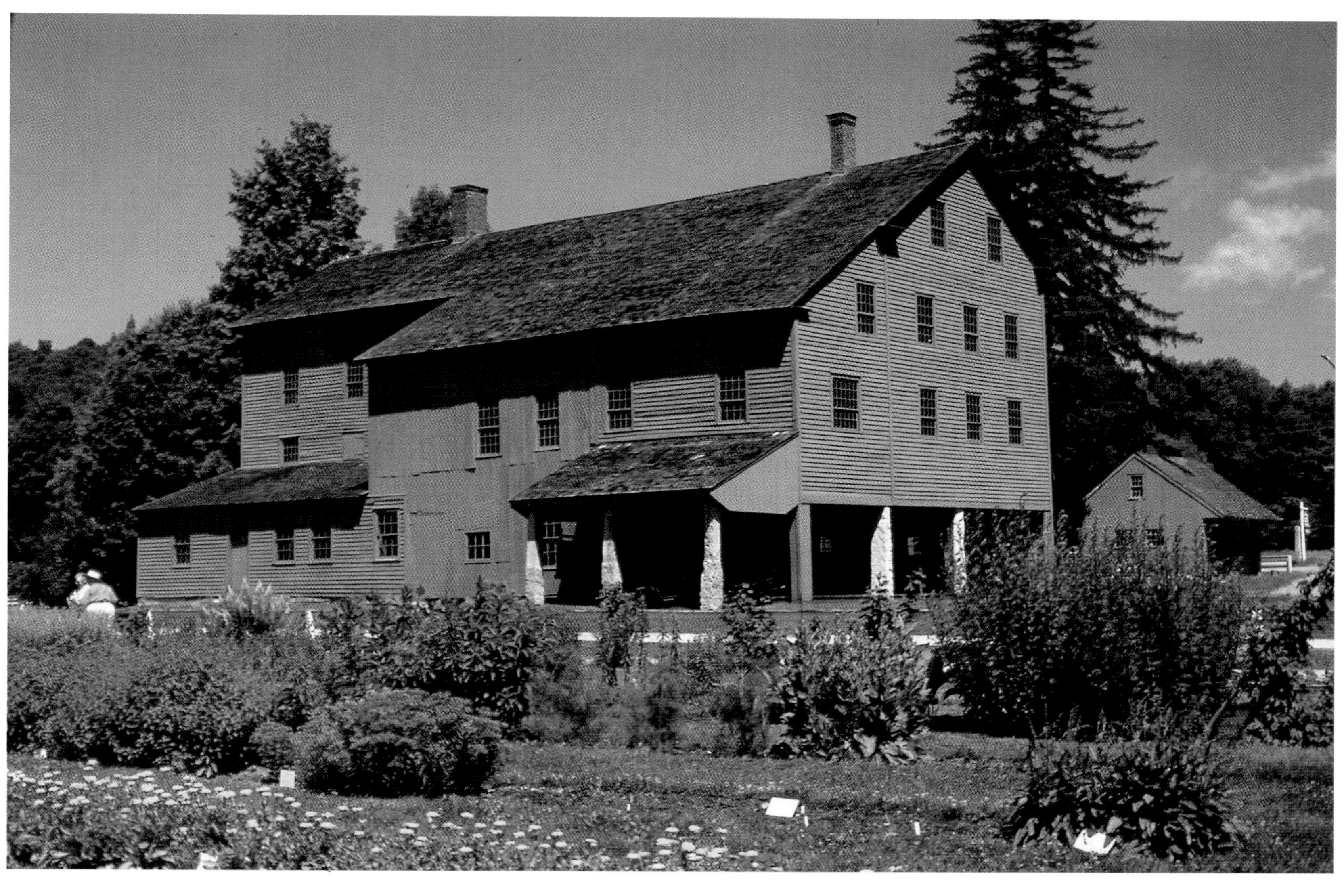

Laundry and Machine Shop, 1790, from herb garden
Hancock Shaker Village, Pittsfield, MA
Photo by Elizabeth Fitzsimmons

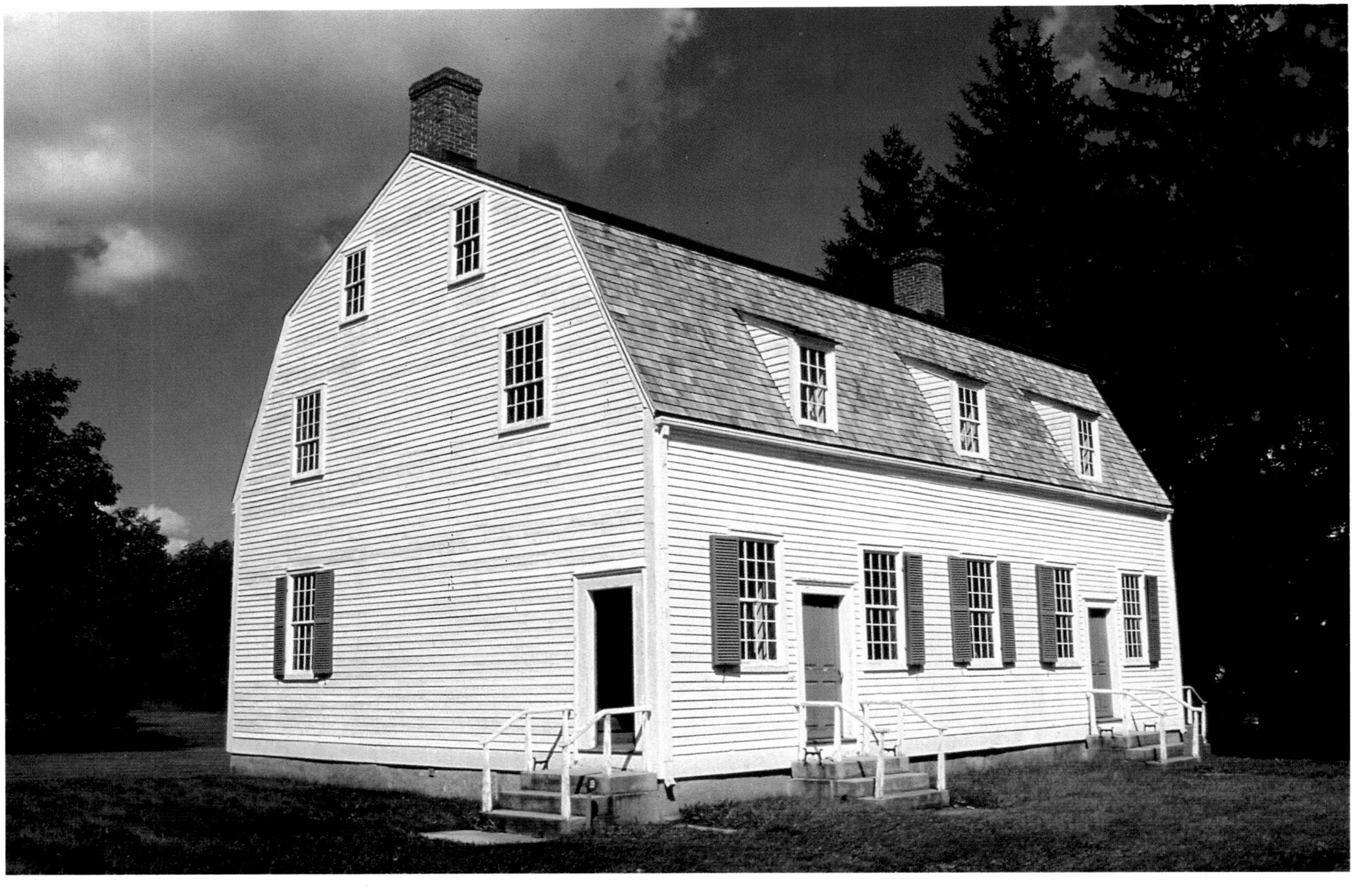

The Meetinghouse, 1793, at Hancock, was moved from the Shaker community at Shirley, MA
Hancock Shaker Village, Pittsfield, MA
Photo by Elizabeth Fitzsimmons

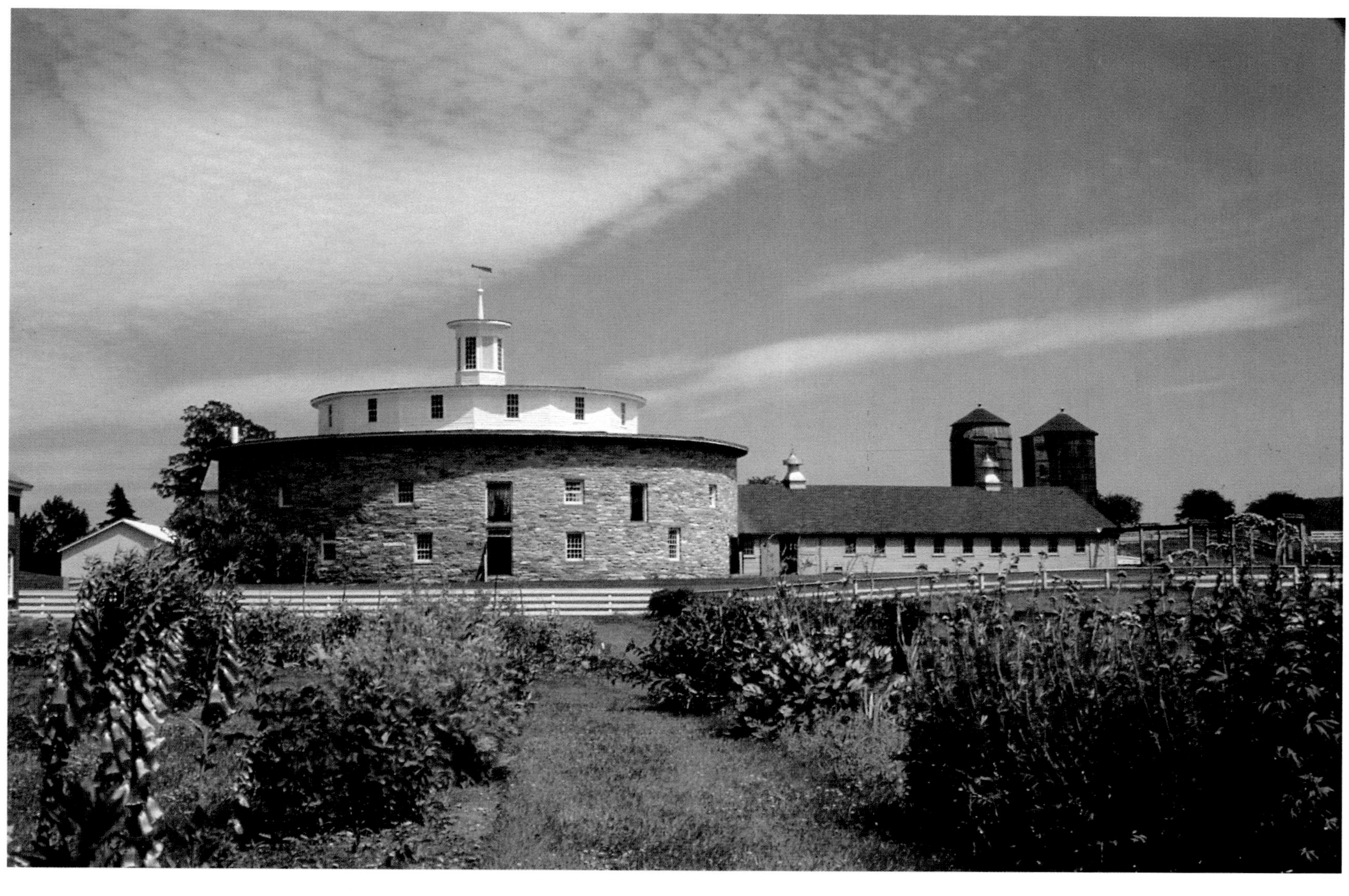

Round Stone Barn, 1826, from herb garden
Hancock Shaker Village, Pittsfield, MA
Photo by Elizabeth Fitzsimmons

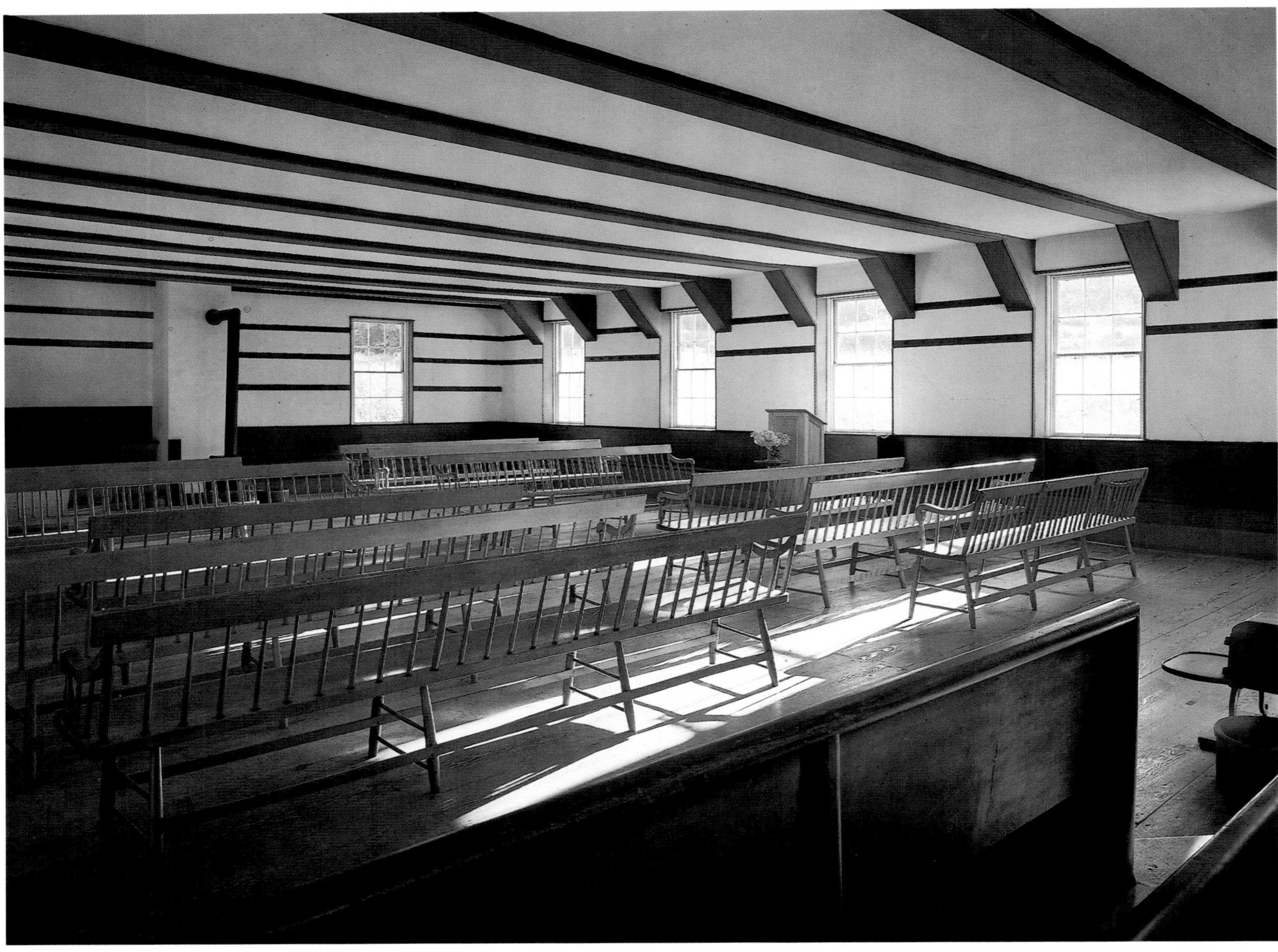

ABOVE AND RIGHT:
Interior views of the Meetinghouse, 1794, built by the Church Family at Sabbathday Lake, ME
Photos by Brian Vanden Brink

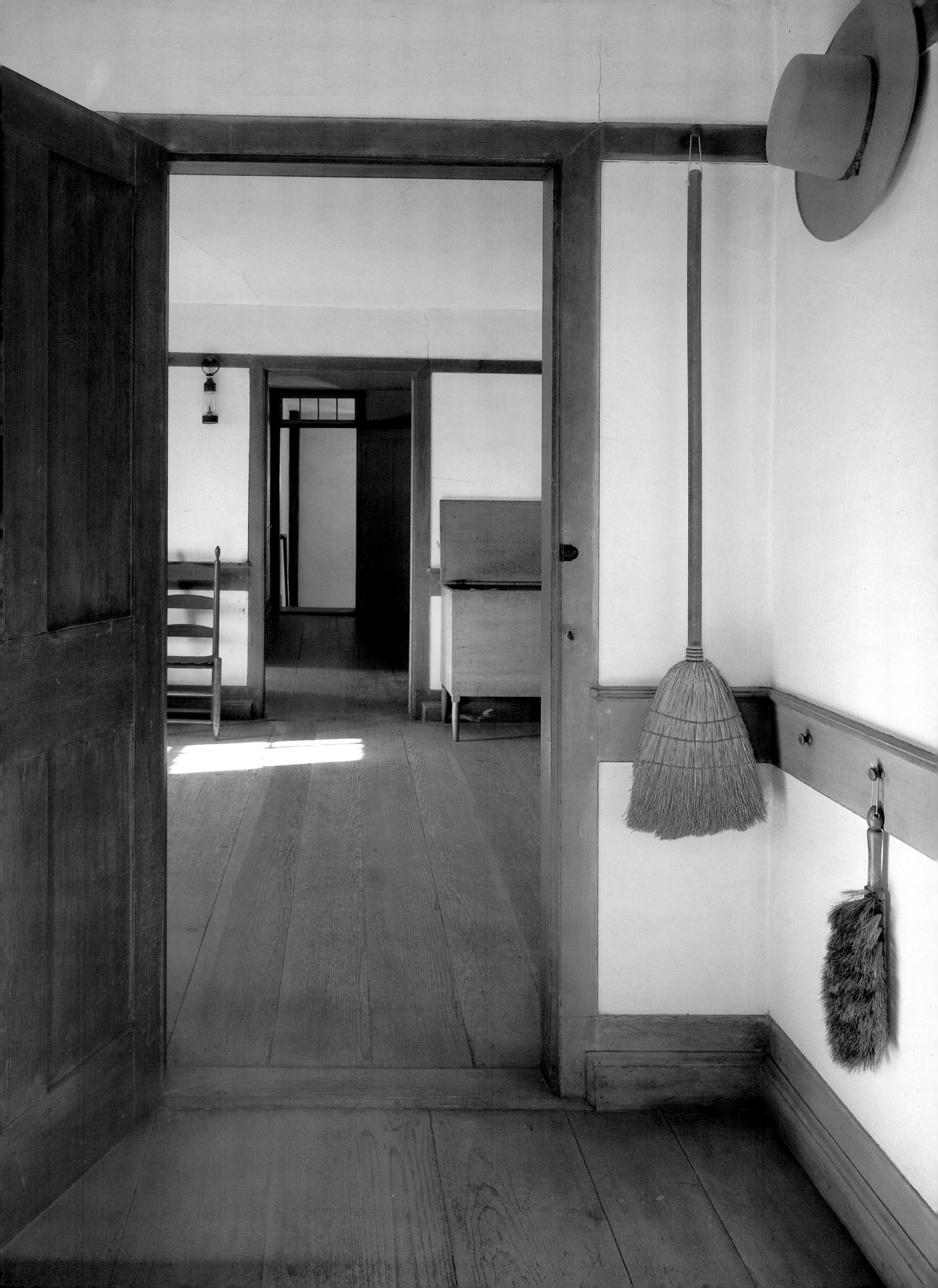

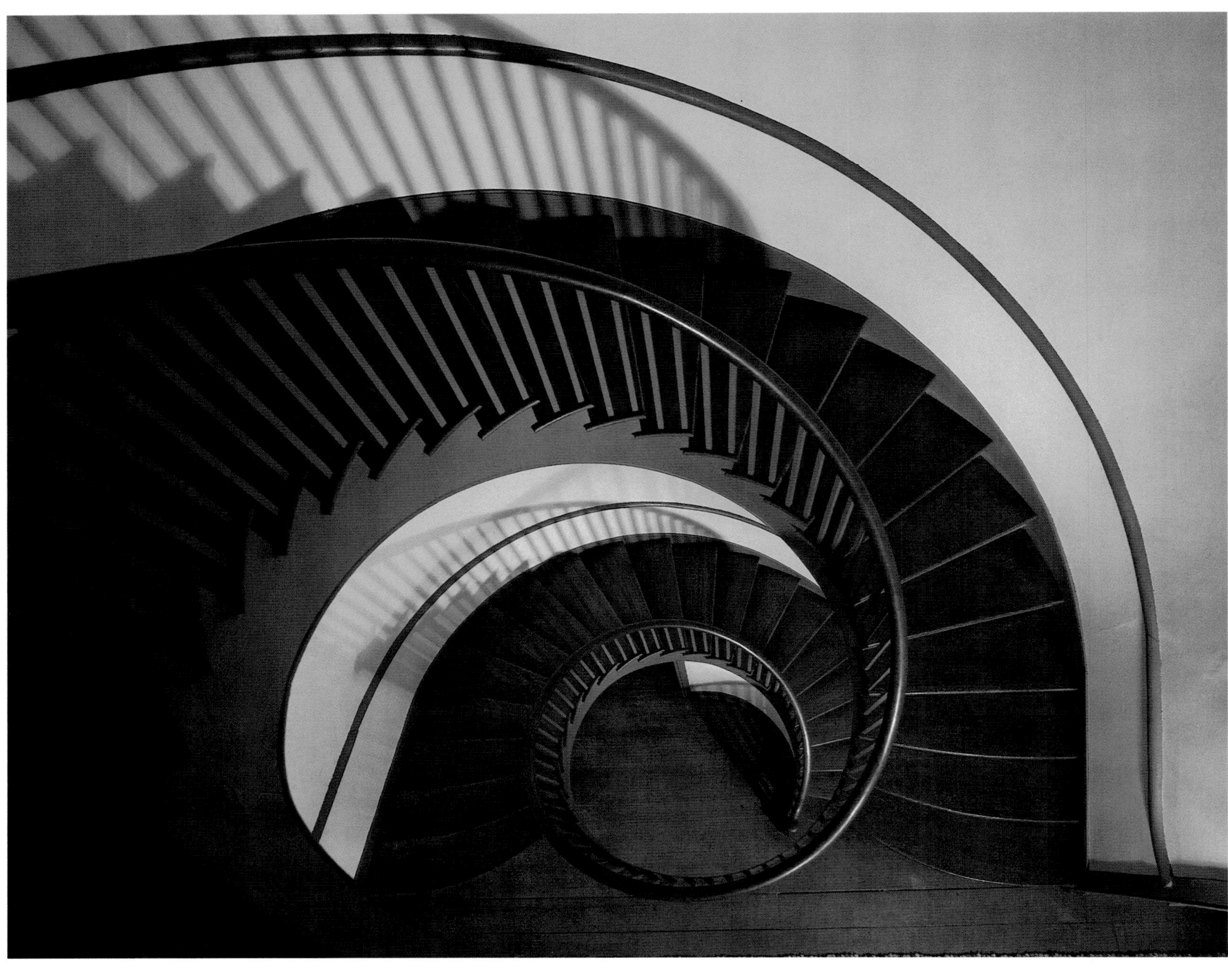

The Trustees' Office at Pleasant Hill, KY, 1839-41, features twin staircases that climb three floors
Photo by James Archambeault

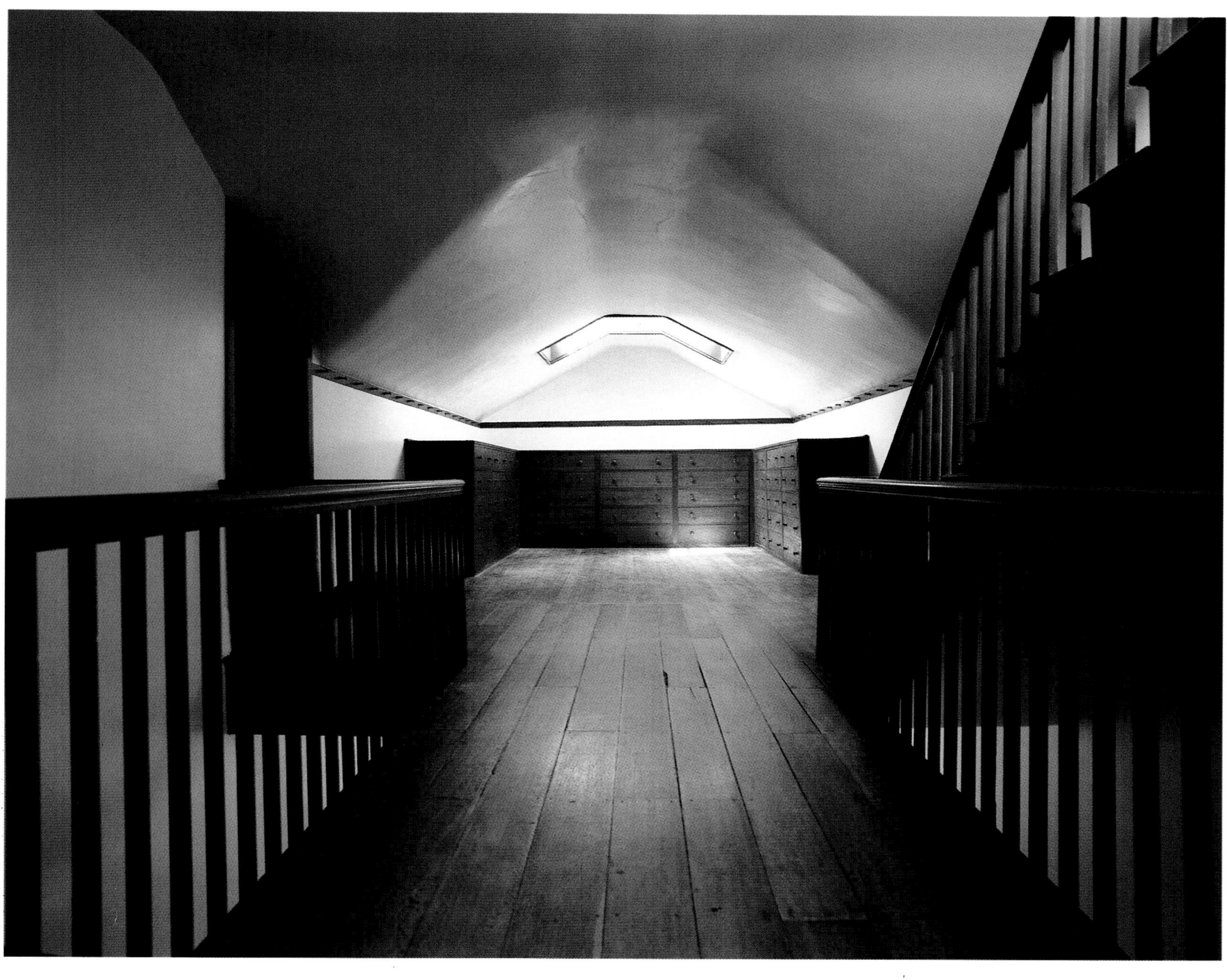

Dormered attic of Pleasant Hill's Centre Family Dwelling, 1824-34, with built-in poplar drawers for storage
Photo by James Archambeault

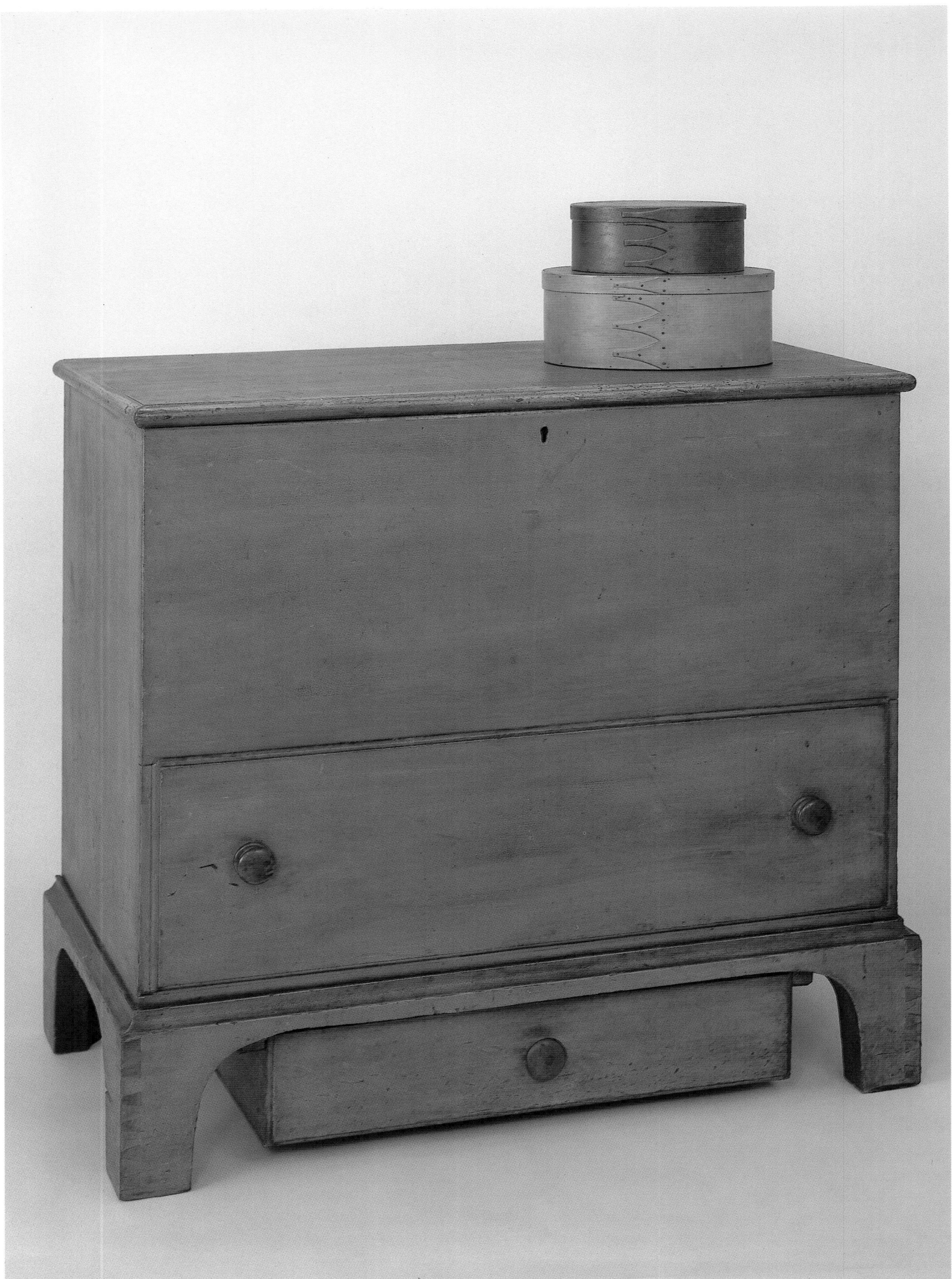

CHAPTER II

FURNITURE FOR LIVING

Among the many appealing quotes attributed to Mother Ann Lee is, "If I come back to earth again, I would like it to be as a chair." Although this is almost certainly an apocryphal aphorism, it is no less telling for what many people today associate with the Shakers: furniture. These pieces are now sold at auctions for many thousands of dollars, and are displayed in museums throughout the world. The gap between Mother Ann's concept and today's reality is only one of the many ironies surrounding Shaker furniture. To understand this, though, Shaker furniture must be defined and distinguished.

The original Shakers simply lived with the furniture they brought with them from the world around them. But even by the early 1780s some Shakers were making some of their own furniture. In part this was because their faith required them to give up all forms of worldly ostentation, and the best way they could do this was to make their own very basic pieces. There is no denying, though, that the basic types and forms of Shaker furniture then as later would derive from that made in the outside world. What distinguishes the Shakers' furniture were the modifications, refinements and details that they added.

Another thing about Shaker furniture that needs to be clarified is that it was not always or in all places the same style. This was inevitable when we consider that at one time or another all of the 20 or so Shaker communities made at least some pieces of furniture. Students of Shaker furniture tend to divide it into three major periods. Furniture made in the years up to about 1820 tended to be rather heavy, painted, and even a bit crude. Pieces made after 1860 tend to reflect the influence of the dominant style of the time, the Victorian style, marked by a darkness in the woods and finishes, a certain massiveness, and a fair amount of decorative elements. True students and collectors of Shaker material culture value furniture from both these periods.

However, it is the furniture made between 1820 and 1860, in what is known as the classical period, that most people consider to be the most typical examples of Shaker furniture. Furthermore, it is primarily the furniture made in the Northeast – the original Shaker villages of New England and upstate New York – that conforms to the strict classical style. Furniture made in the western communities tended to reflect more local traditions. The classical Shaker furniture of the Northeast, in turn, tended to draw on the traditions prevalent there, both in the design and techniques of construction.

Classical Shaker furniture falls into two basic types – that used in shops or for work, and that used for domestic living. The former includes the various worktables and counters, spinning wheels and looms, sewing stands, shelves and drying racks. The best known pieces in the latter category include chairs (including rocking chairs), benches and settees, tables, beds, stands, desks, cabinets, and chests. Also included among this type are clocks, mirrors, screens, cradles, stools, and commodes. There are a number of features that characterize classical Shaker furniture. White pine was the wood most commonly used, but hard woods (maple, walnut, cherry, ash, and oak among others) were used for many of the finer pieces. In order to let the natural wood grain show, shellacs, varnish, and light stains were used, but paint was also used; during the classical period, paint was usually thinned and used more like a stain or wash. The subtle turning of legs and supporting members was another characteristic, as were such methods of joining as the exposed dovetailing and mortise-and-tenon.

All these features, however admirably executed, do not make Shaker furniture totally different from at least some furniture made elsewhere in America. There are several elements, however, that the Shakers did seem to introduce: large wooden casters or rollers on beds, the ball-and-socket on the back post of some sidechairs that allowed for tilting back on the chair, certain shapes of table legs and bracing, drawers in unexpected locations, twin pieces such as double-desks or sewing stands for two, and colored tape used for woven chair seats.

Although most Shaker furniture of all periods and locales was handmade by individual craftsmen, this does not mean that they did not take advantage of tools or technology. They bought lathes, saws, and various tools as well as some pieces of hardware, and devised new or improved tools and gadgets.

Of all the Shaker furniture, it is the simple slat-back sidechair that became the best known. By the 1870s, these chairs were so widely admired that the New Lebanon, New York, community began to mass produce them and sell them to the outside world – even through catalogues and known retail outlets. They continued selling these chairs into the 1930s in what was effectively a factory operation to earn money to support the dwindling Shaker community. Meanwhile, in the years after the 1860s, some Shaker villages went in another direction, and instead of anonymous workmen replicating a traditional style, they supported known individuals who designed individual pieces that reflected the Victorian styles of the outer world. Henry Green of the Alfred, Maine, village is probably the best known of these master furniture makers. This final period also produced a number of unusual, one-of-a-kind pieces, indicative of a relaxing of the traditional laws throughout all aspects of Shaker practice.

What finally characterizes Shaker furniture is its unadorned simplicity. But it would be wrong to imagine that this was some self-conscious aesthetic goal on the part of the craftsmen. Shakers were exhorted to strive for simplicity. One of their several written laws was, "(Whatever is fashioned, let) it be plain and simple, and of the good and substantial quality. . . unembellished by any superfluities, which add nothing to its goodness or durability." This advice was rooted in the Shakers' stress on practicality, which in turn was rooted in their religious faith. Indeed, the final irony of the fate of Shaker furniture may be that in their search to eliminate aesthetic elements, the Shakers produced work that we today consider examples of simple beauty.

Low chest with drawers and oval boxes
Hancock Shaker Village, Pittsfield, MA
Photo by Paul Rocheleau

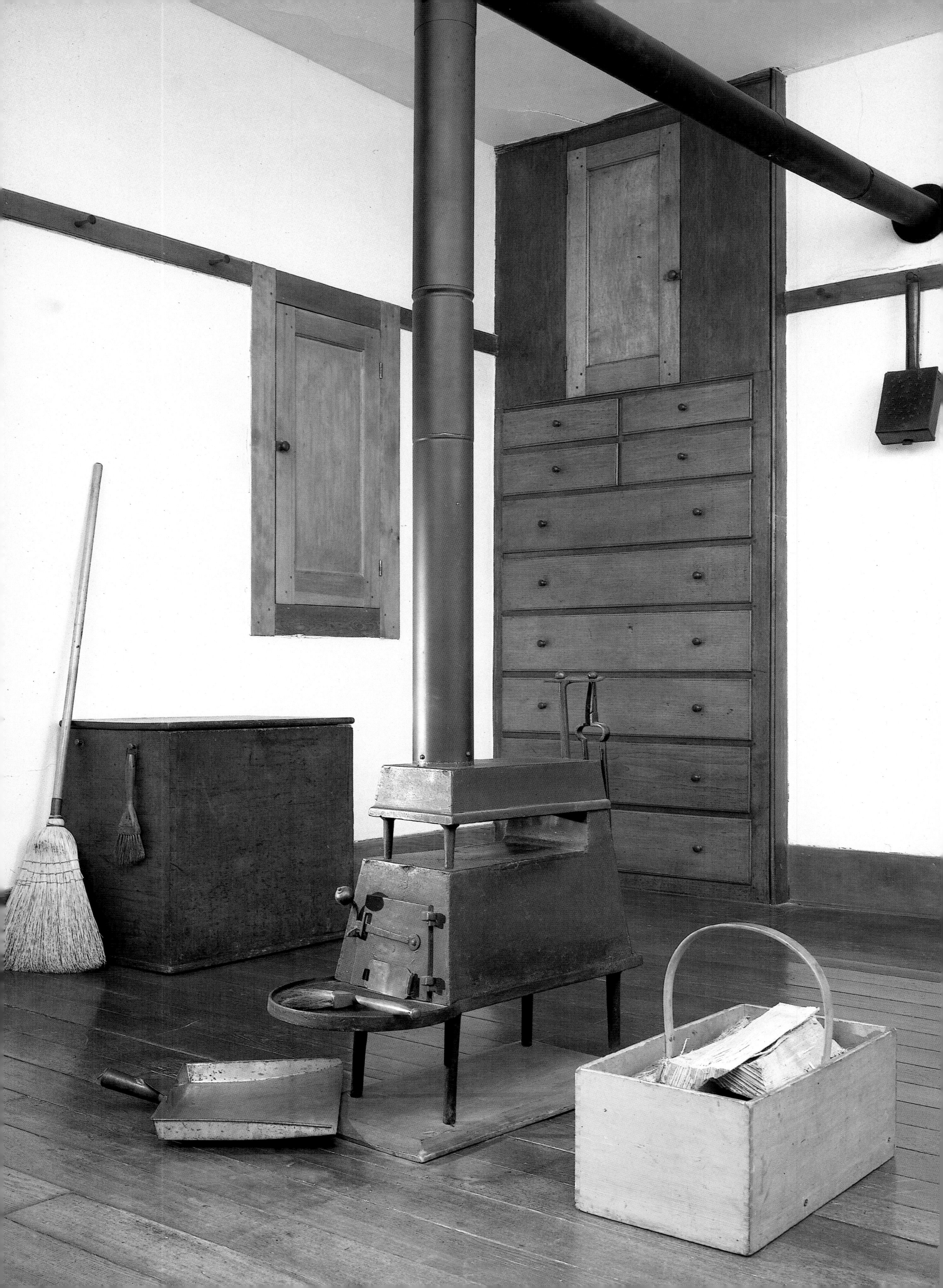

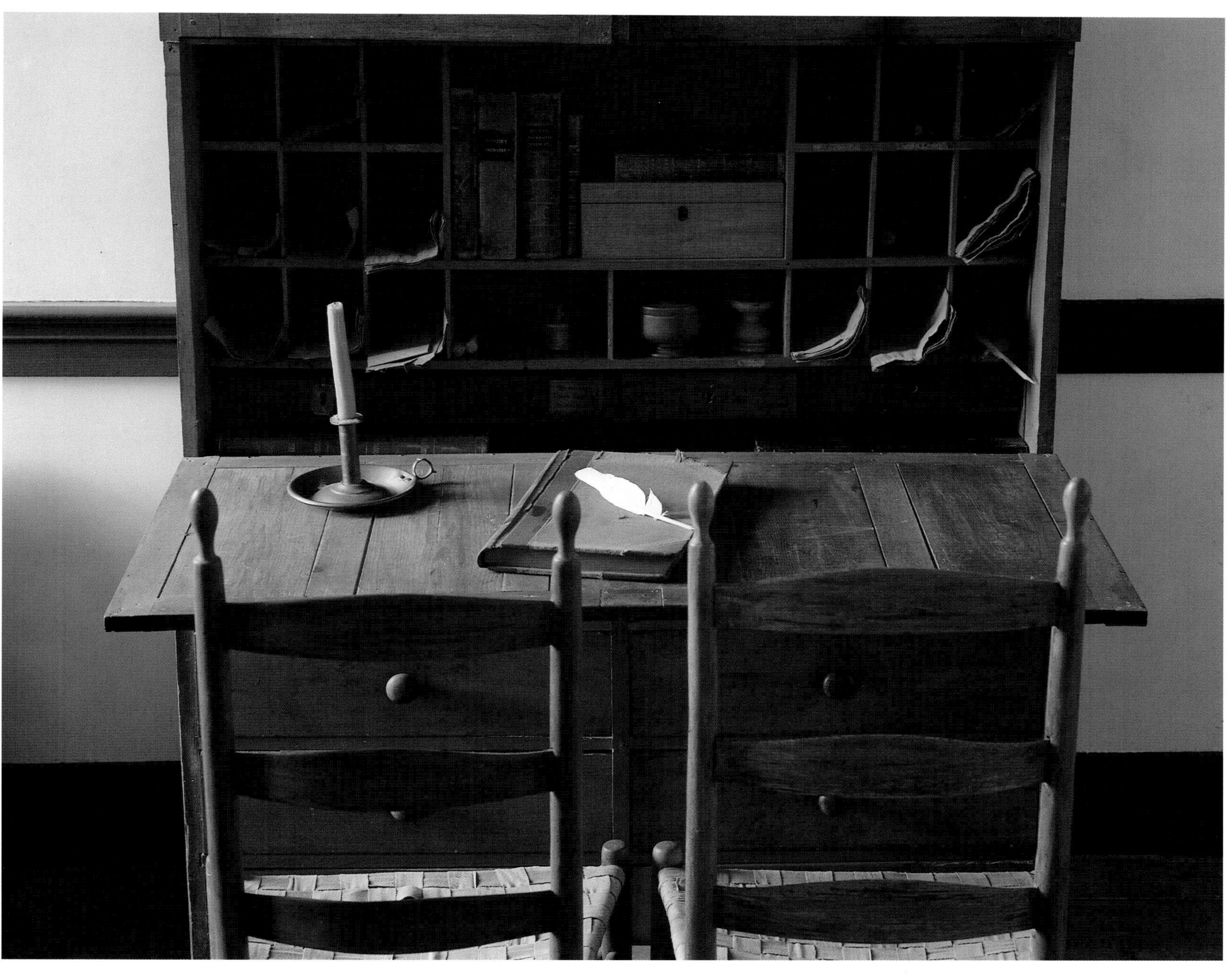

LEFT:
Built-in cupboards with wood stove and accessories, Brick Dwelling
Hancock Shaker Village, Pittsfield, MA
Photo by Paul Rocheleau

ABOVE:
Writing desk, Pleasant Hill, KY
Photo by James Archambeault

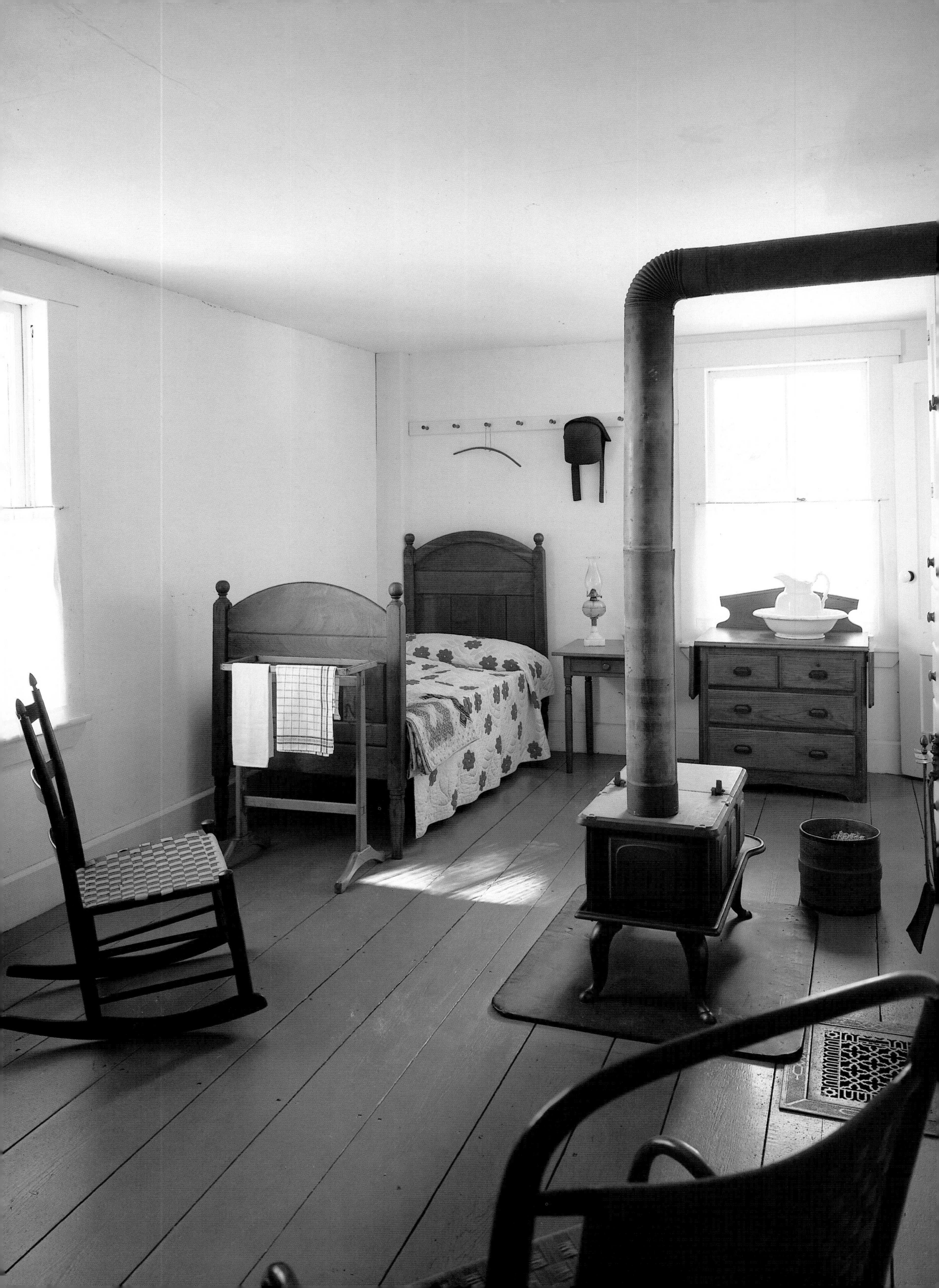

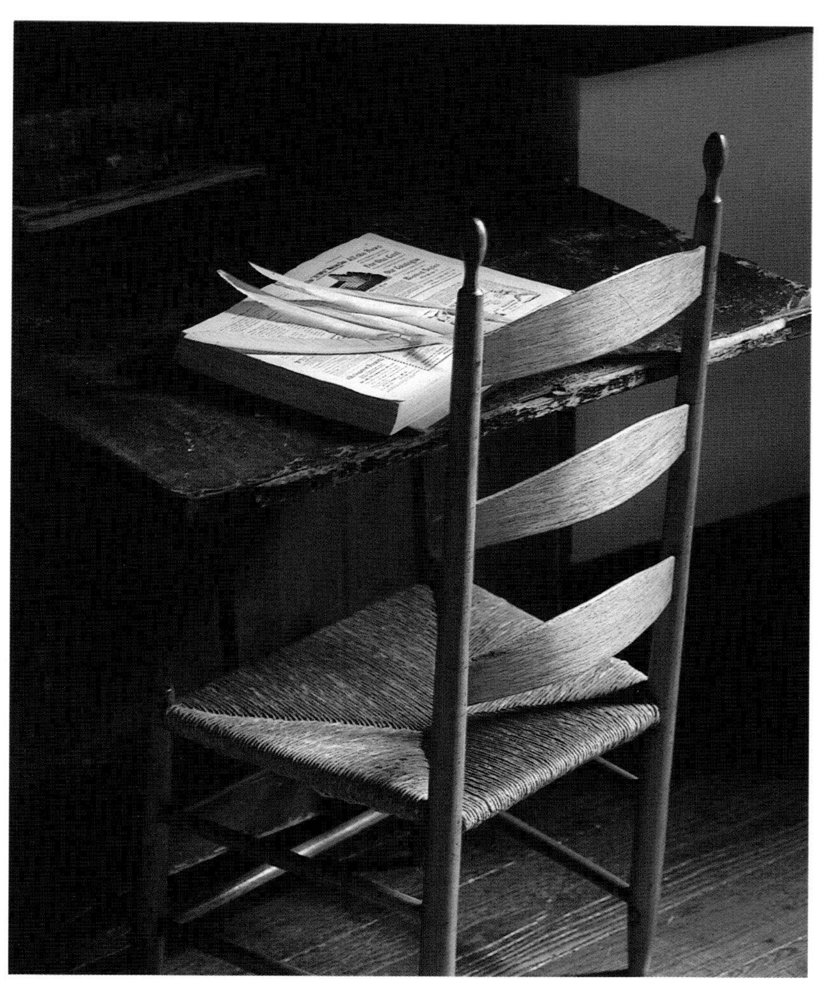

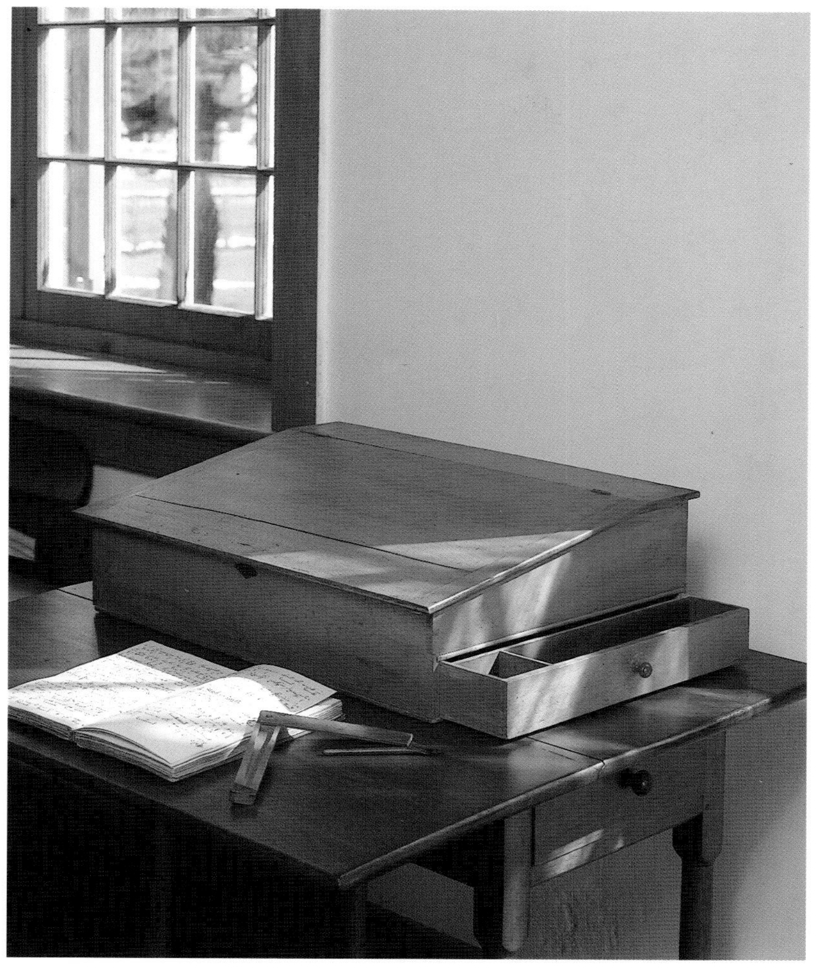

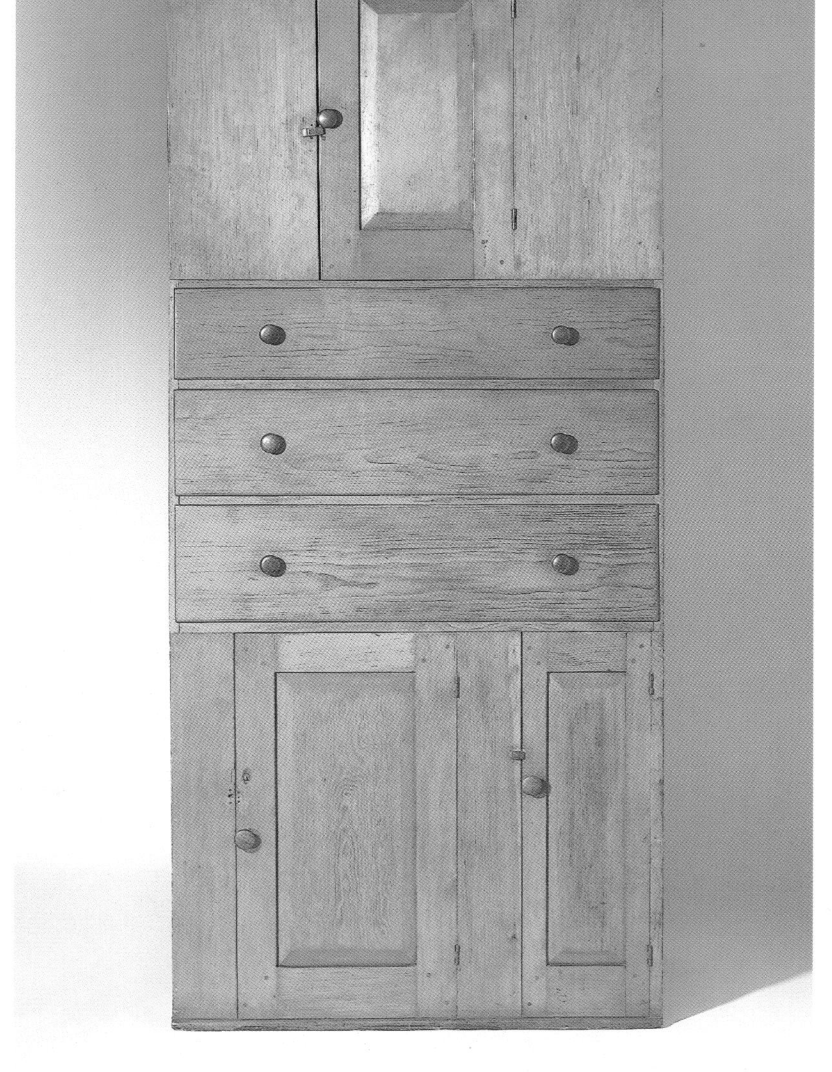

LEFT:
Shaker "retiring" room at Sabbathday Lake, ME
Photo by Brian Vanden Brink

ABOVE LEFT:
Desk and rush seat chair, Pleasant Hill, KY
Photo by James Archambeault

ABOVE RIGHT:
Shaker writing box with side drawer
Hancock Shaker Village, Pittsfield, MA
Photo by Paul Rocheleau

RIGHT:
Casepiece with cupboards at bottom and top, drawers in middle
Hancock Shaker Village, Pittsfield, MA
Photo by Paul Rocheleau

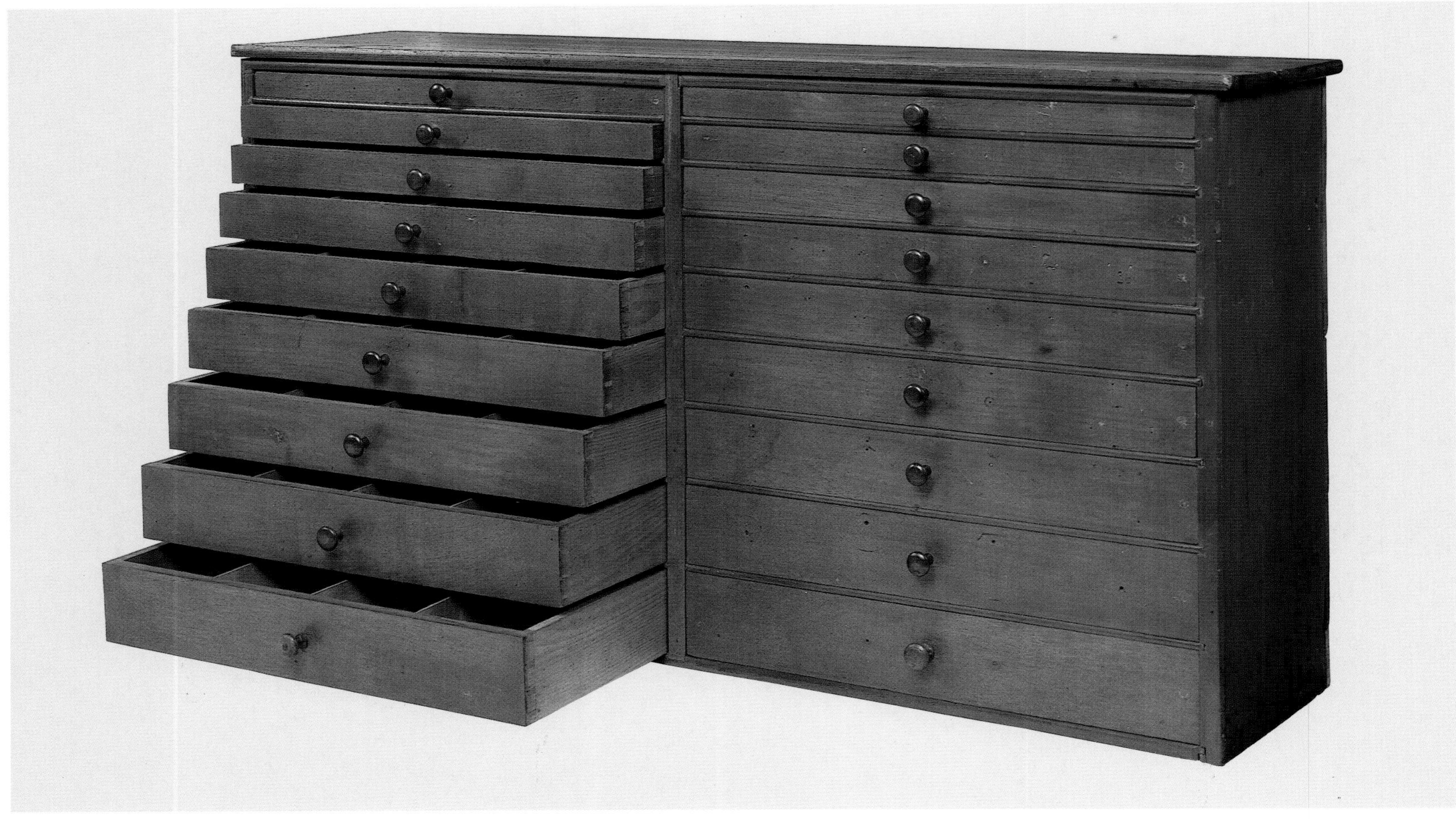

ABOVE:
Case of drawers, c. 1825-50, from the Shaker community at New Lebanon, NY
The Shaker Museum and Library, Old Chatham, NY
Photo by Paul Rocheleau

ABOVE RIGHT:
Rocking chairs with arms
Hancock Shaker Village, Pittsfield, MA
Photo by Paul Rocheleau

RIGHT:
Double dropleaf table and side chairs with tilters
Hancock Shaker Village, Pittsfield, MA
Photo by Paul Rocheleau

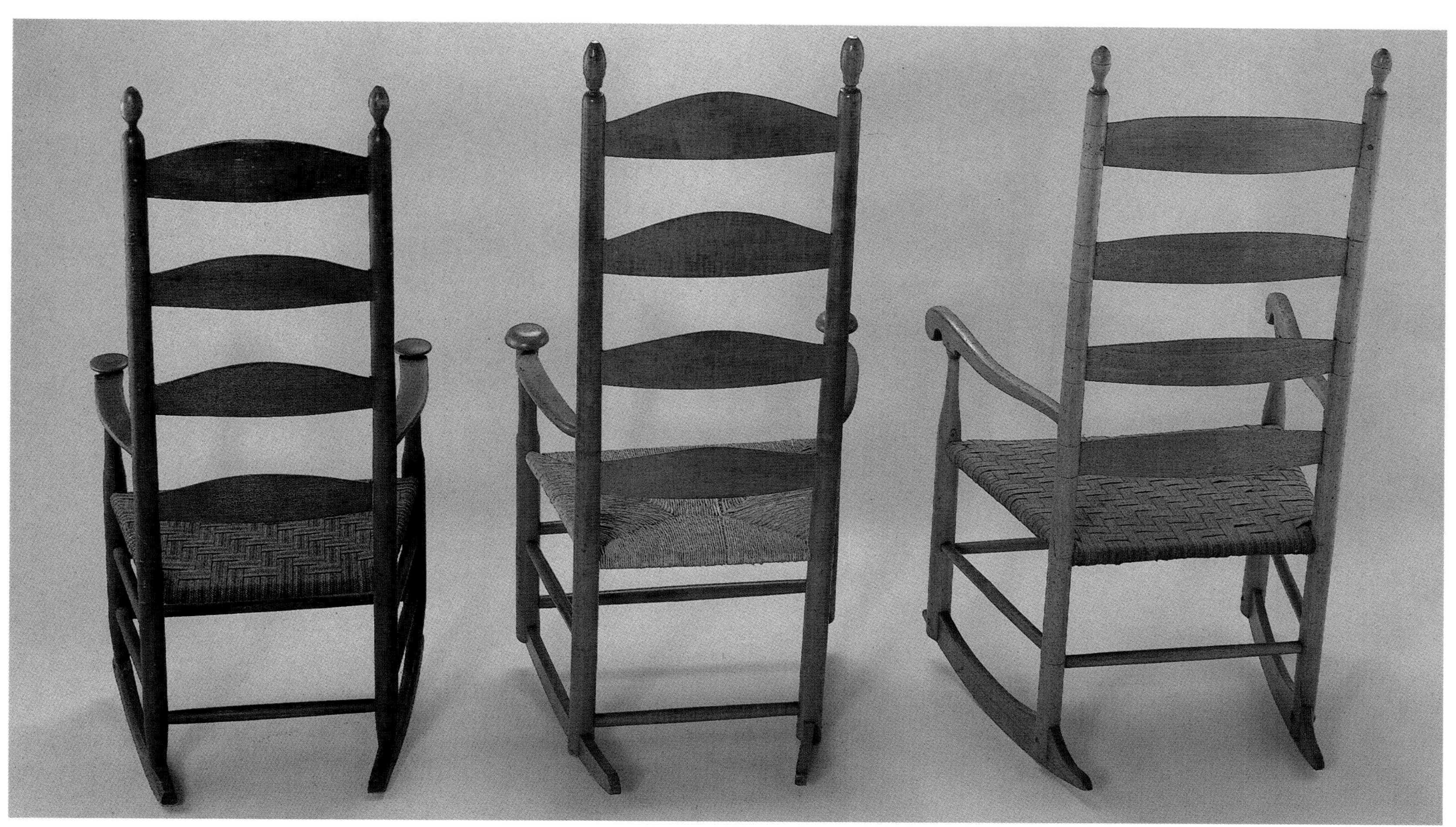

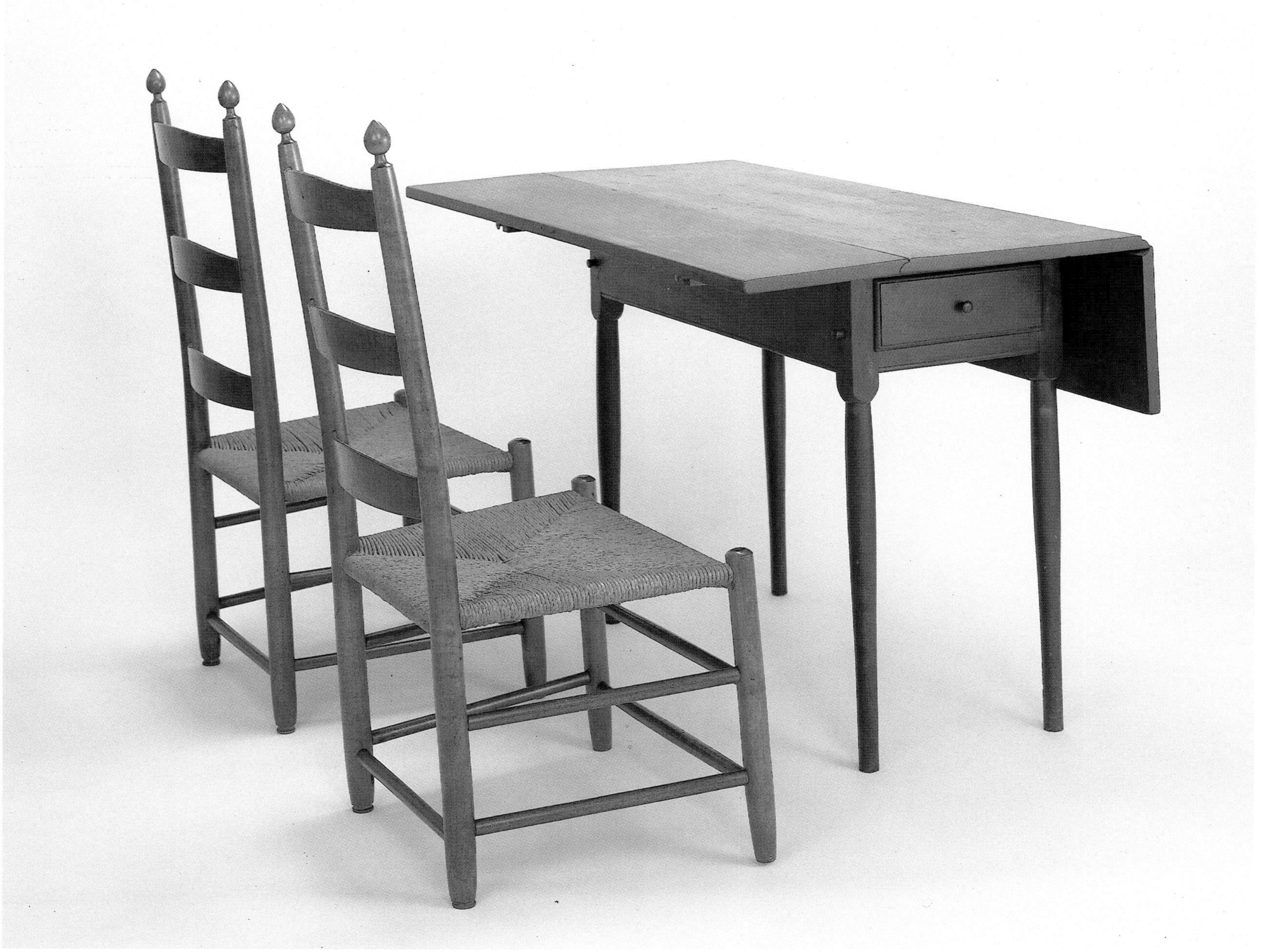

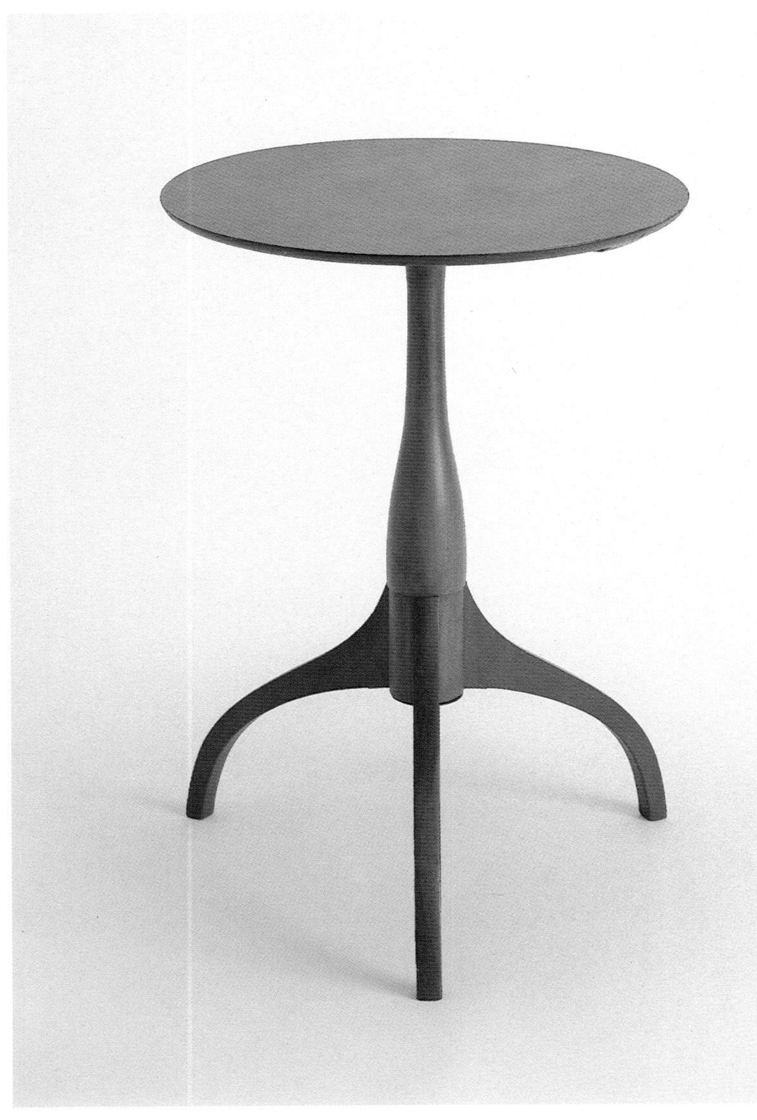

LEFT:
Tripod stand, c. 1820-30, from Mount Lebanon, NY
Hancock Shaker Village, Pittsfield, MA
Photo by Paul Rocheleau

BOTTOM:
Green bed in Brethren's Retiring Room
Hancock Shaker Village, Pittsfield, MA
Photo by Paul Rocheleau

RIGHT:
Sewing desks and table swift
Hancock Shaker Village, Pittsfield, MA
Photo by Michael Fredericks

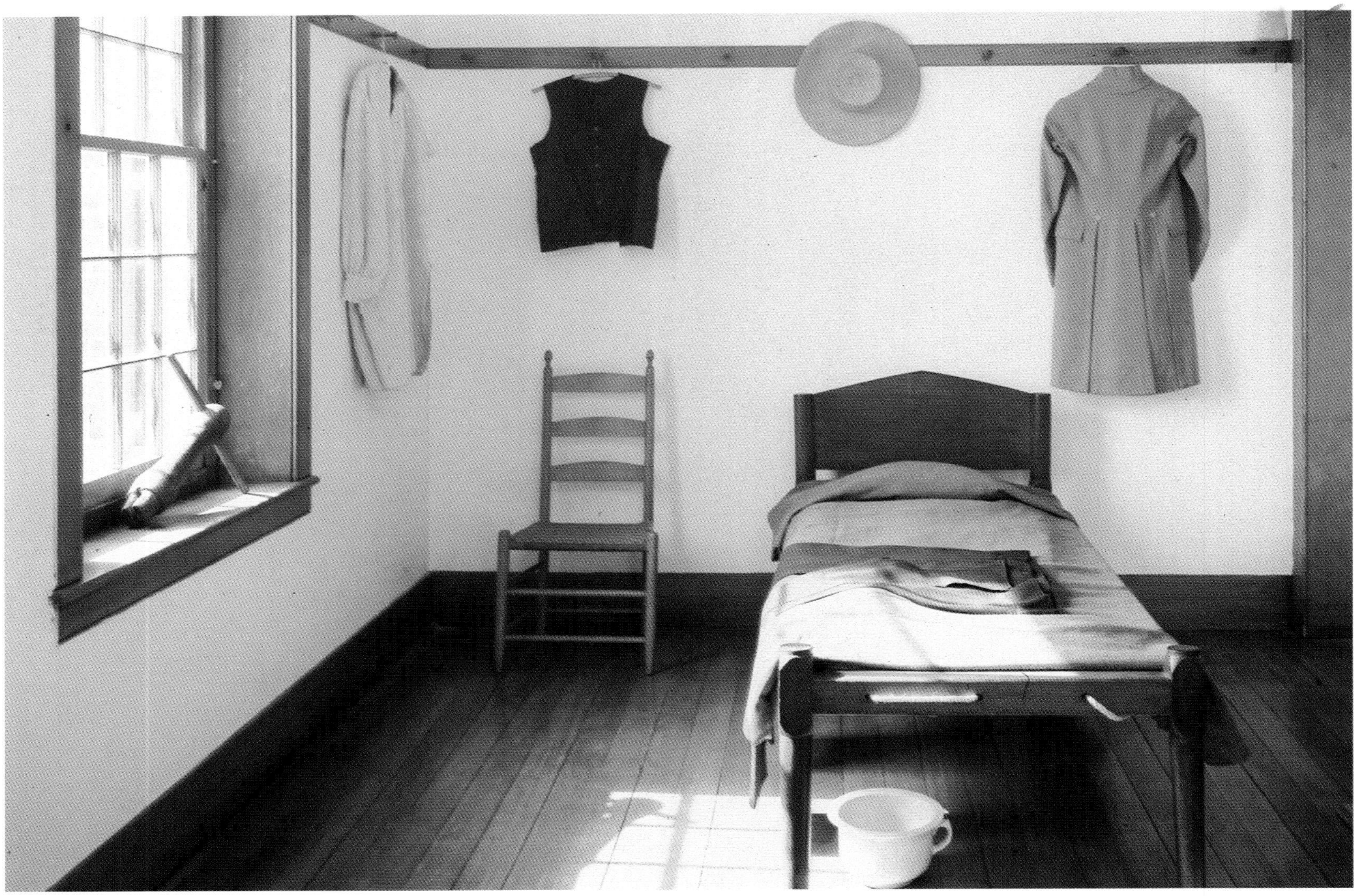

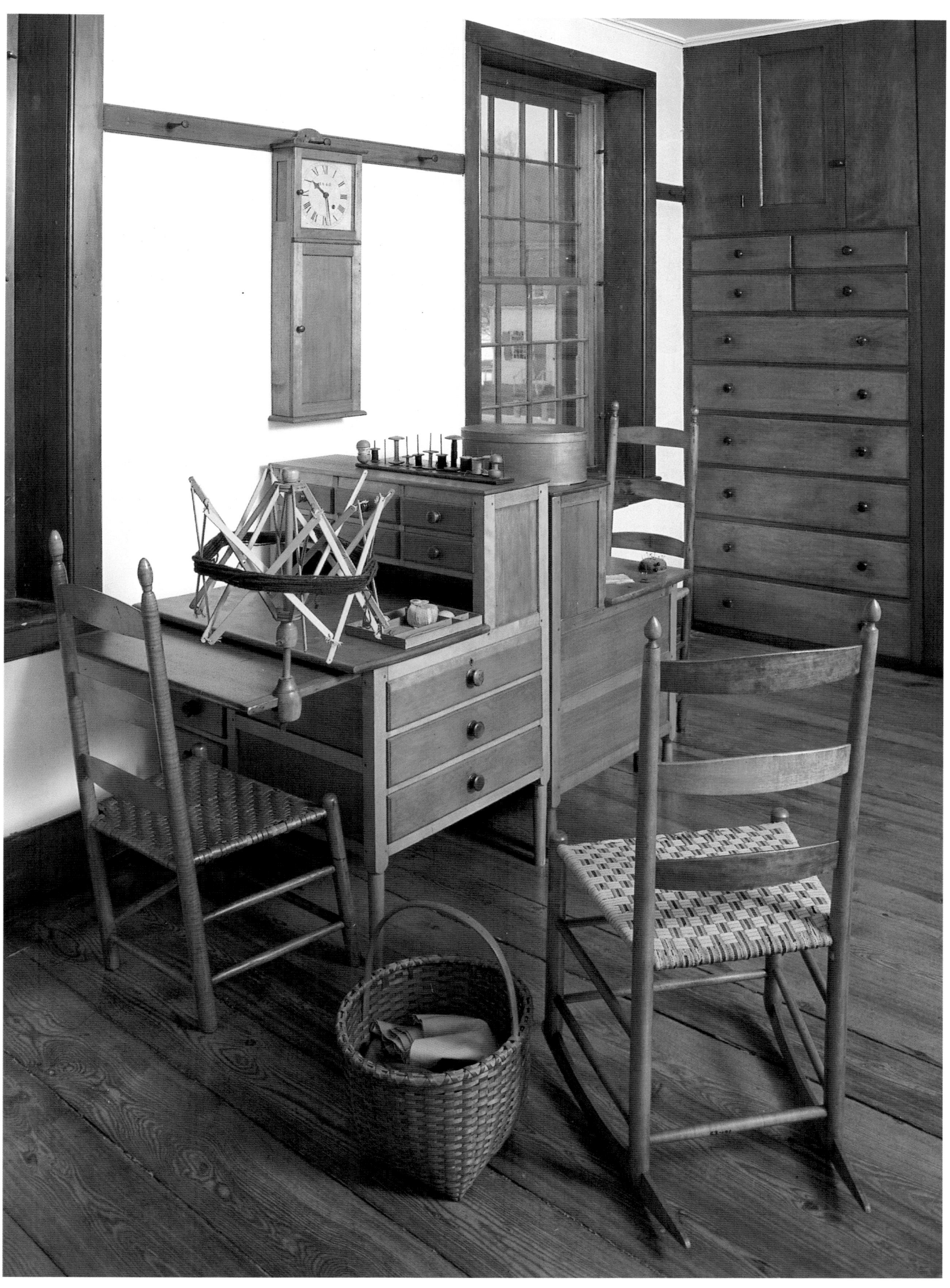

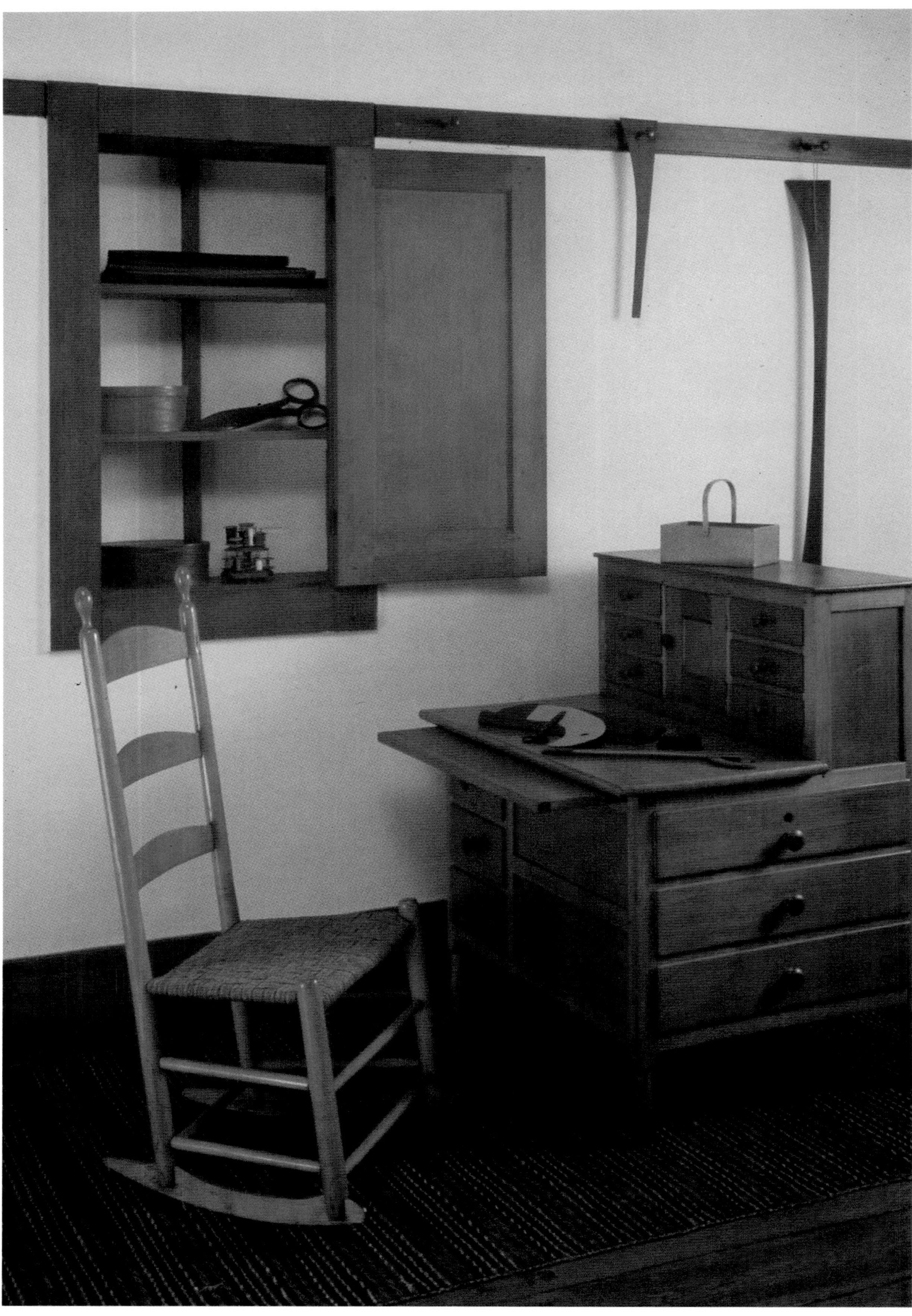

ABOVE:
Sisters' sewing desk
Hancock Shaker Village, Pittsfield, MA
Photo by Paul Rocheleau

ABOVE RIGHT:
Retiring room at Hancock Shaker Village, Pittsfield, MA
Photo by Lilo Raymond

RIGHT:
Elders' Room with double desk
Hancock Shaker Village, Pittsfield, MA
Photo by Michael Fredericks

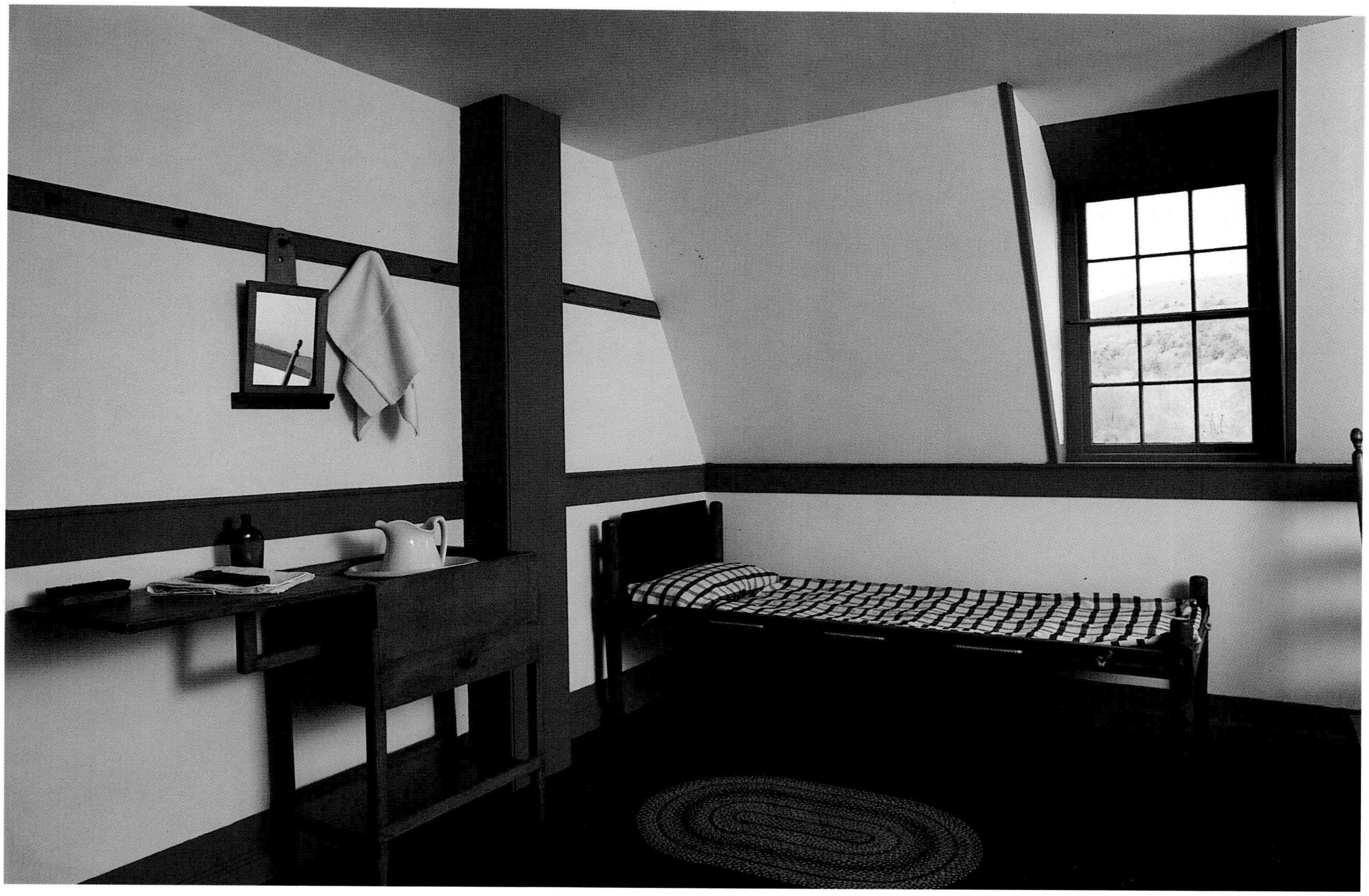

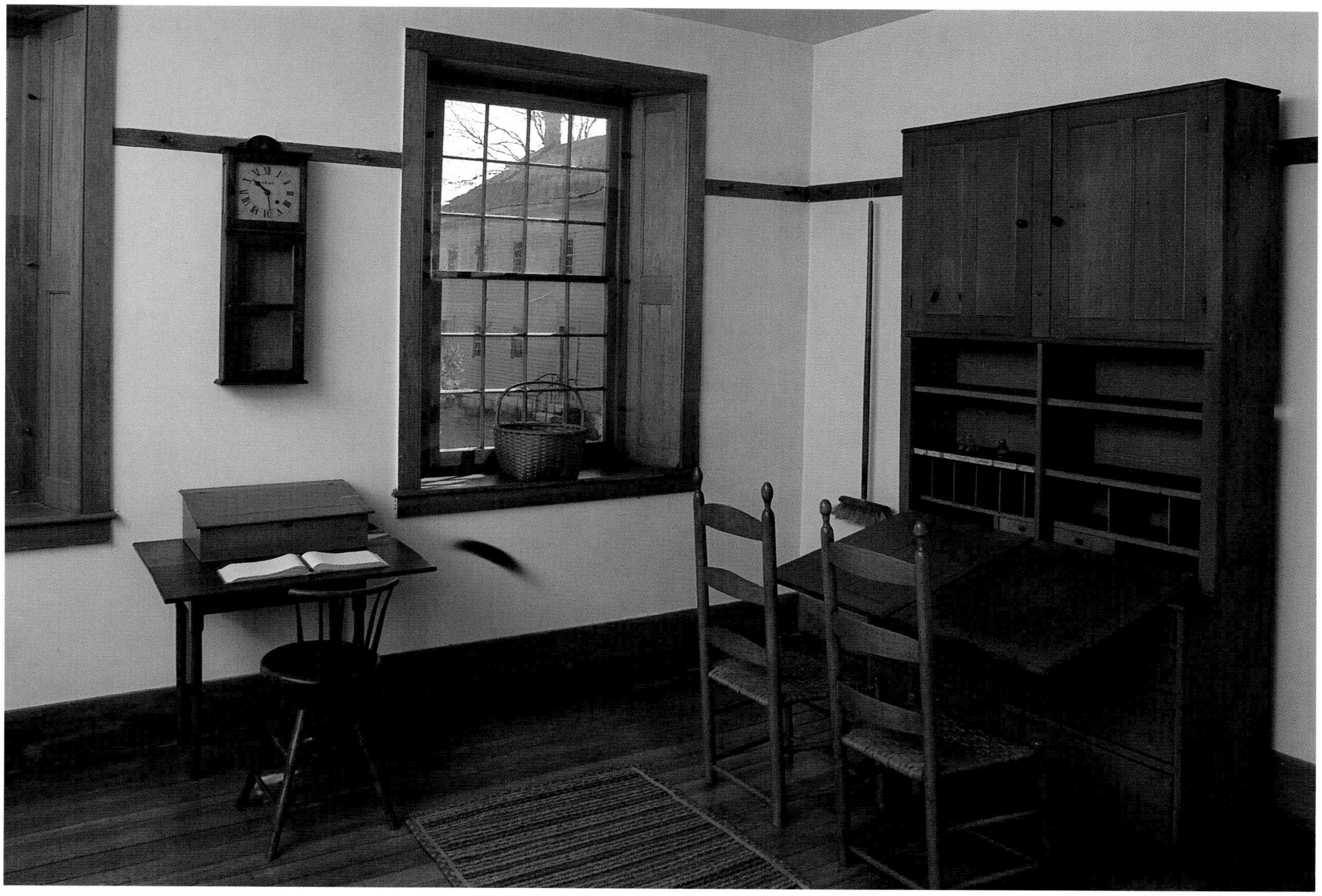

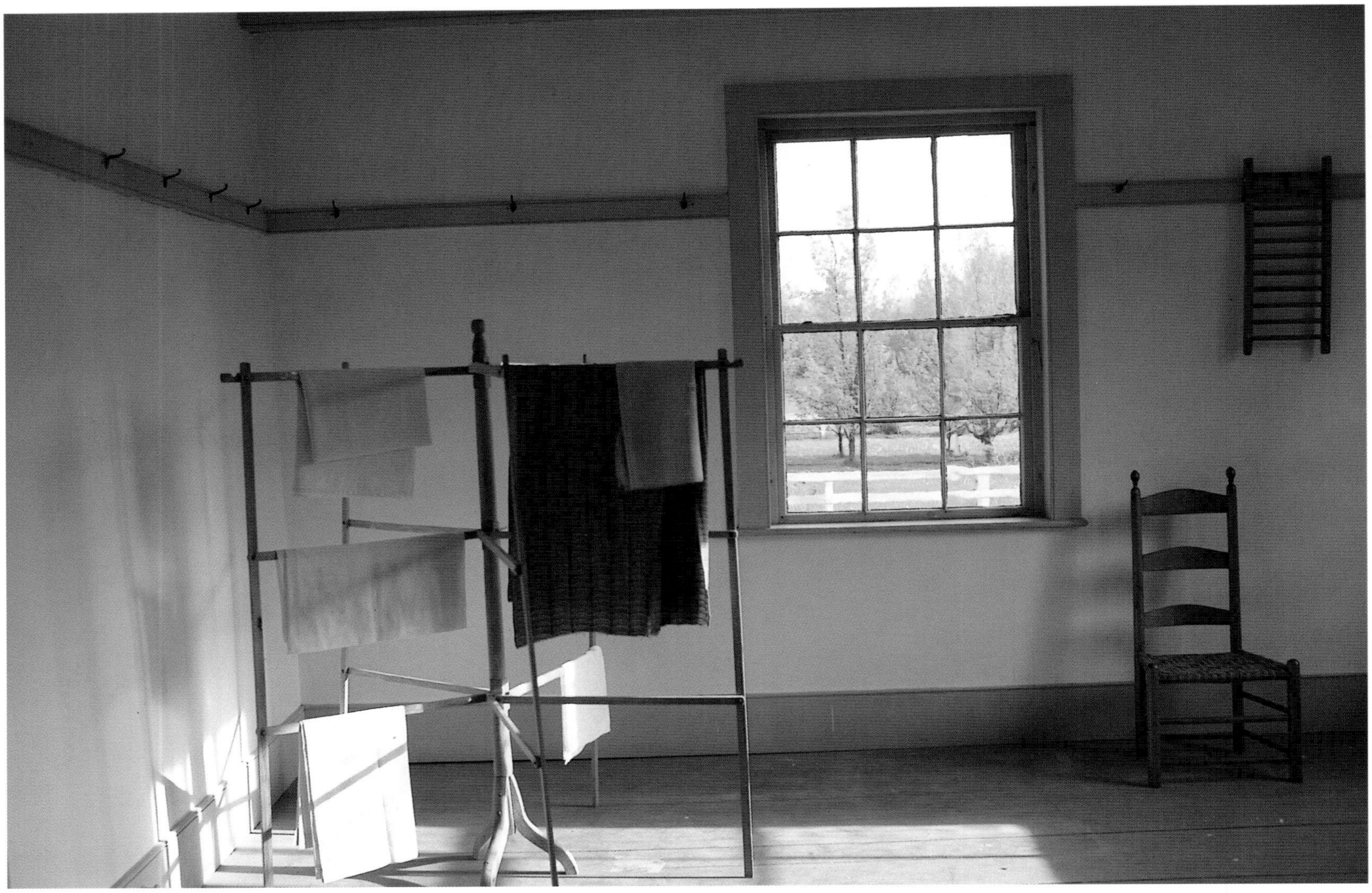

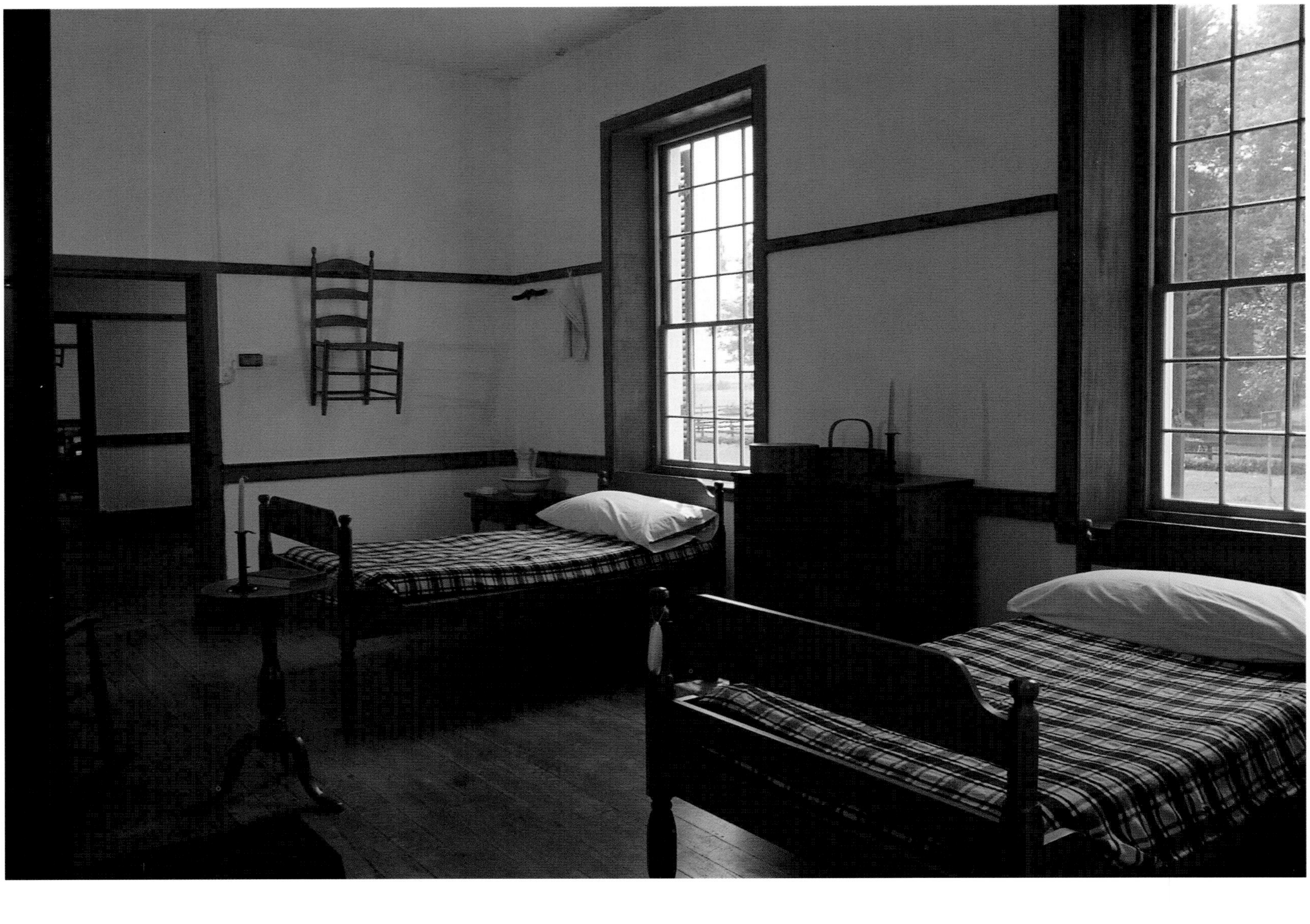

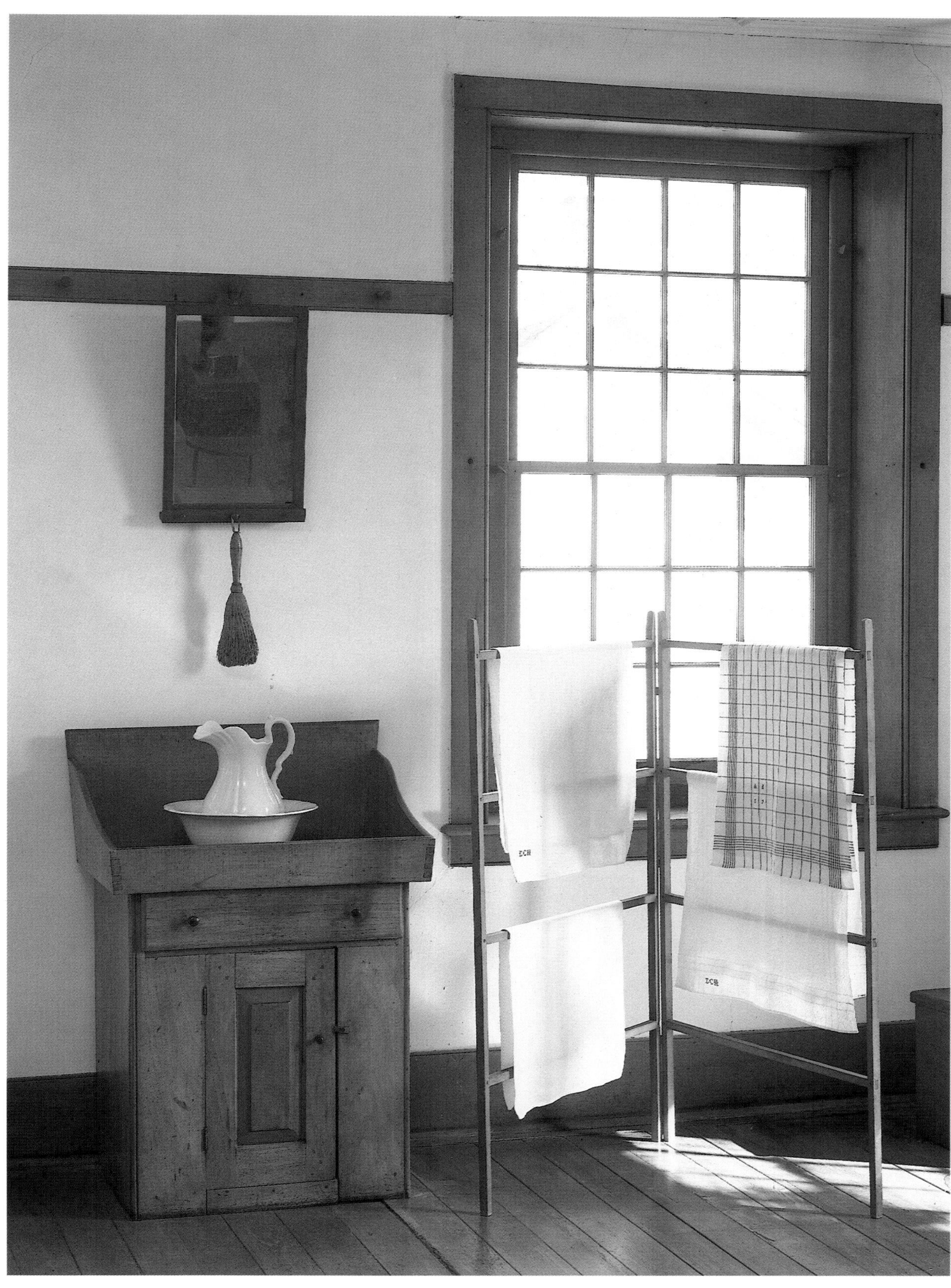

ABOVE LEFT:
Towel rack and room with Shaker pegs at Hancock, MA
Photo by Lilo Raymond

LEFT:
Sisters' Retiring Room, Centre Family, South Union, KY
Photo courtesy Shakertown at South Union, KY

ABOVE:
Washstand and towel rack
Hancock Shaker Village, Pittsfield, MA
Photo by Paul Rocheleau

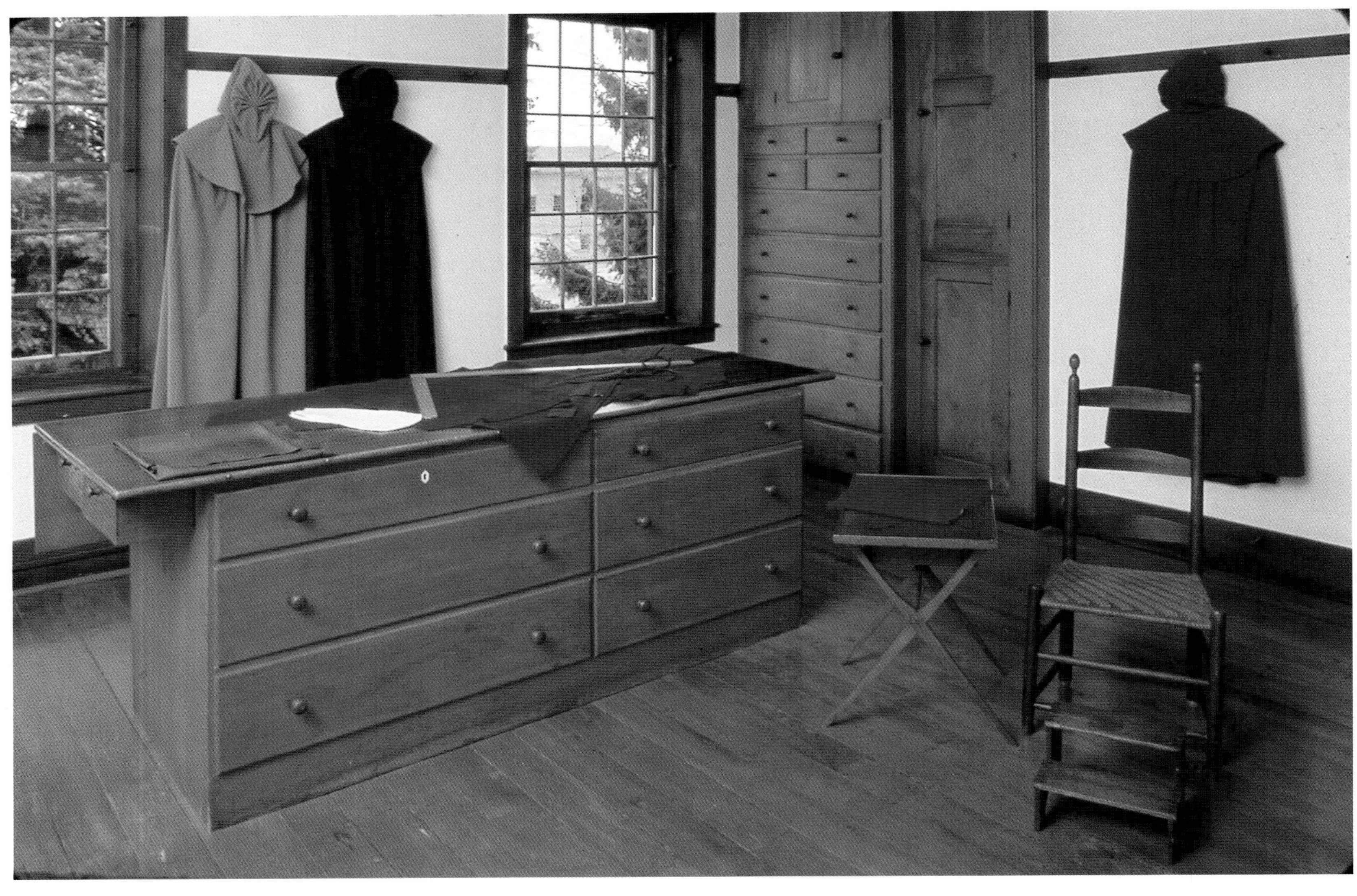

ABOVE:
Cloak Room, Brick Dwelling, featuring tailoring counter
Hancock Shaker Village, Pittsfield, MA
Photo by Michael Fredericks

RIGHT:
Two tall cupboards with angled feet and leaded trim around doors, c. 1820, Mount Lebanon, NY
Private Collection
Photo by Paul Rocheleau

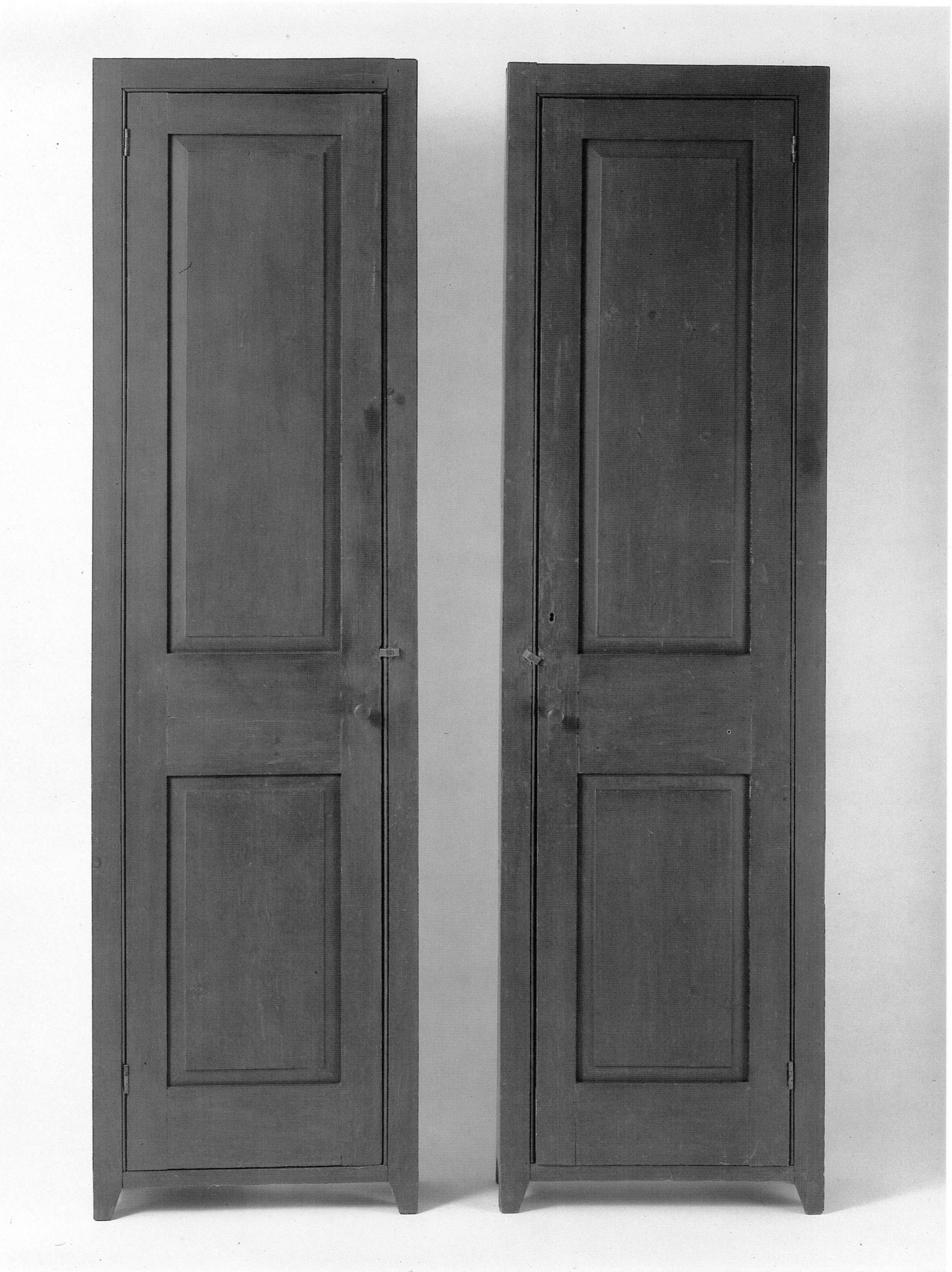

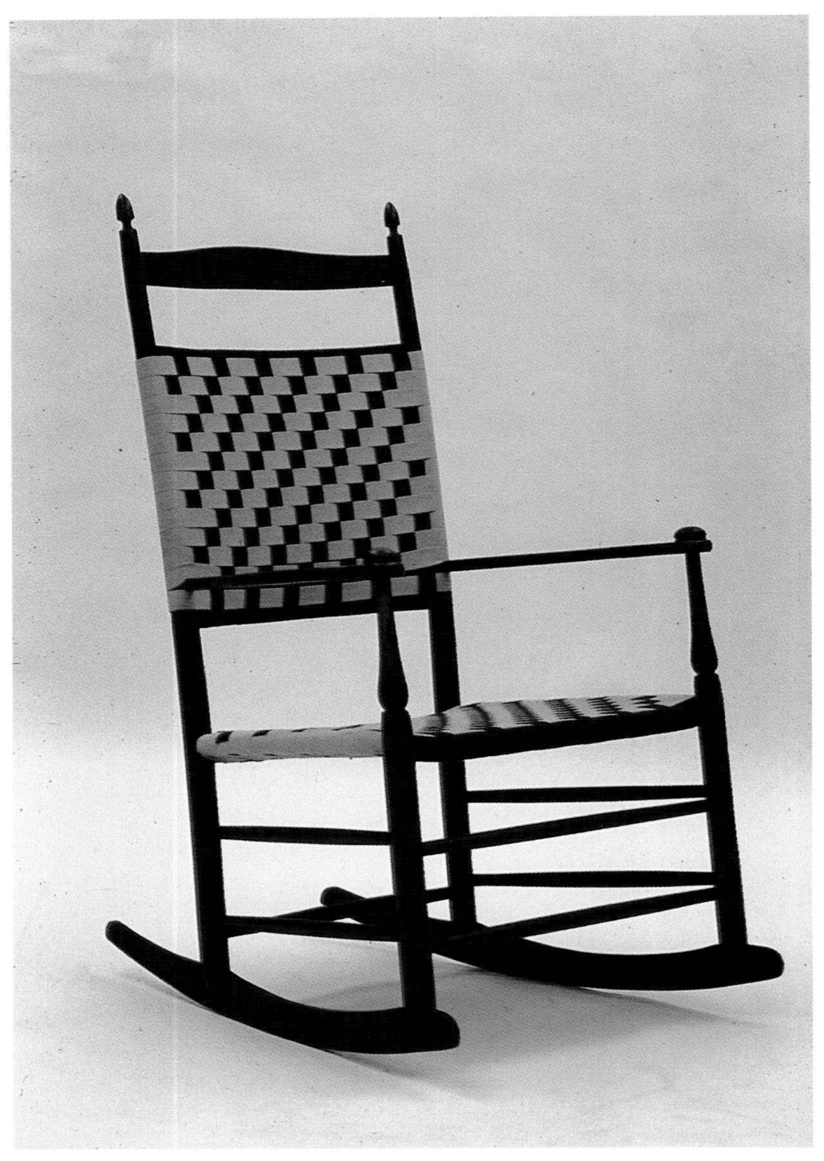

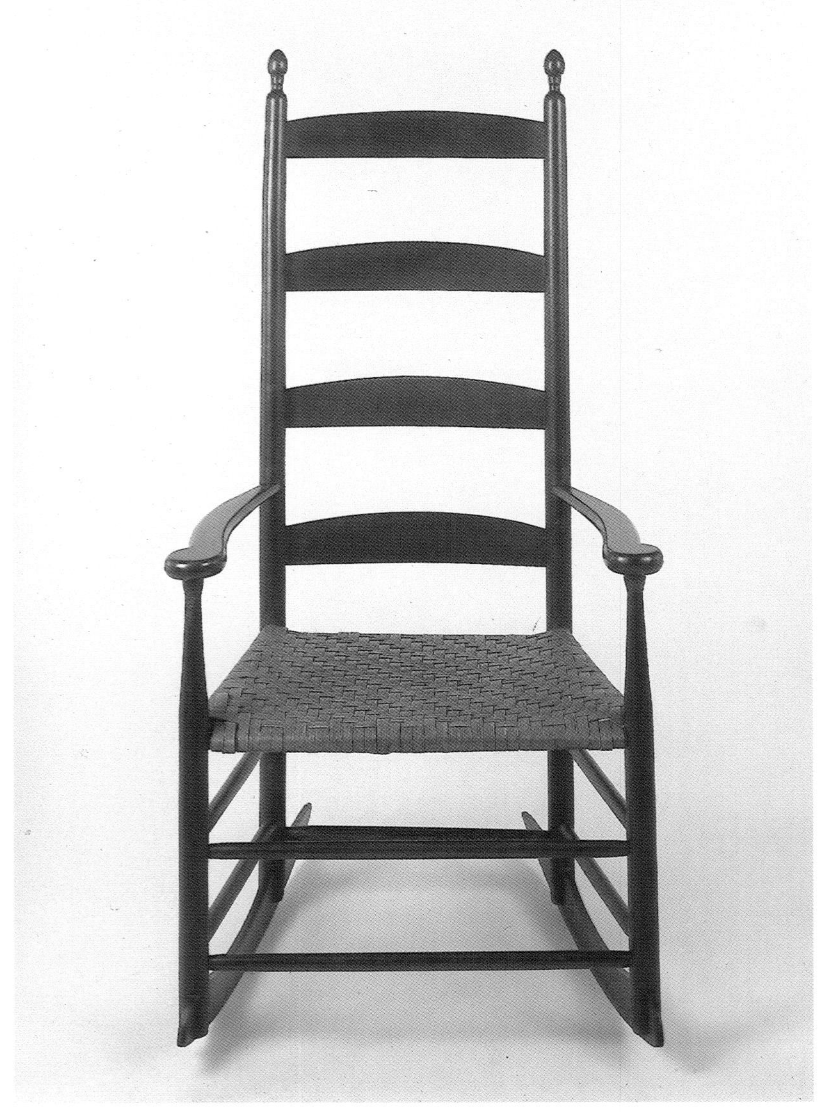

ABOVE:
Black rocking chair with arms
Hancock Shaker Village, Pittsfield, MA

ABOVE RIGHT:
Rocking chair, c. 1840-50, Mount Lebanon, NY
Private Collection
Photo by Paul Rocheleau

ABOVE FAR RIGHT:
Cherry candlestand, ca. 1830, marked "meeting room, stand"
Photo courtesy Shakertown at South Union, KY

RIGHT:
Tilt top umbrella-legged stand, c. 1830, Harvard, MA
Private Collection
Photo by Paul Rocheleau

FAR RIGHT:
Tall shelf clock, cherry, c. 1794, Canterbury, NH
Private Collection
Photo by Paul Rocheleau

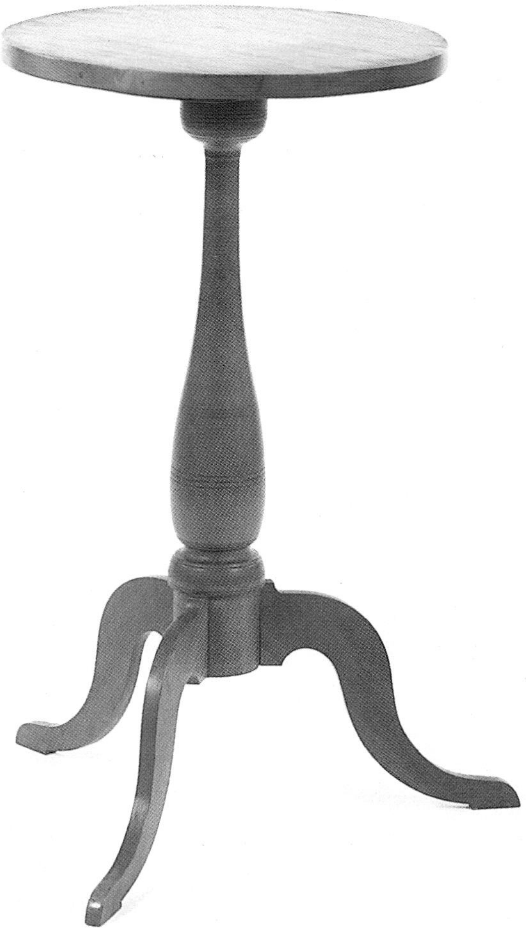

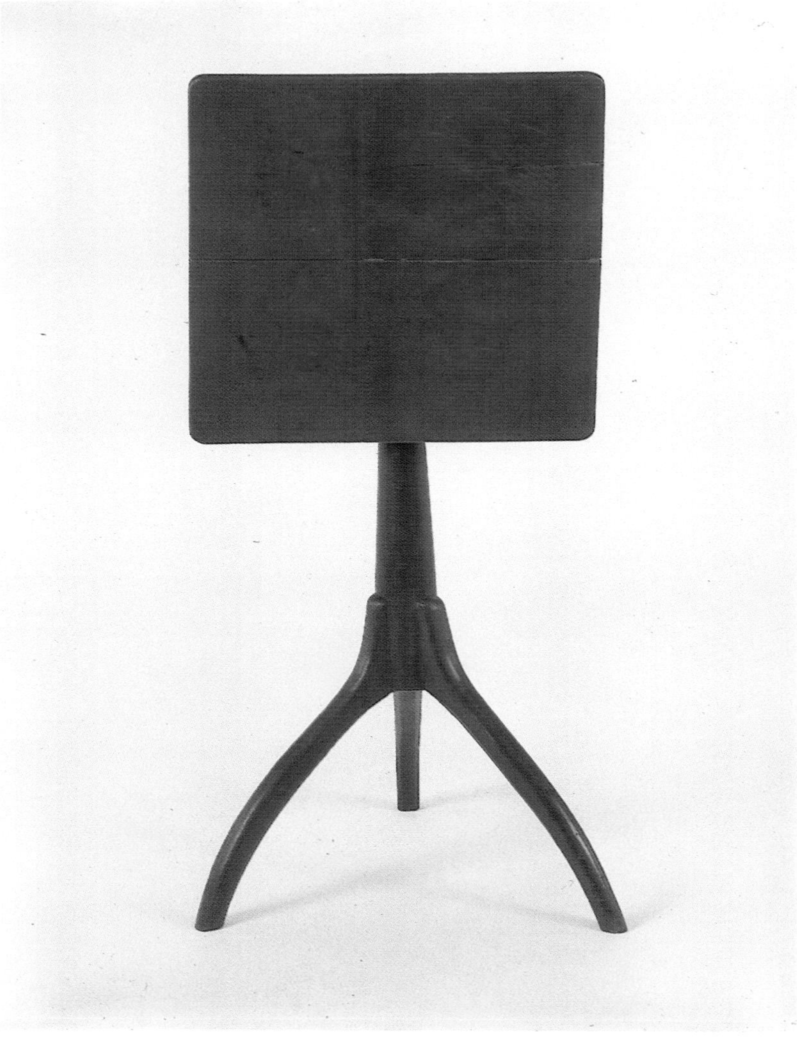

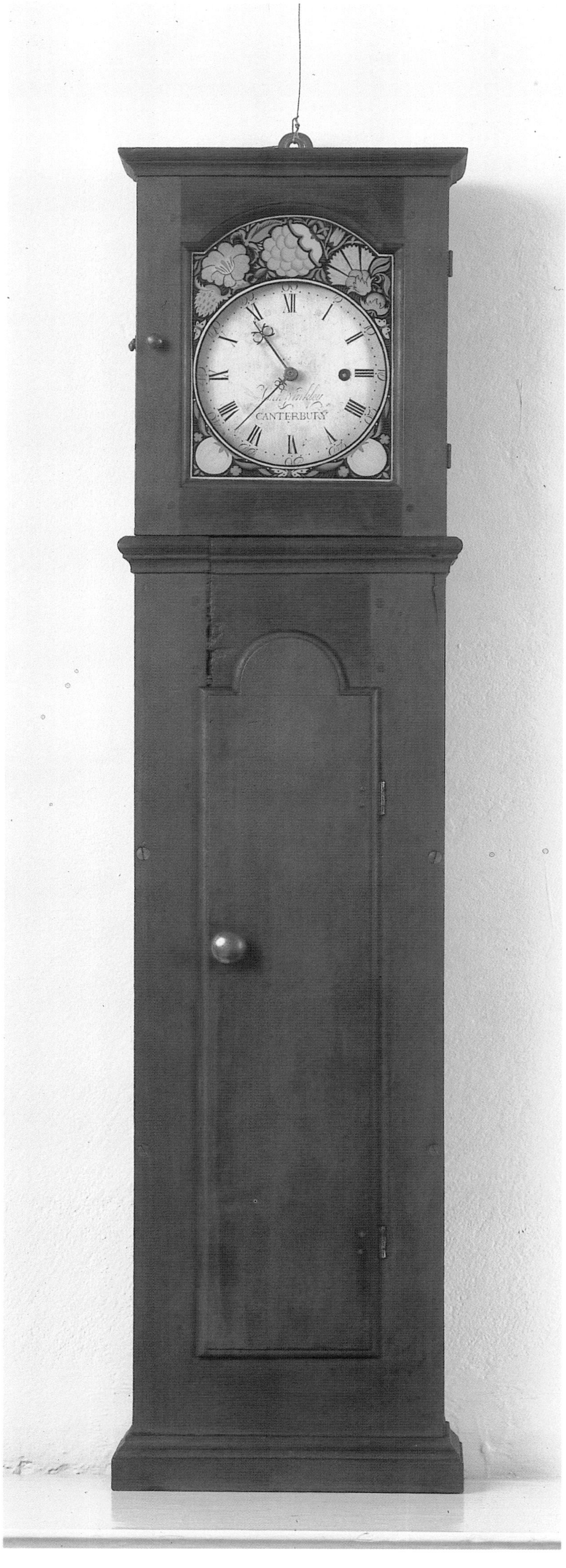

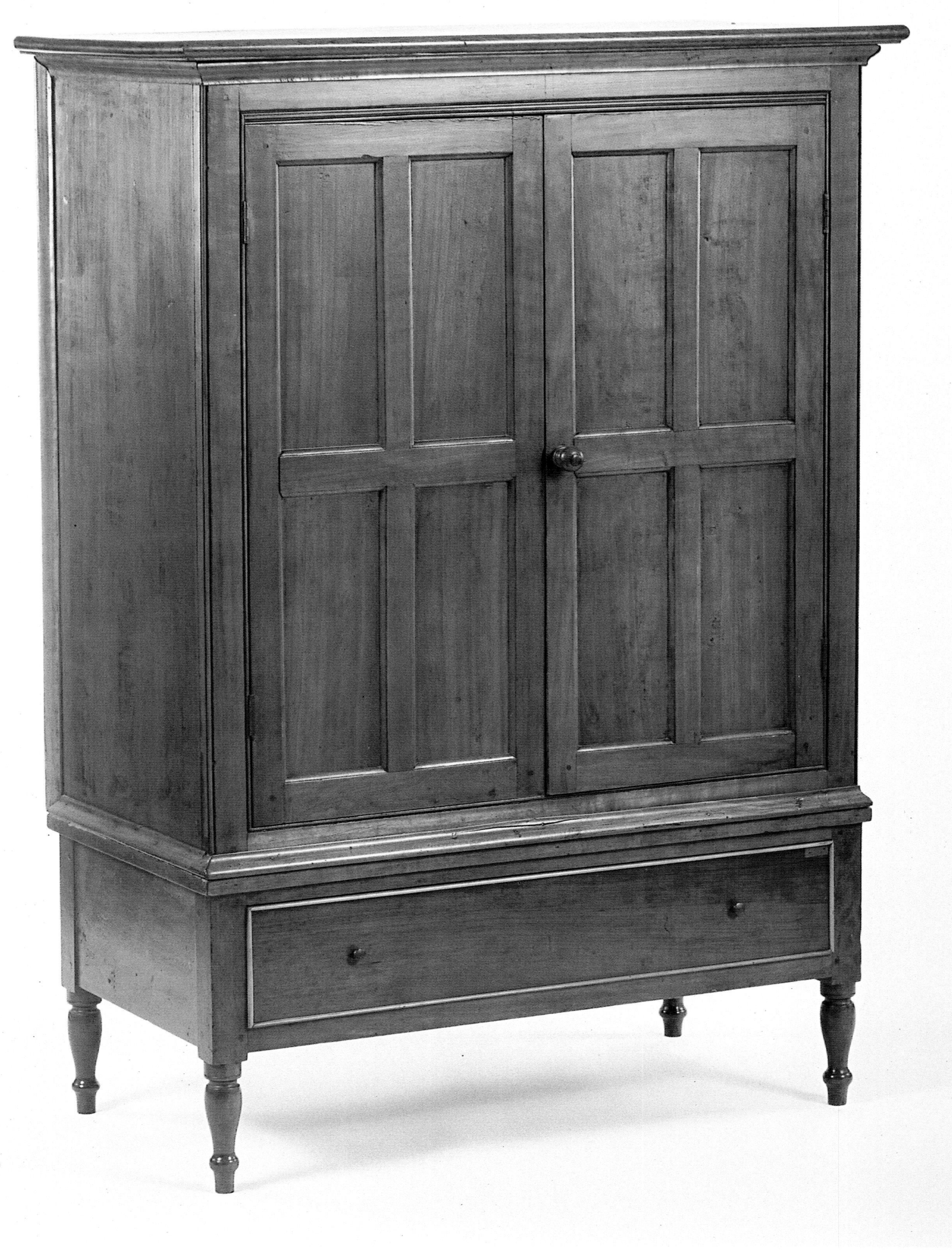

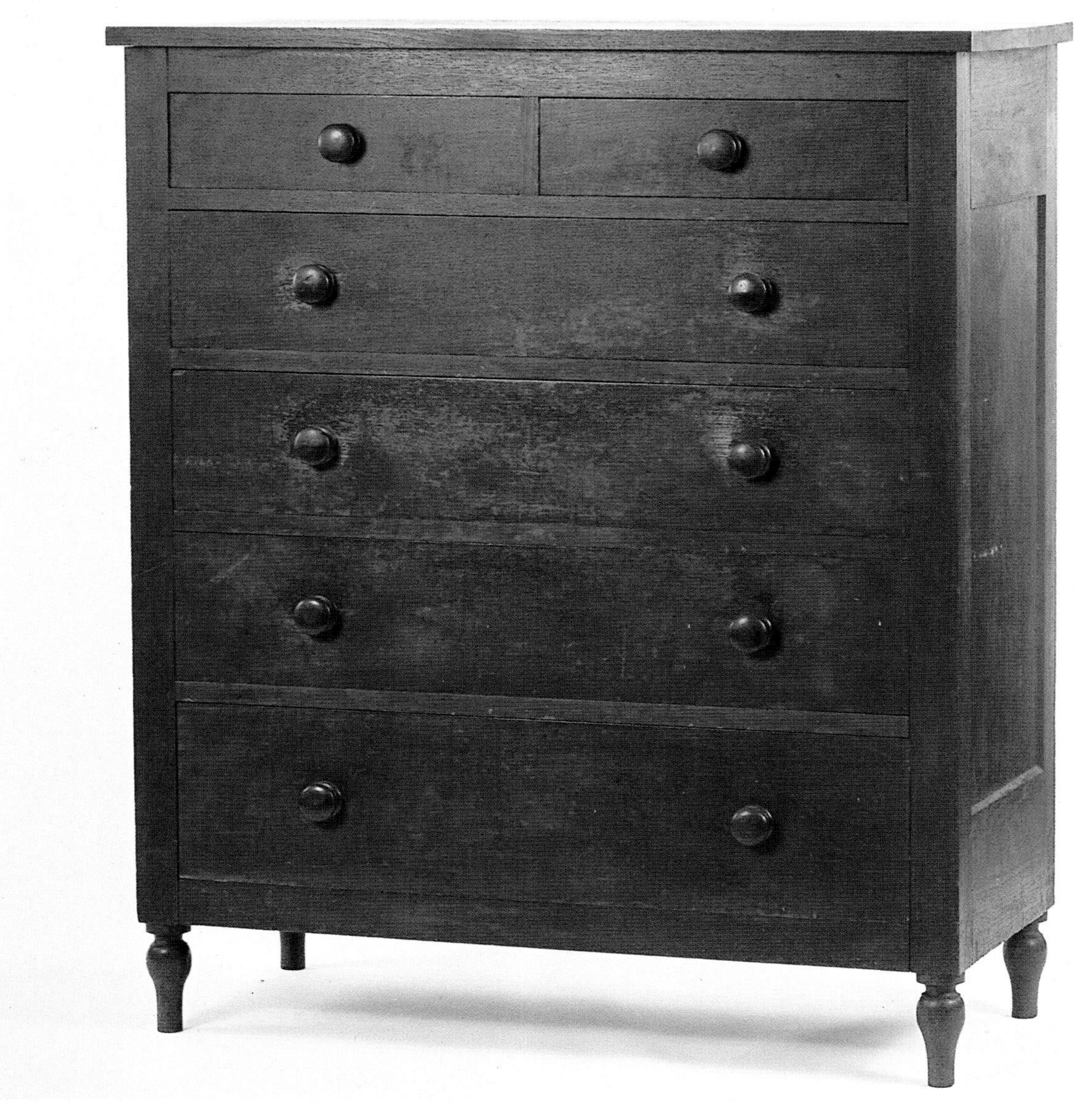

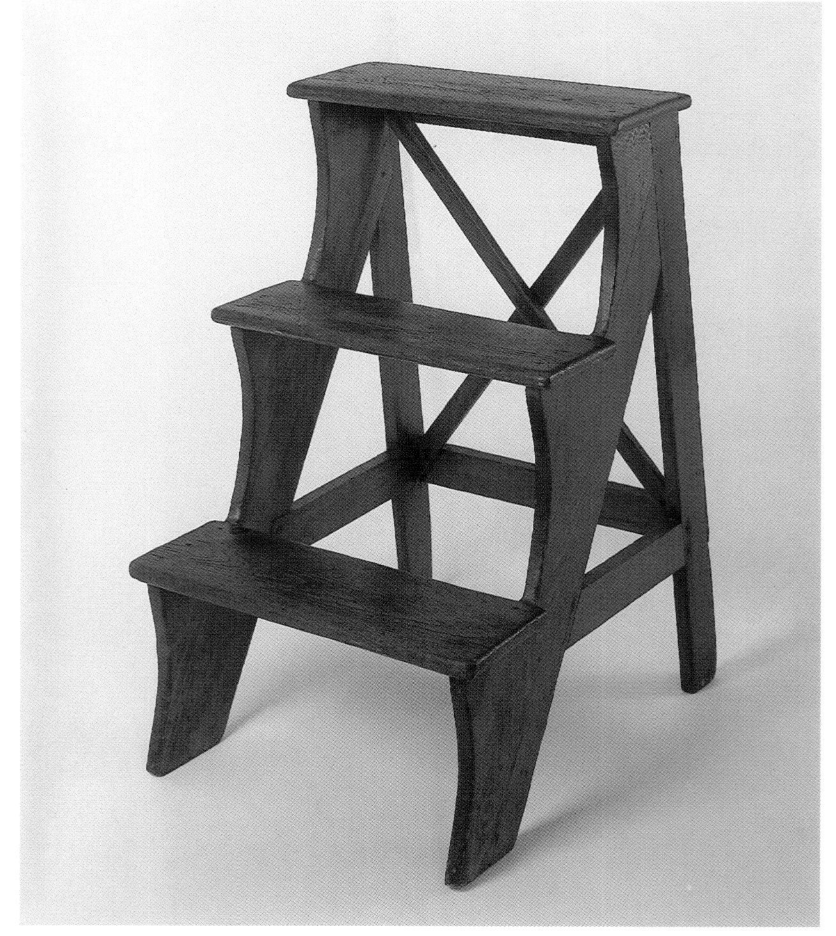

LEFT:
Cherry linen press, ca. 1840
Photo courtesy Shakertown at South Union, KY

ABOVE:
Chest of drawers, walnut, ca. 1840
original finish, typical South Union form and design
Photo courtesy Shakertown at South Union, KY

RIGHT:
Step stool, pine, c. 1830-50, Enfield, NH
Private Collection
Photo by Paul Rocheleau

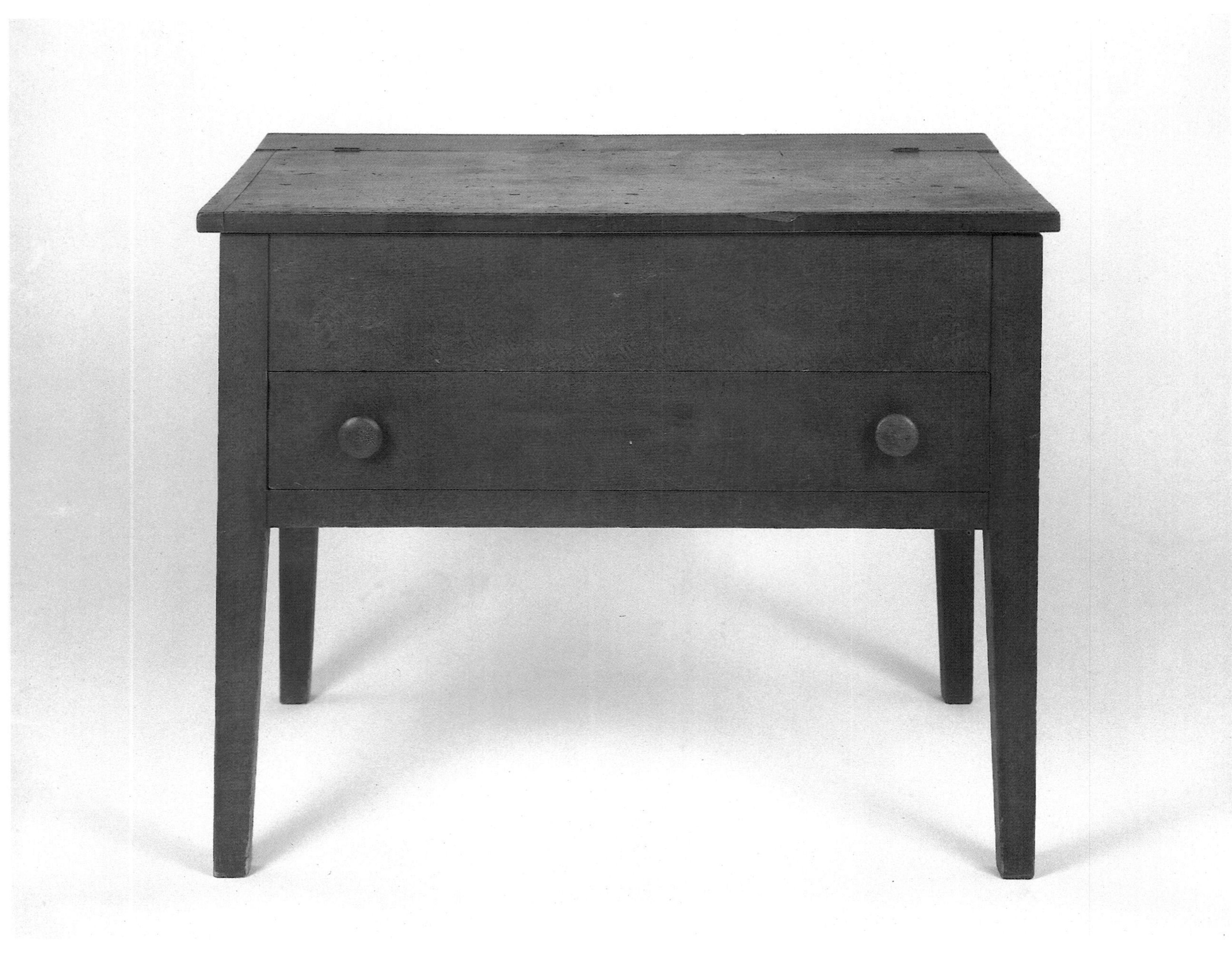

ABOVE:
Lift-top chest with tall tapered legs, c. 1840, Enfield, NH
Private Collection
Photo by Paul Rocheleau

ABOVE RIGHT:
Raised lift-top blanket chest with butter churn and three baskets, c. 1830, Alford, MA
Private Collection
Photo by Paul Rocheleau

RIGHT:
Child's work counter with side extensions, two round boxes and hog-scraper candlestick
Private Collection
Photo by Paul Rocheleau

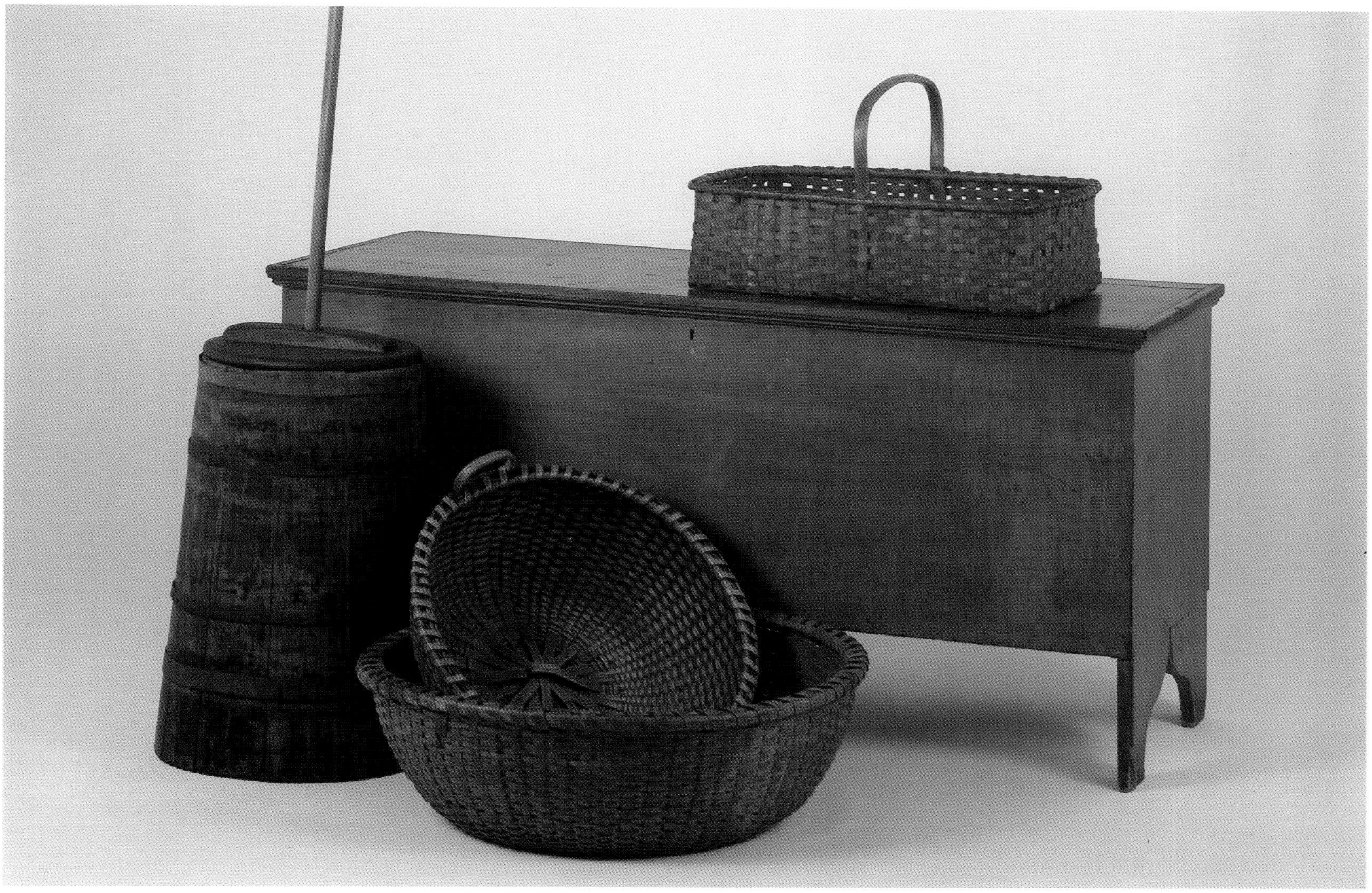

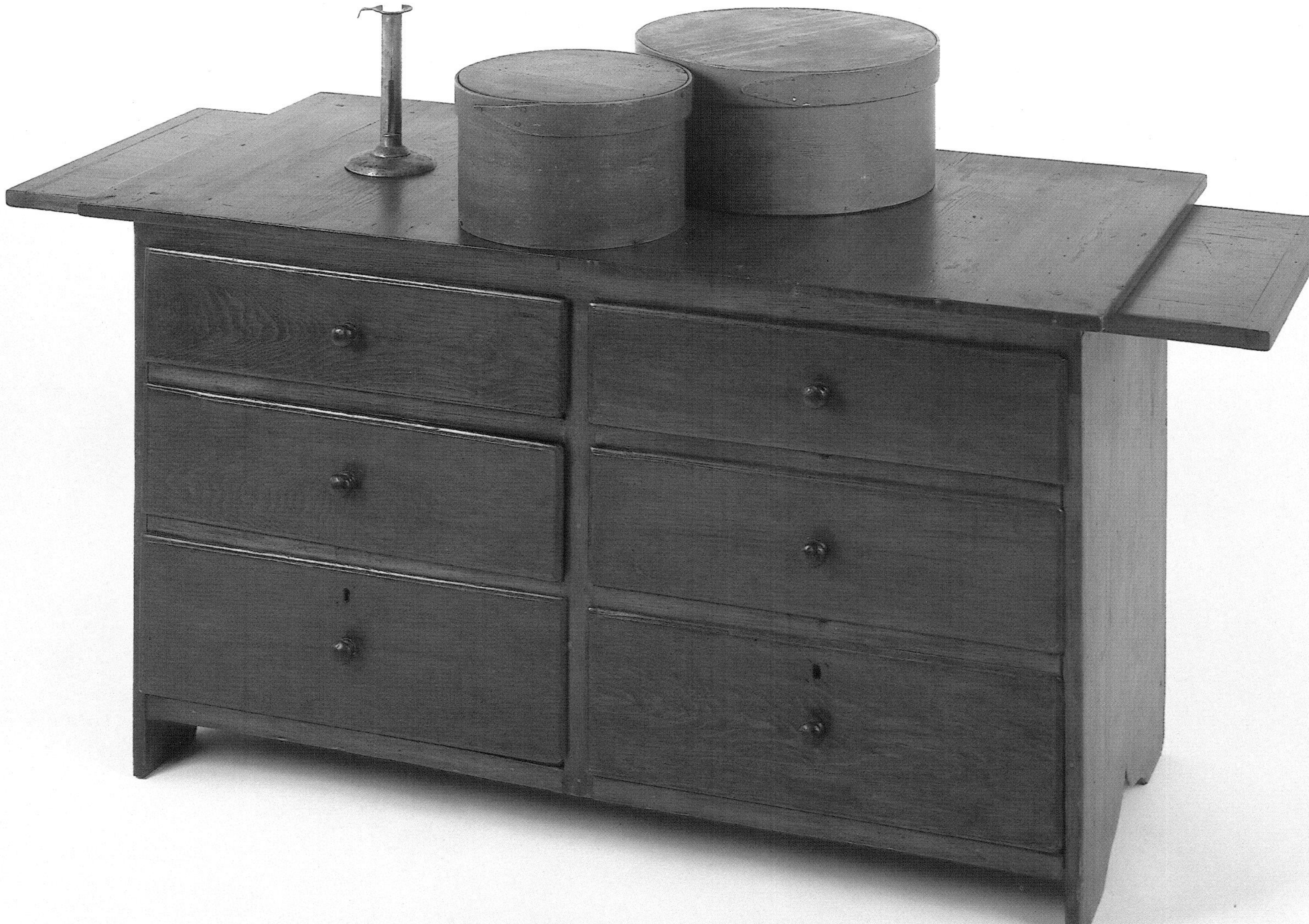

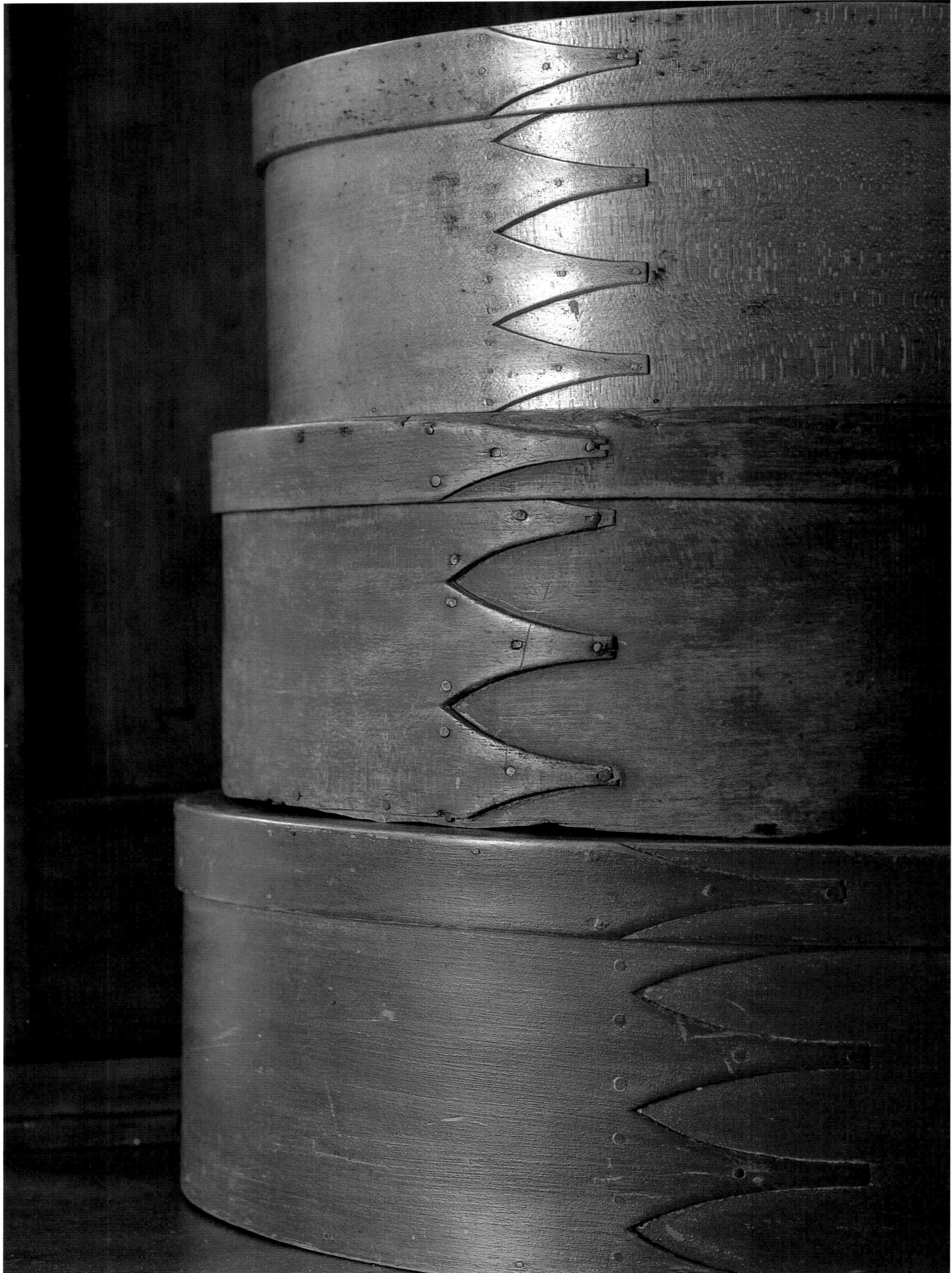

CHAPTER III

FINE HANDWORK

Today, the handicrafts of the Shakers are often displayed as works of art. It is not uncommon to see their work, for instance, set alongside the most delicate of Japanese craftswork as though both stem from some common tradition. "Shaker style" thereby comes to assume the status of one of the most subtle and self-conscious aesthetics known. This may help us to look closely at the Shakers' production but it can also be misleading. For to truly appreciate the Shakers' fine handwork, we must understand its historical context.

From the outset, the goal of the first American Shakers was to form self-sufficient communities. This was not a matter of economic theory or even of necessity. It came out of their desire to isolate themselves from the "polluted" world around them. Yet the Shakers came from that world – they knew its ways and its skills. As people who grew up largely in the late eighteenth century and throughout the nineteenth century, and mainly in rural or small-town America, they started with a strong predilection for doing things frugally and doing things for themselves.

So it was that the Shakers tended to make most of the objects of everyday life for themselves. Many specialized metal tools had to be bought, but some communities made their own tinware – pitchers, funnels, dustpans, and such. As in every village of that period, there was usually a blacksmith who worked iron into everything from horseshoes to clothes irons.

Among the many items the Shakers made were their clothes. When they first moved into their villages, of course, they wore the clothing of the outside world, and in fact there was little attempt to require them to adopt any uniform. The sole proviso was to keep it simple, to abandon all the decorations that suggested frivolity and vanity – to avoid, what a later Shaker called, "body-deforming dresses." But as the decades of the nineteenth century rolled on and as the Shakers began to expand their Millennial Laws – that is, the regulations that increasingly governed all aspects of their lives – there was an attempt both to retain traditional clothing and to keep it uniform throughout all communities. In effect, the approved clothing was that of rural Americans circa 1800; by the 1890s, though, many Shaker communities were abandoning this tradition.

During the workday, men and women were allowed to wear a variety of standard clothes, as long as they were modest and simple. Shakers were encouraged to produce and wear only high quality clothing – long-lasting and well-made. For church services and other formal gatherings they were expected to wear almost a uniform. For women this meant ankle-length dresses, bonnets, and cloaks; for men this meant basic black suits and broad-brimmed hats. In 1849, a Shaker elder from Ohio and Kentucky actually published a large illustrated volume, *The Tailor's Division System*, showing how to make traditional Shakers' men's clothing. Women's bonnets, some of which were made of quilted textiles, others of straw and lined with some cloth material, became almost a trademark of the Shakers, and they often sold them to the outside world. The distinctive women's cloaks and capes also came to be admired, and were made in quantity and sold to the outside world.

Wool was taken from the sheep that the Shakers kept in great flocks and was used in several ways. Some of it was dyed and sold in skeins to the outside word. Some of it was used for knit goods – mittens, stockings, "footens," sweaters and such. Some of it was woven on the looms they themselves built; the wool was then used for clothing, blankets, towels, and other items. Some Shakers wove small rugs but this was not a major product as colorful rugs were regarded as an unnecessary luxury. Another use for their wool was for hundreds of yards of brightly-dyed tapes that were used to weave the seats of their slat-back chairs.

Some other textiles – cotton and linen – obviously had to be brought in from outside, but in at least one community, that of South Union, Kentucky, they raised silkworms and made their own silk. This was then used to make fine scarfs and handkerchiefs. Such a product would seem to run counter to the usual Shaker prohibition on items of luxury and adornment, but this is only one of several instances where there was not complete adherence and uniformity among all Shakers over two centuries.

Most villages produced their own leather and then made their own footwear and other leather goods, from belts to bridles. Since all shoes were custom made, Shakers actually enjoyed a luxury denied to all but a few in our own time. A wooden shoe form, or last, found at one Shaker village actually has a leather "bump" attached to the site of a toe so that the shoemaker could customize that individual's shoe to accommodate a bunion.

Wood was widely worked for all kinds of products. Many kitchen aids were carved or turned from wood – scoops, rolling pins and such. So, too, were buckets and pails of many sizes and shapes. Although made with only the most ordinary uses in mind, many of these items today strike us as elegant objects. Another of the most admired Shaker products these days are their baskets. Woven from splints, or strips, of ash, oak, poplar, or willow, these baskets came in a variety of sizes and types. One special type were the delicate sewing baskets lined with fine satin or kid leather; these was to hold pin cushions (also handmade), scissors, and emery (for sharpening needles).

Perhaps the most distinctive of the Shaker handicrafts are the oval wooden boxes used to hold all manner of objects and substances. They came in a wide range of sizes and were made so that they could "nest" in each other for storage. They were made of thin sheets of wood – usually maple for the sides, and pine for top and bottom. Aside from their simple elegance, these boxes are distinguished by the "finger" or "swallowtail" joint" by which the band of wood was attached by copper rivets to the side; this allowed the wood to shrink or swell with changes in the temperature and humidity. In their combination of form and function, of tradition and innovation, of technology and artistry, of simplicity and sophistication, and above all of unself-consciousness and deliberation, these boxes truly embody Shaker style.

Stack of boxes, Pleasant Hill, KY
Photo by James Archambeault

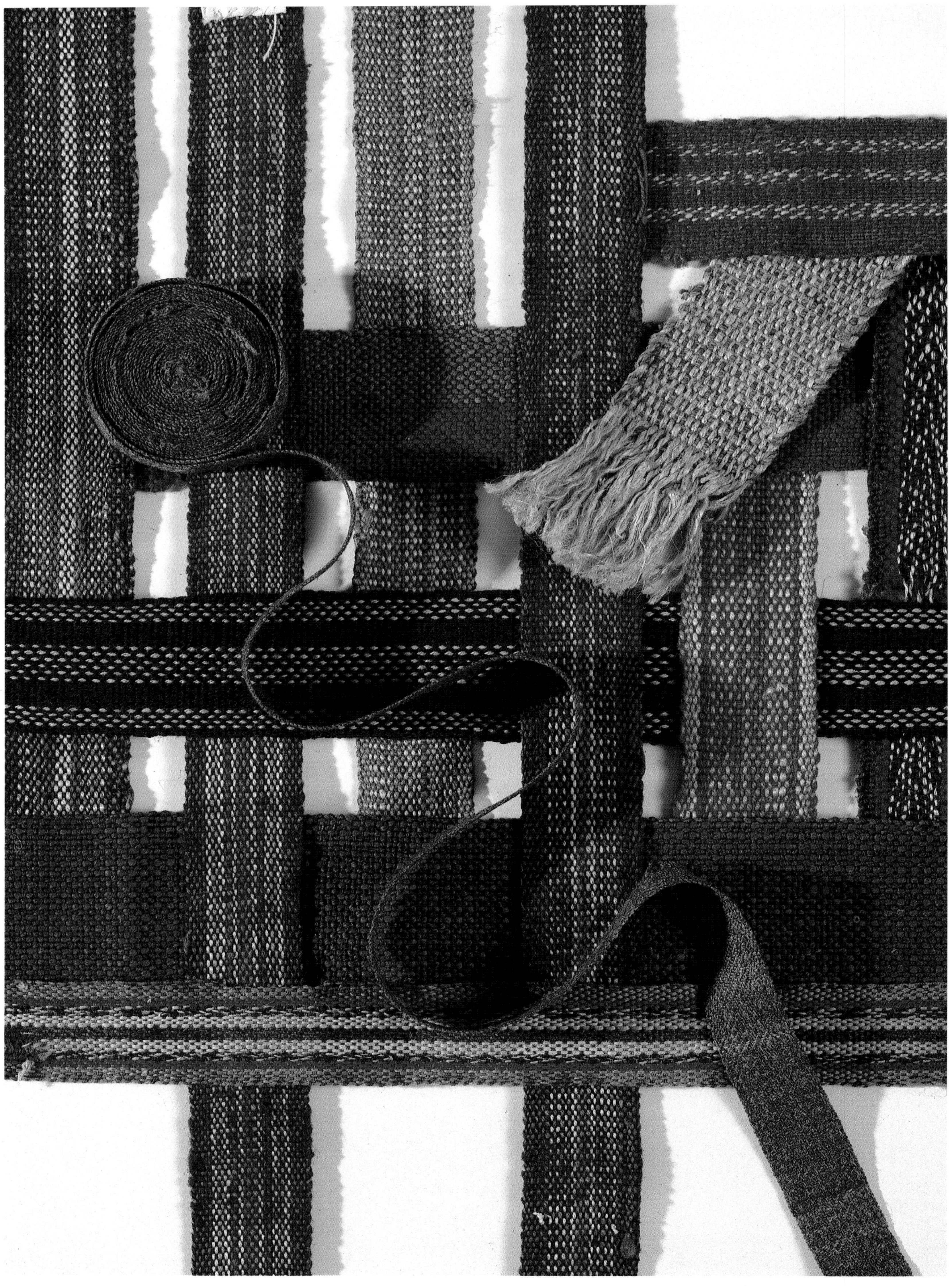

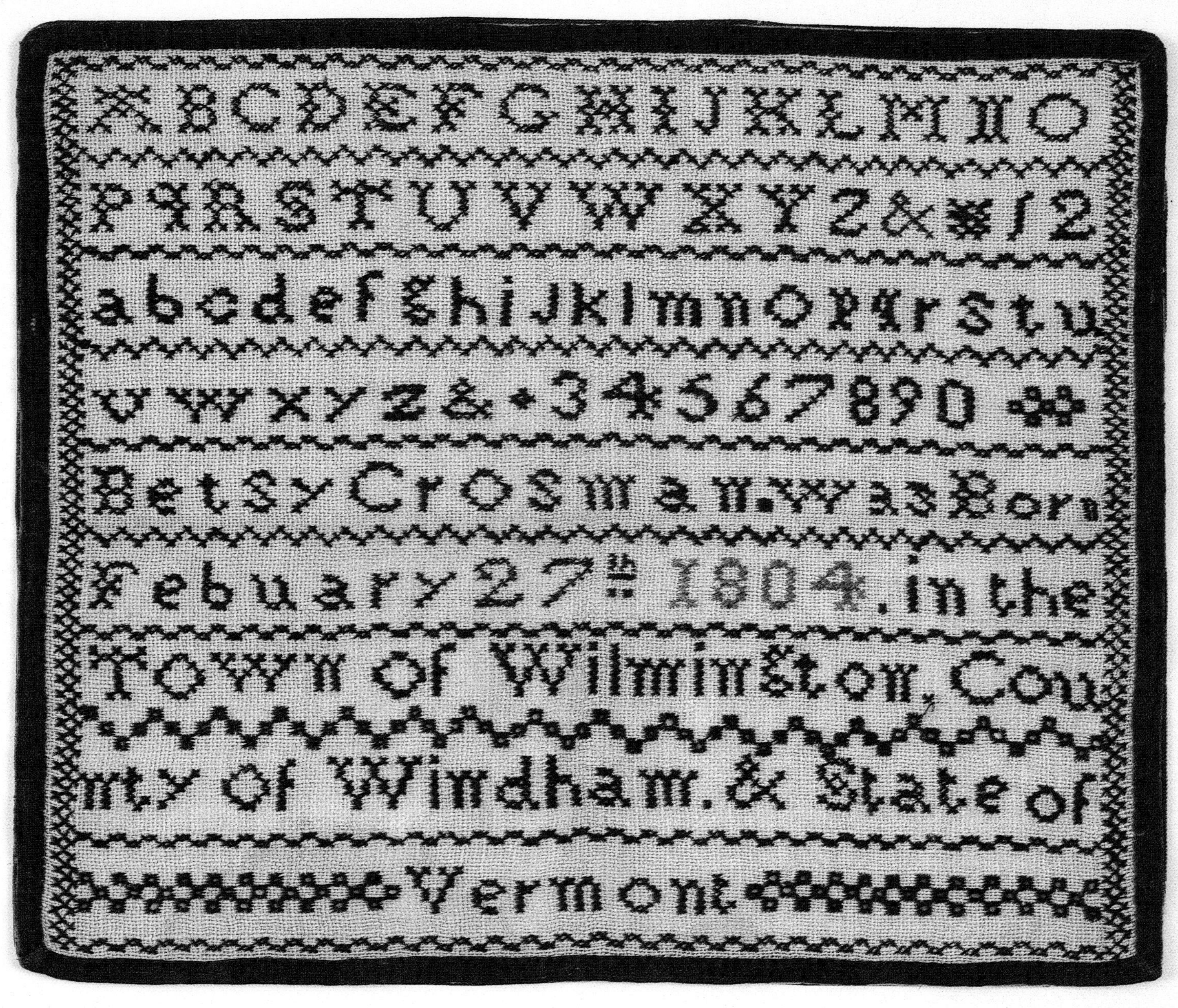

LEFT:
Samples of chair tapes
Hancock Shaker Village, Pittsfield, MA
Photo by Paul Rocheleau

ABOVE:
Betsy Crosman Sampler
Hancock Shaker Village, Pittsfield, MA
Photo by Paul Rocheleau

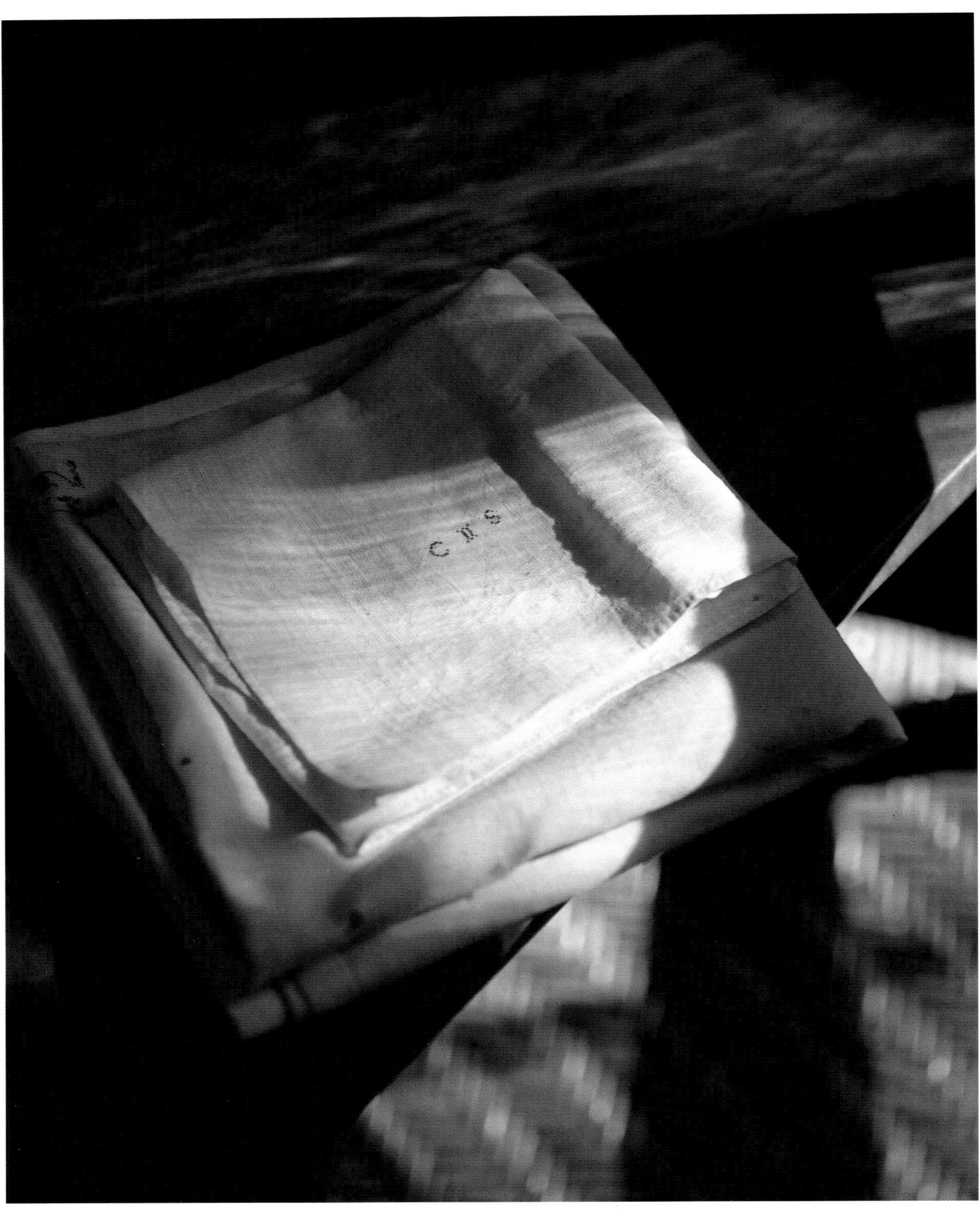

ABOVE:
Embroidered handkerchiefs at Pleasant Hill, KY
Photo by James Archambeault

ABOVE RIGHT:
Rag carpet and spit box, c. 1850-75
probably from New Lebanon, NY
Hancock Shaker Village, Pittsfield, MA
Photo by Paul Rocheleau

RIGHT:
Sisters' neckerchiefs
Hancock Shaker Village, Pittsfield, MA
Photo by Paul Rocheleau

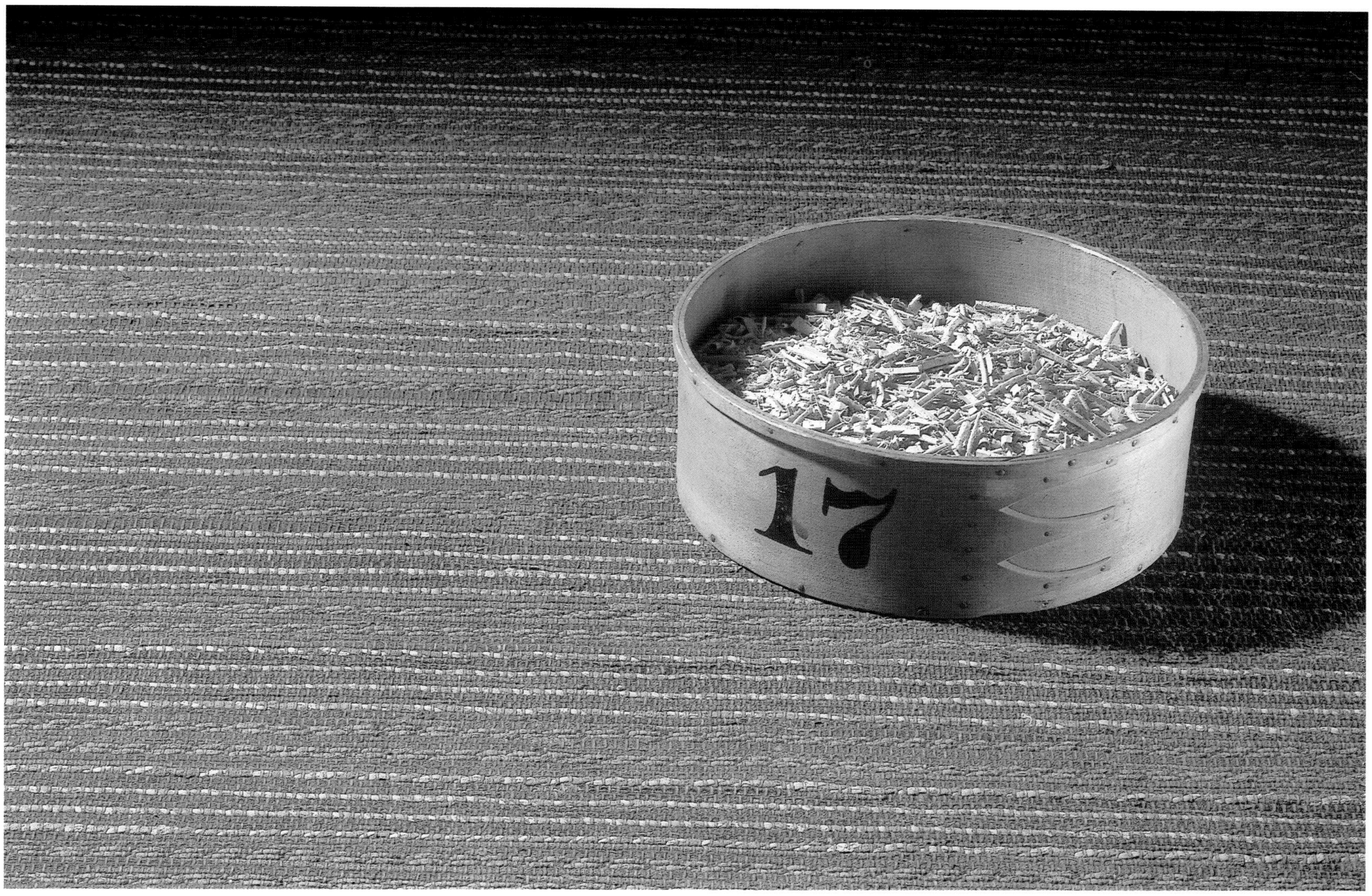

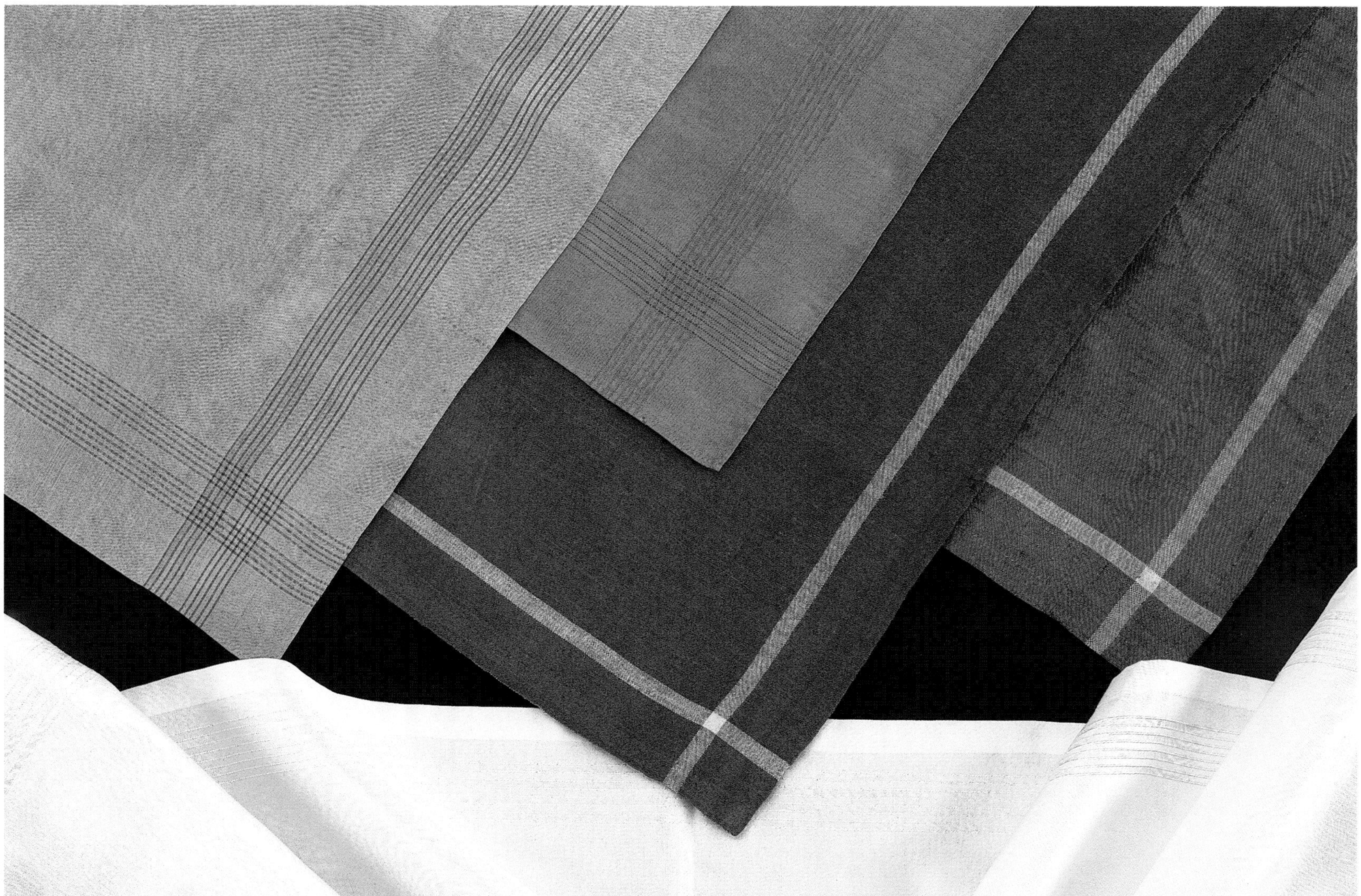

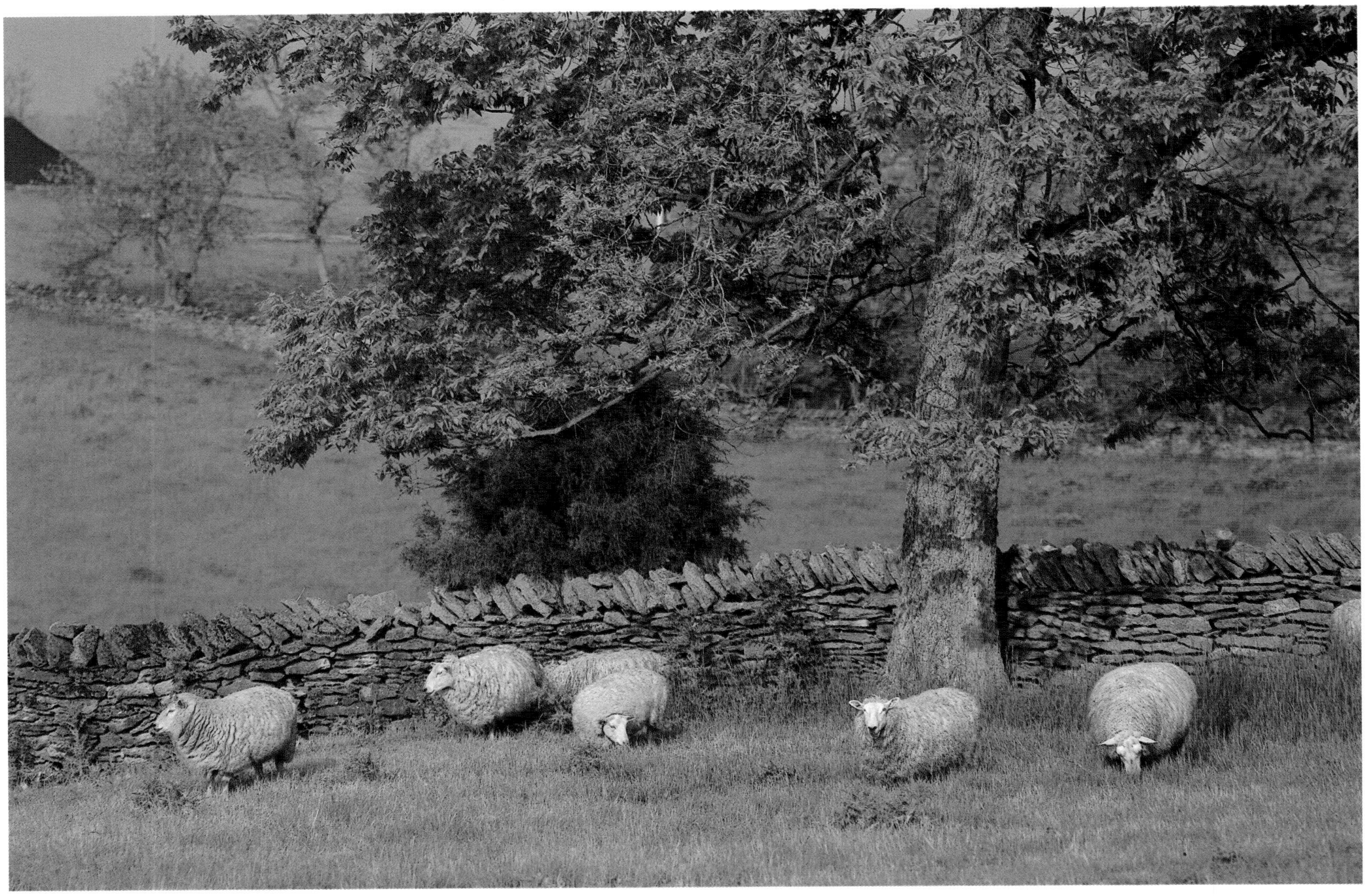

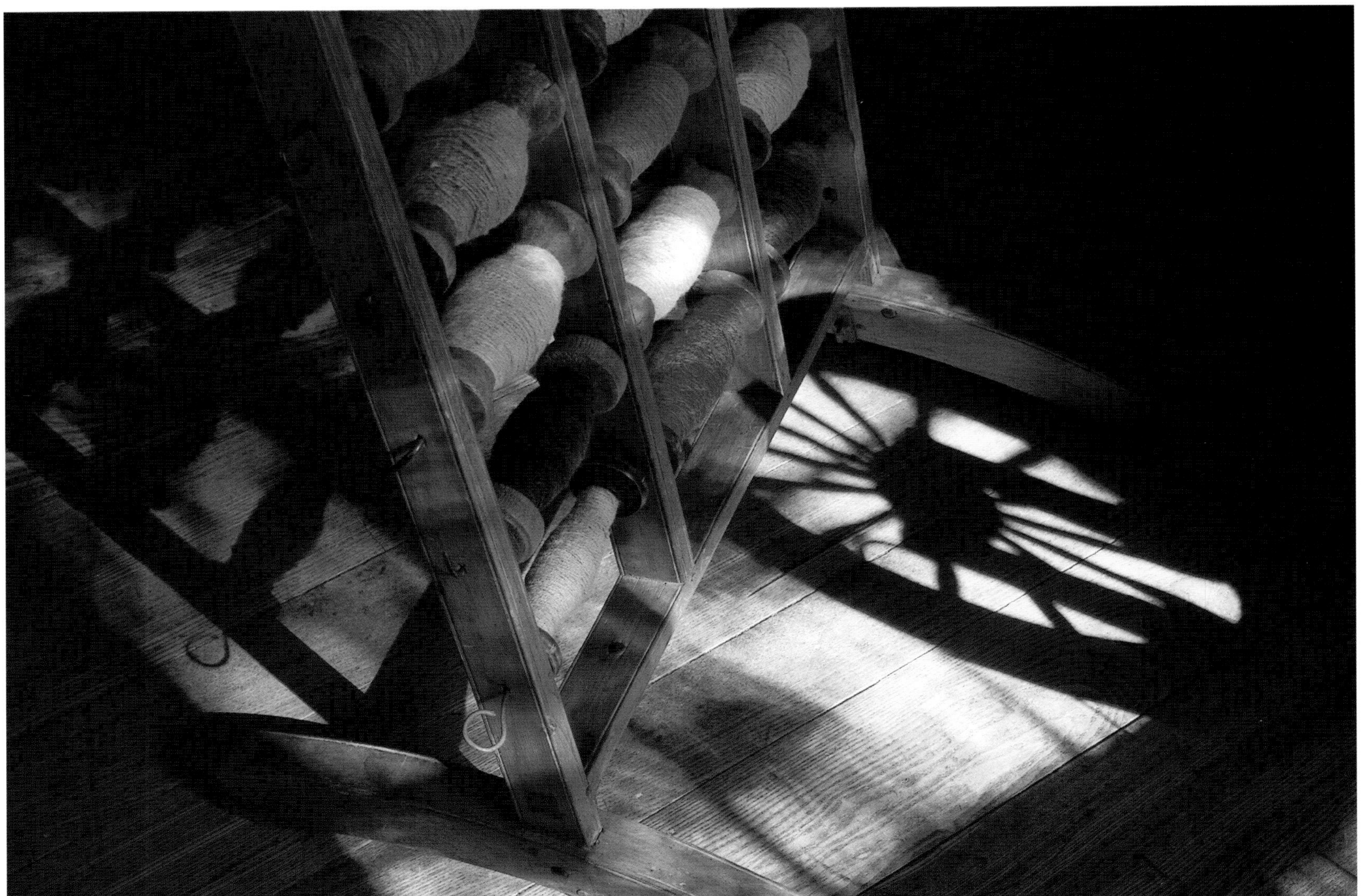

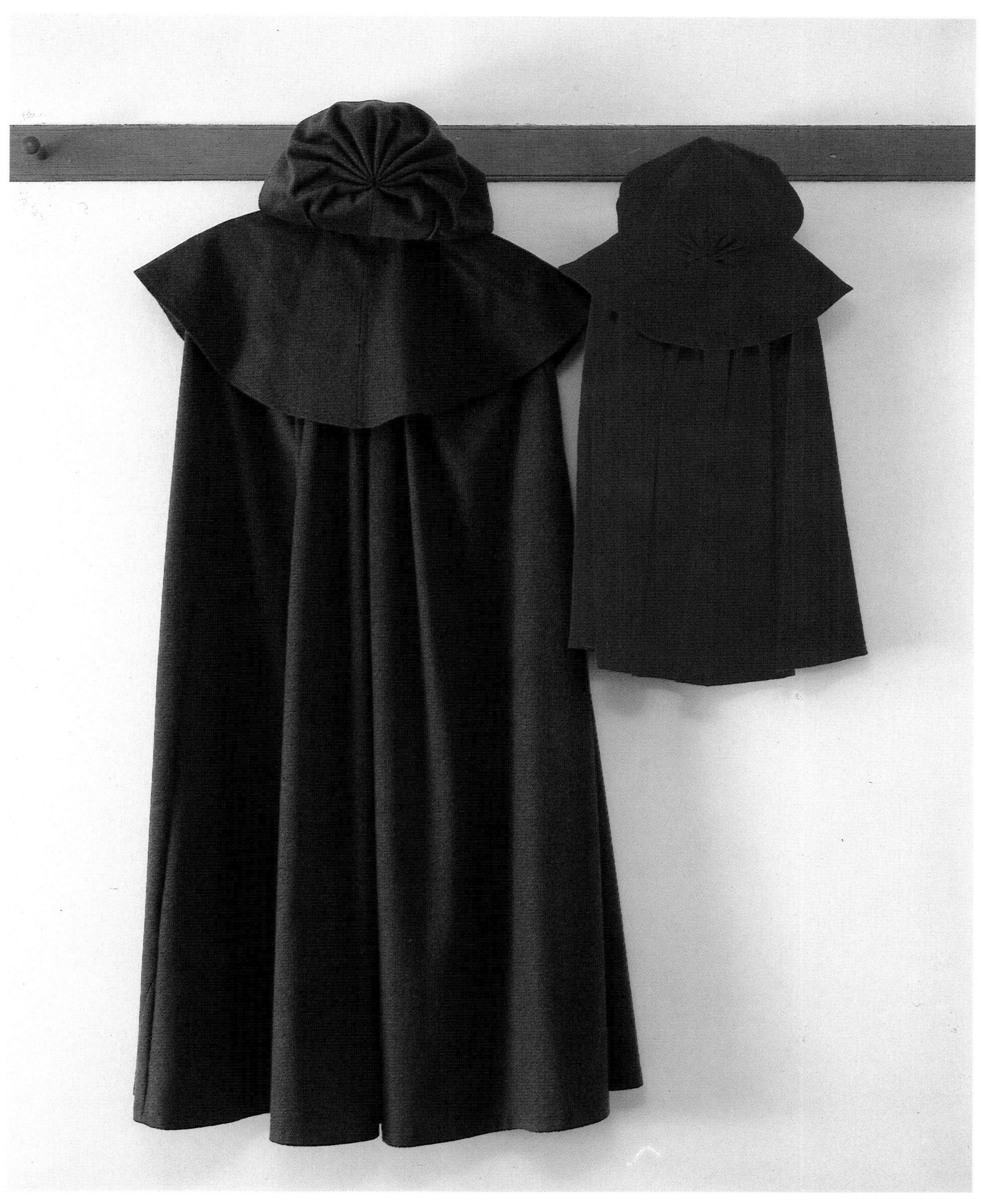

ABOVE LEFT:
Border Leicester sheep, raised since the 1820s at Pleasant Hill, KY, produce fine, long fleece
Photo by James Archambeault

LEFT:
Scarne holds spools of dyed yarn, Pleasant Hill, KY
Photo by James Archambeault

ABOVE:
Shaker cloaks hang on pegs
Hancock Shaker Village, Pittsfield, MA
Photo by Paul Rocheleau

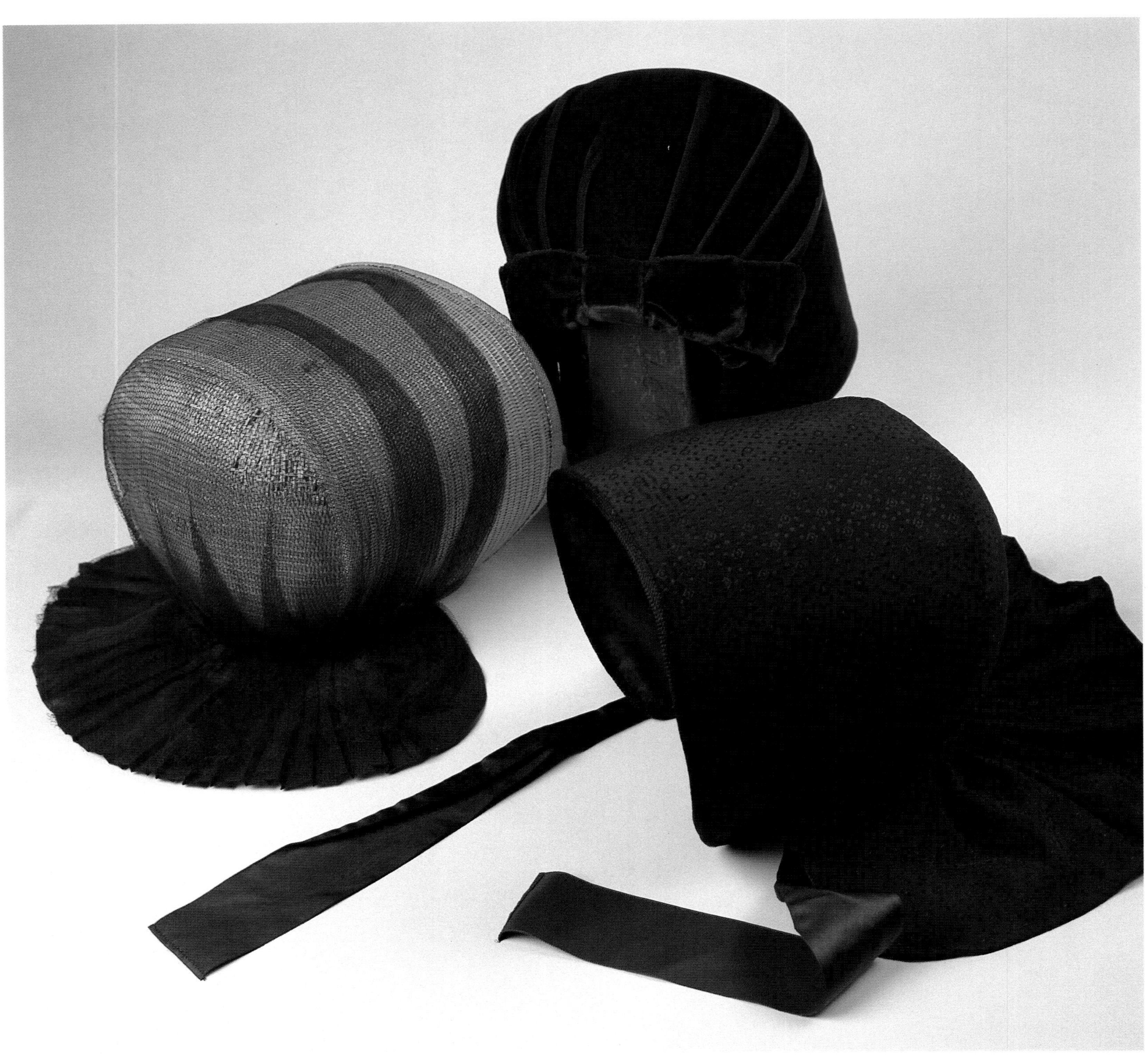

ABOVE:
Bonnet grouping, blue felt and straw woven, Canterbury, NH
Photo by Todd Buchanan

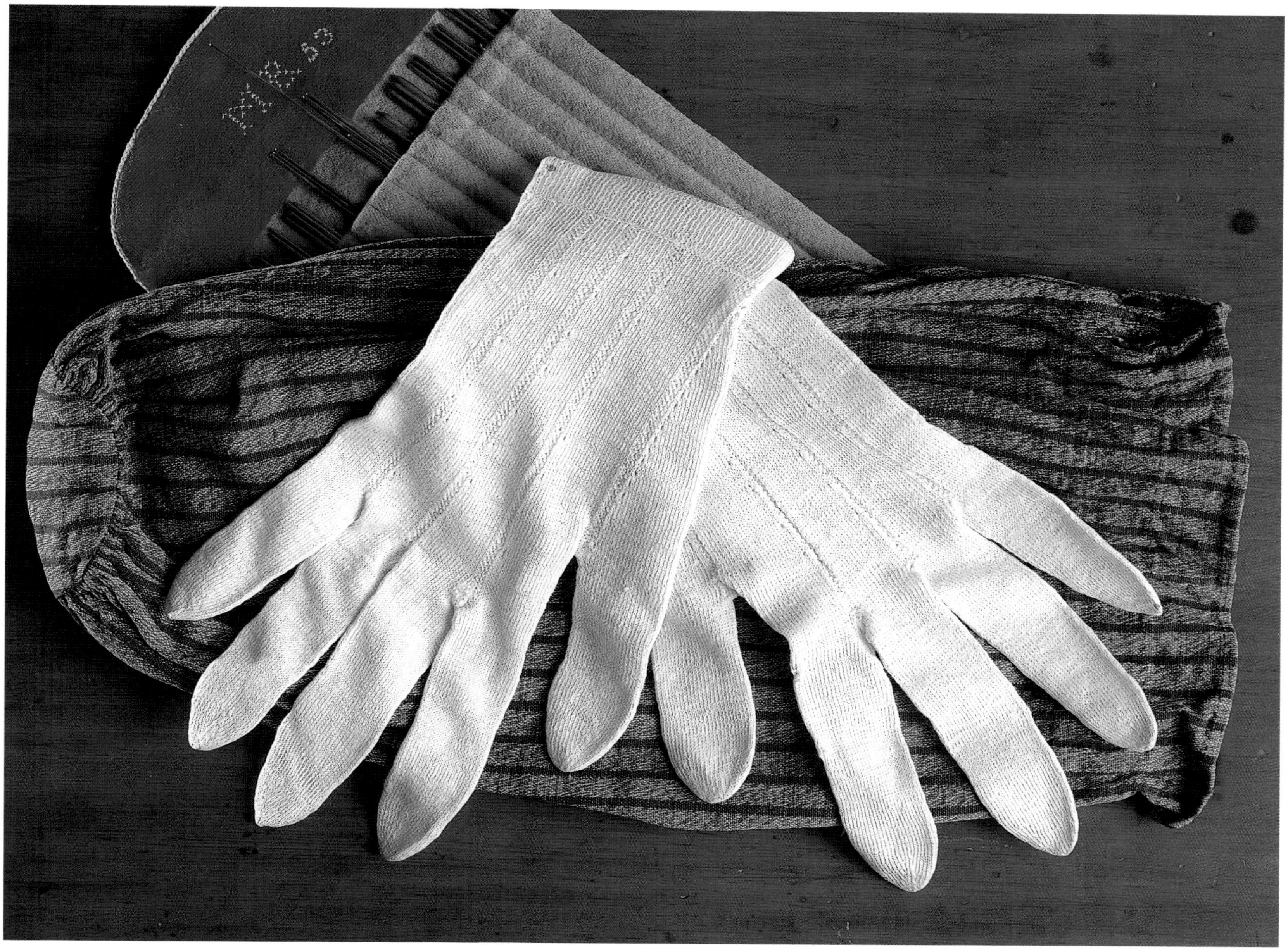

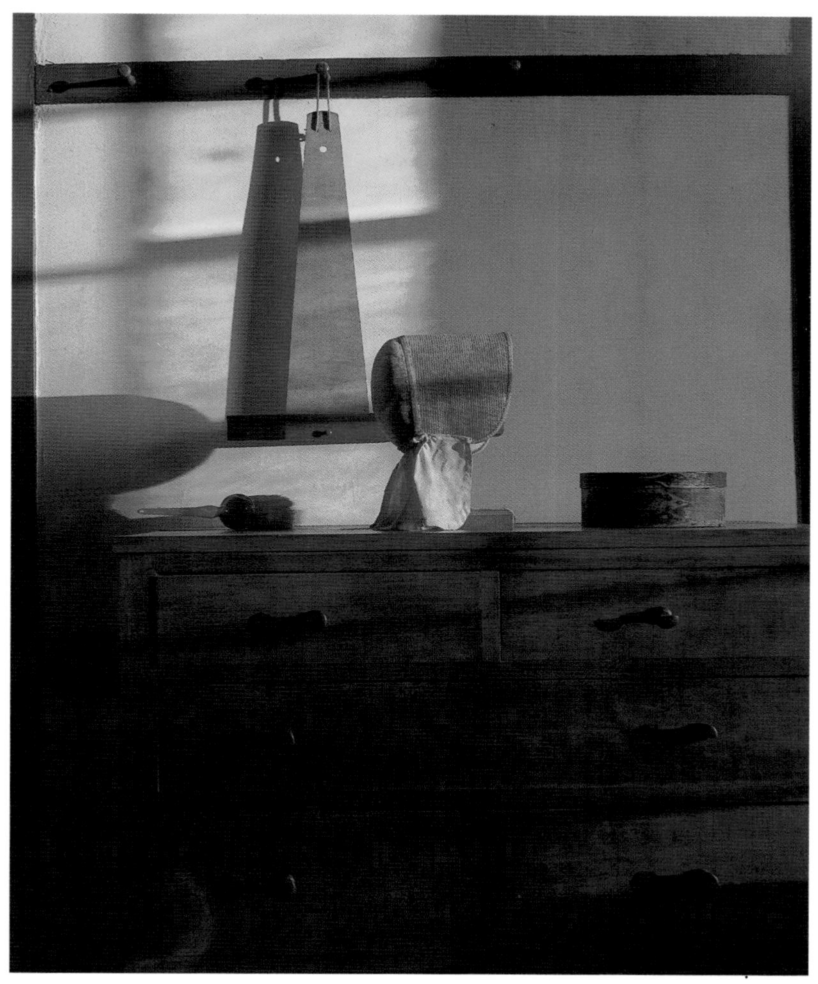

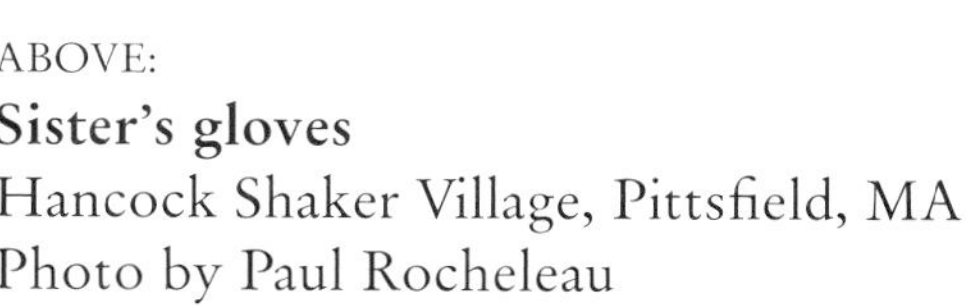

ABOVE:
Sister's gloves
Hancock Shaker Village, Pittsfield, MA
Photo by Paul Rocheleau

RIGHT:
Sister's bonnet at Pleasant Hill, KY
Photo by James Archambeault

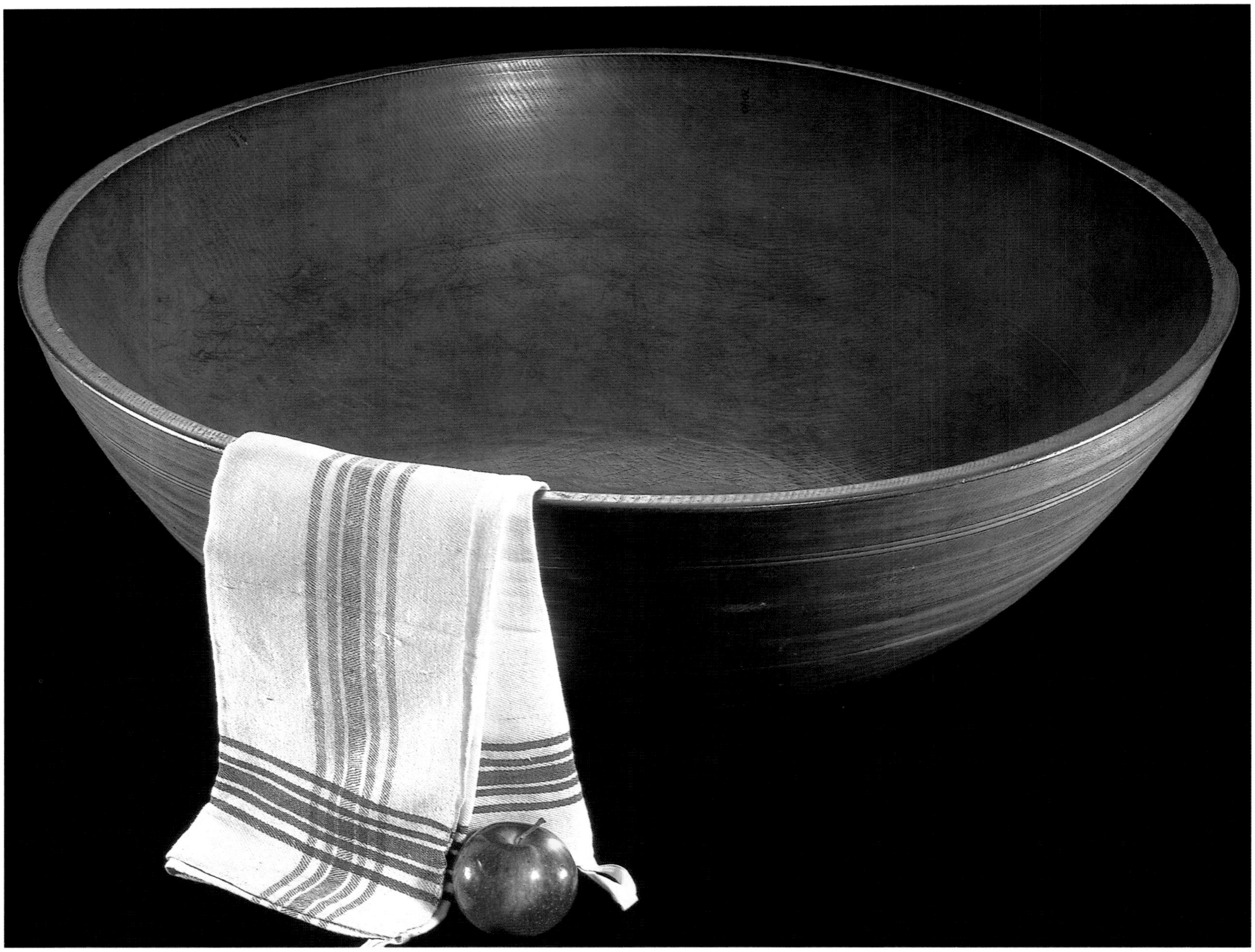

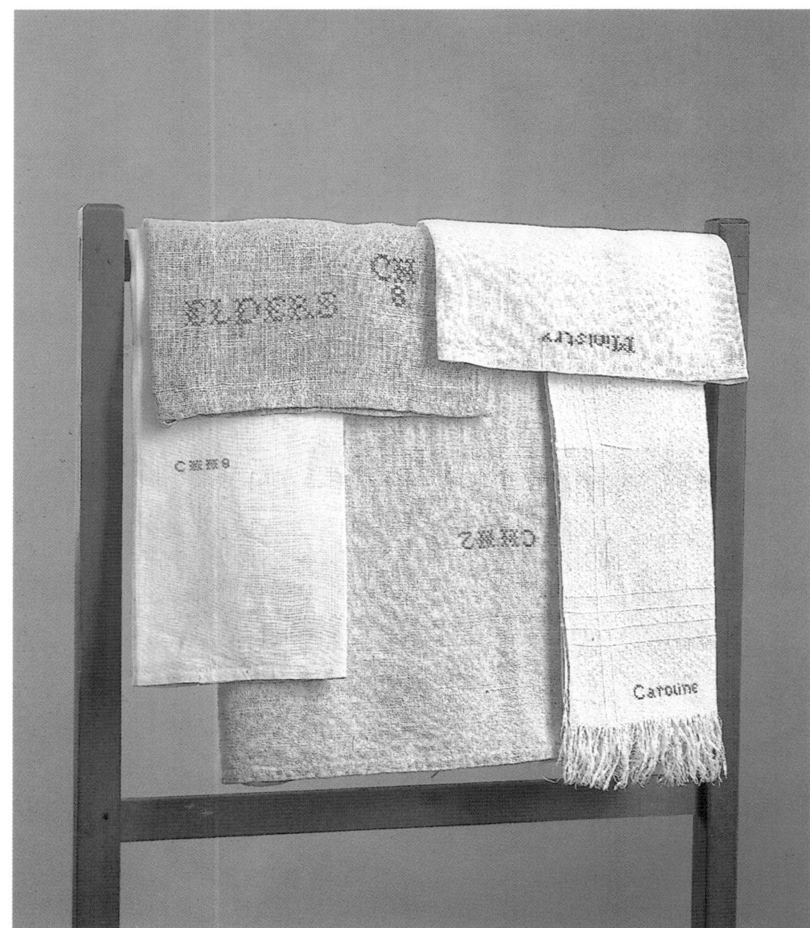

ABOVE:
Bowl, ash, c. 1825-50, New Lebanon, NY
The Shaker Museum and Library, Old Chatham, NY
Photo by Paul Rocheleau

LEFT:
Embroidered towels on rack
Hancock Shaker Village, Pittsfield, MA

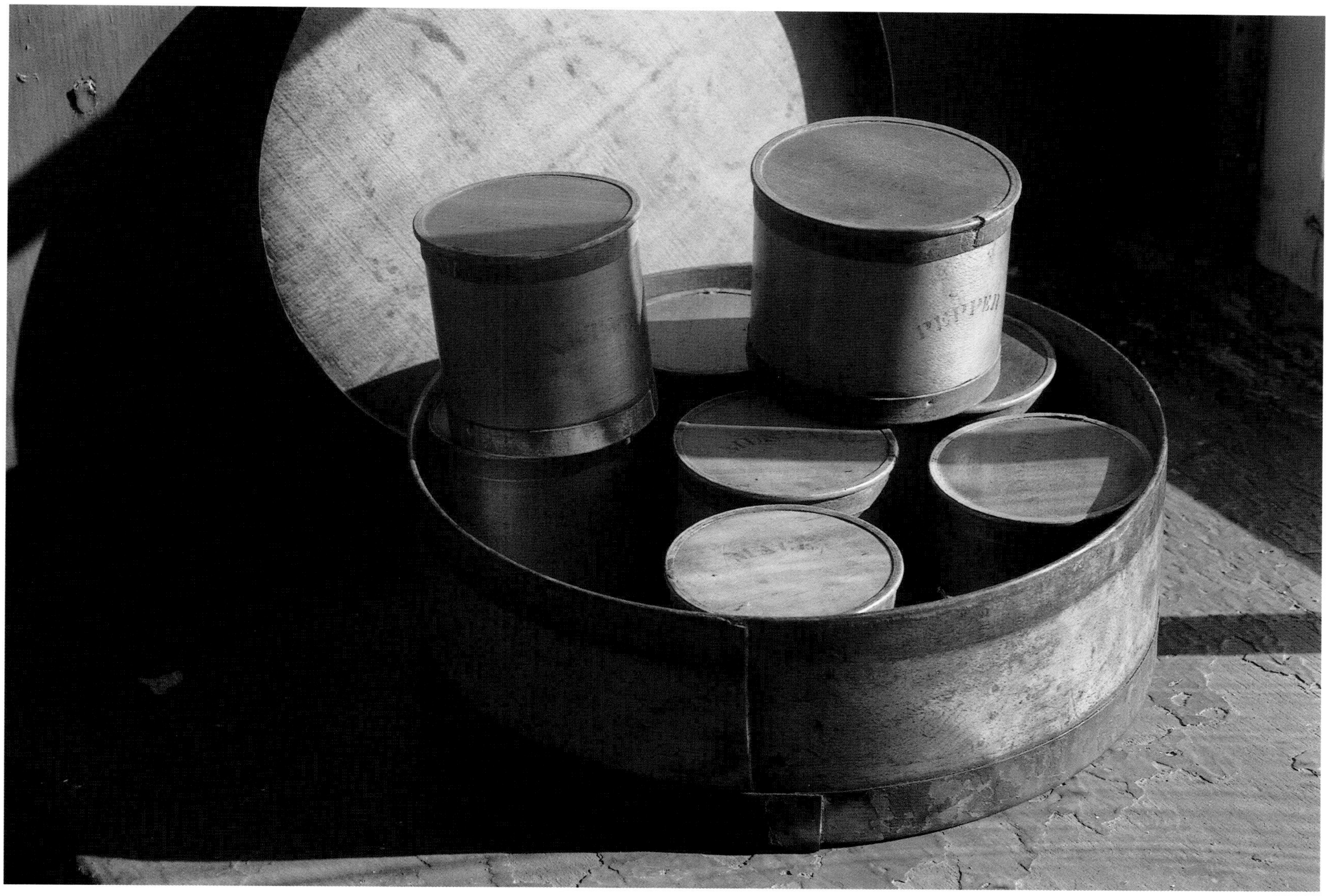

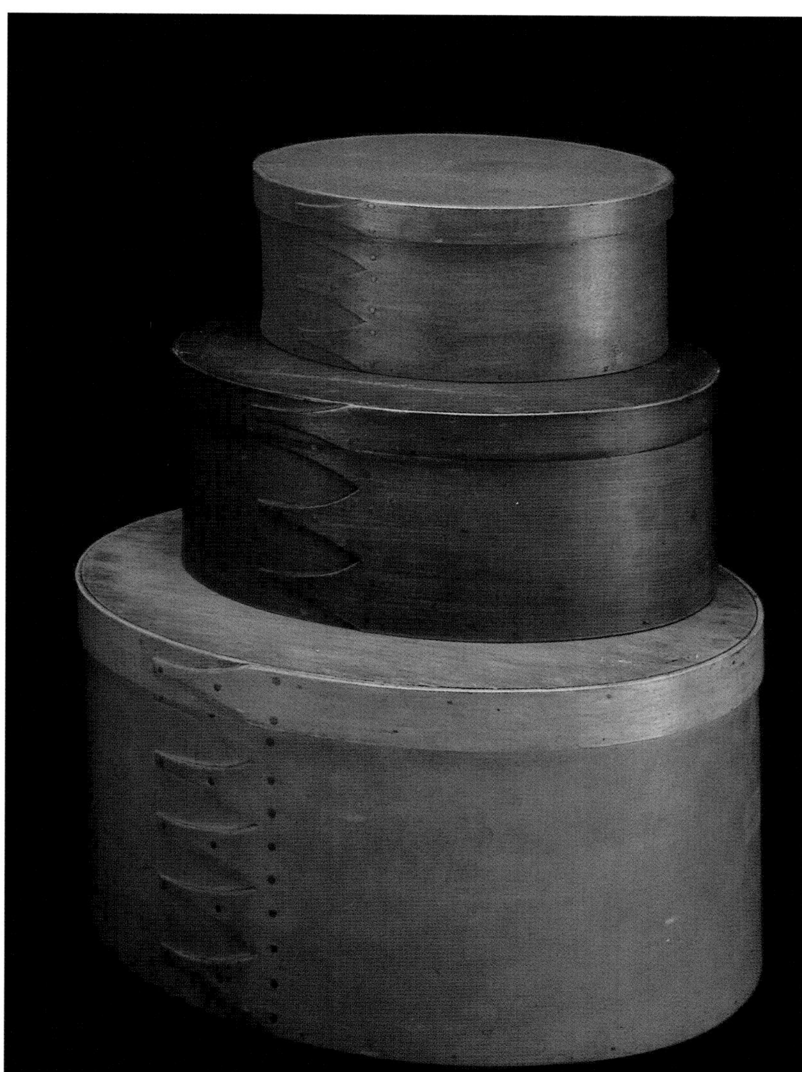

ABOVE:
Set of round spice boxes at Pleasant Hill, KY
Photo by James Archambeault

RIGHT:
Stack of three colored oval boxes
Hancock Shaker Village, Pittsfield, MA
Photo by Paul Rocheleau

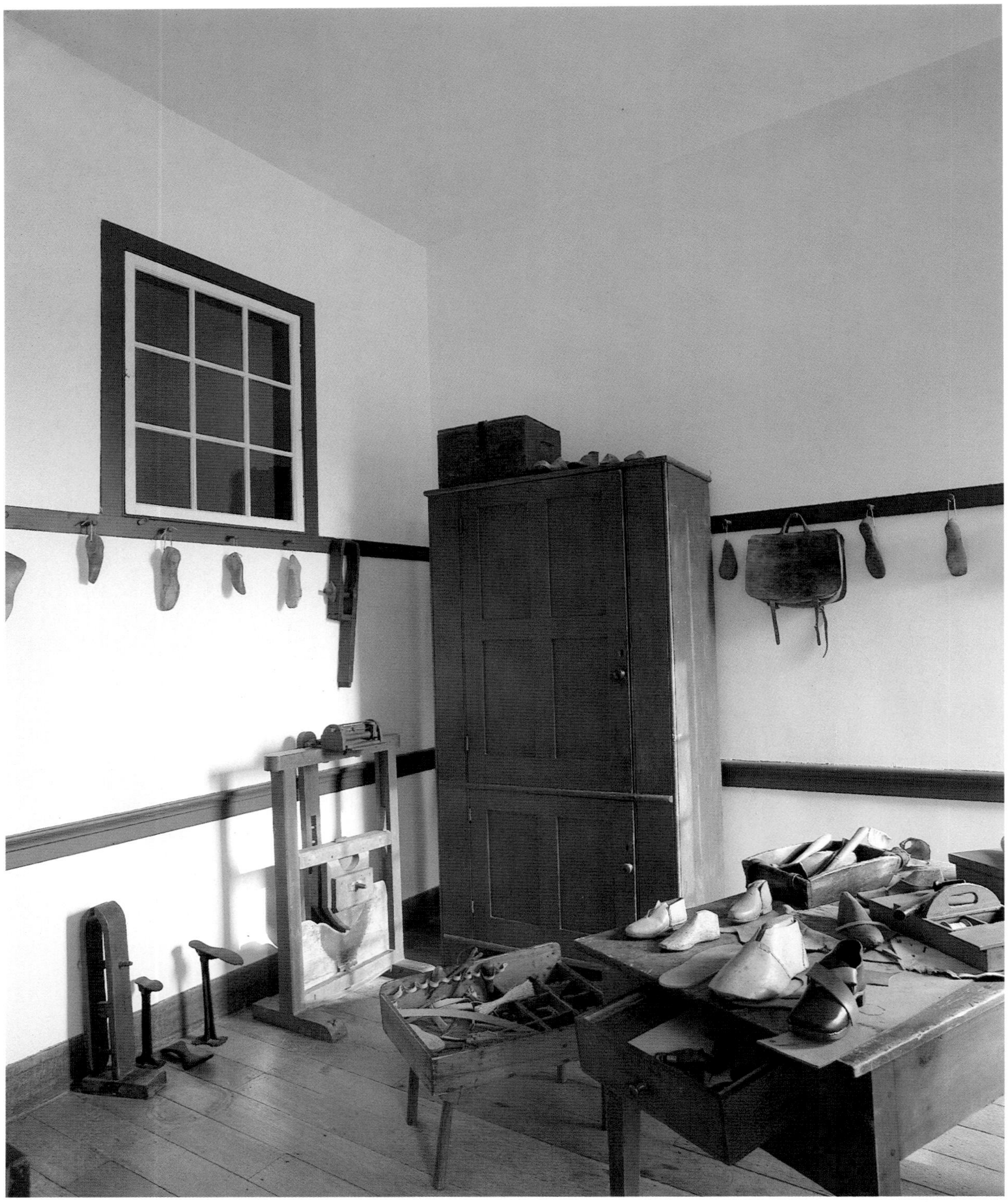

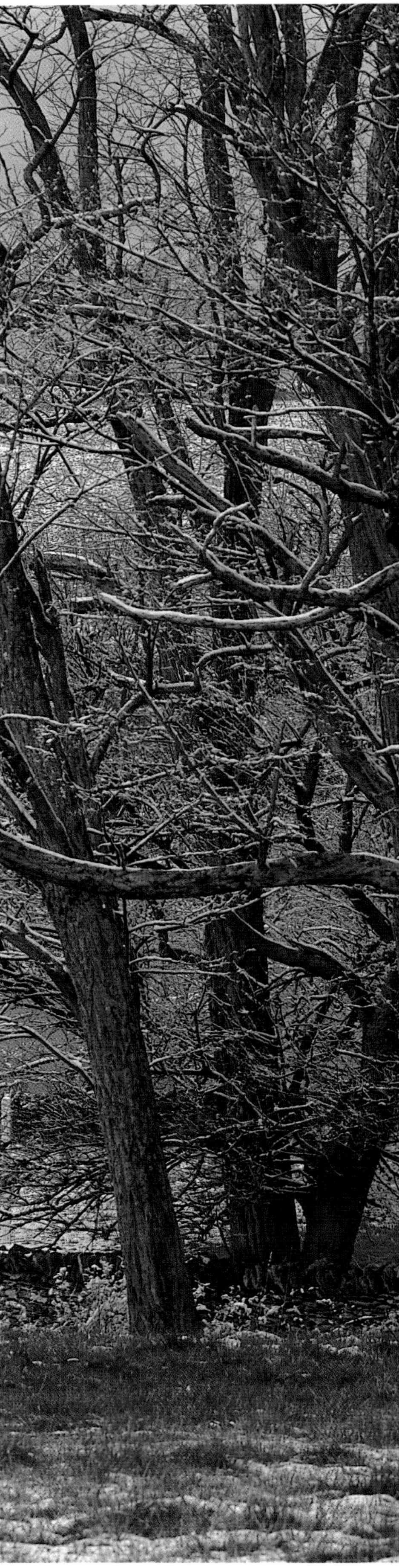

Cobblers shop, Pleasant Hill, KY
Photo by James Archambeault

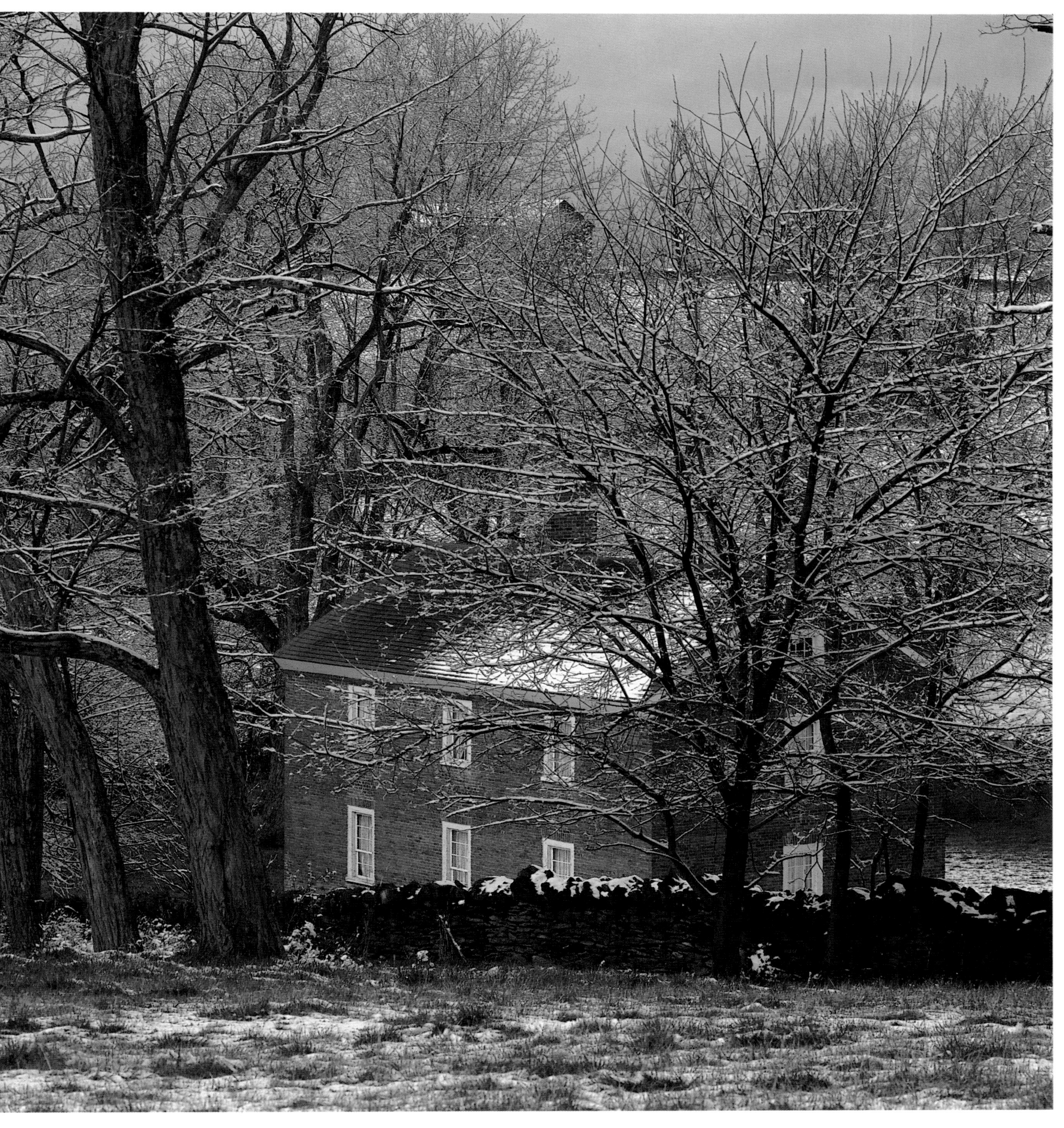

Tanyard Brick Shop, 1823, Pleasant Hill, KY, processed hides for cobblers and harness makers
Photo by James Archambeault

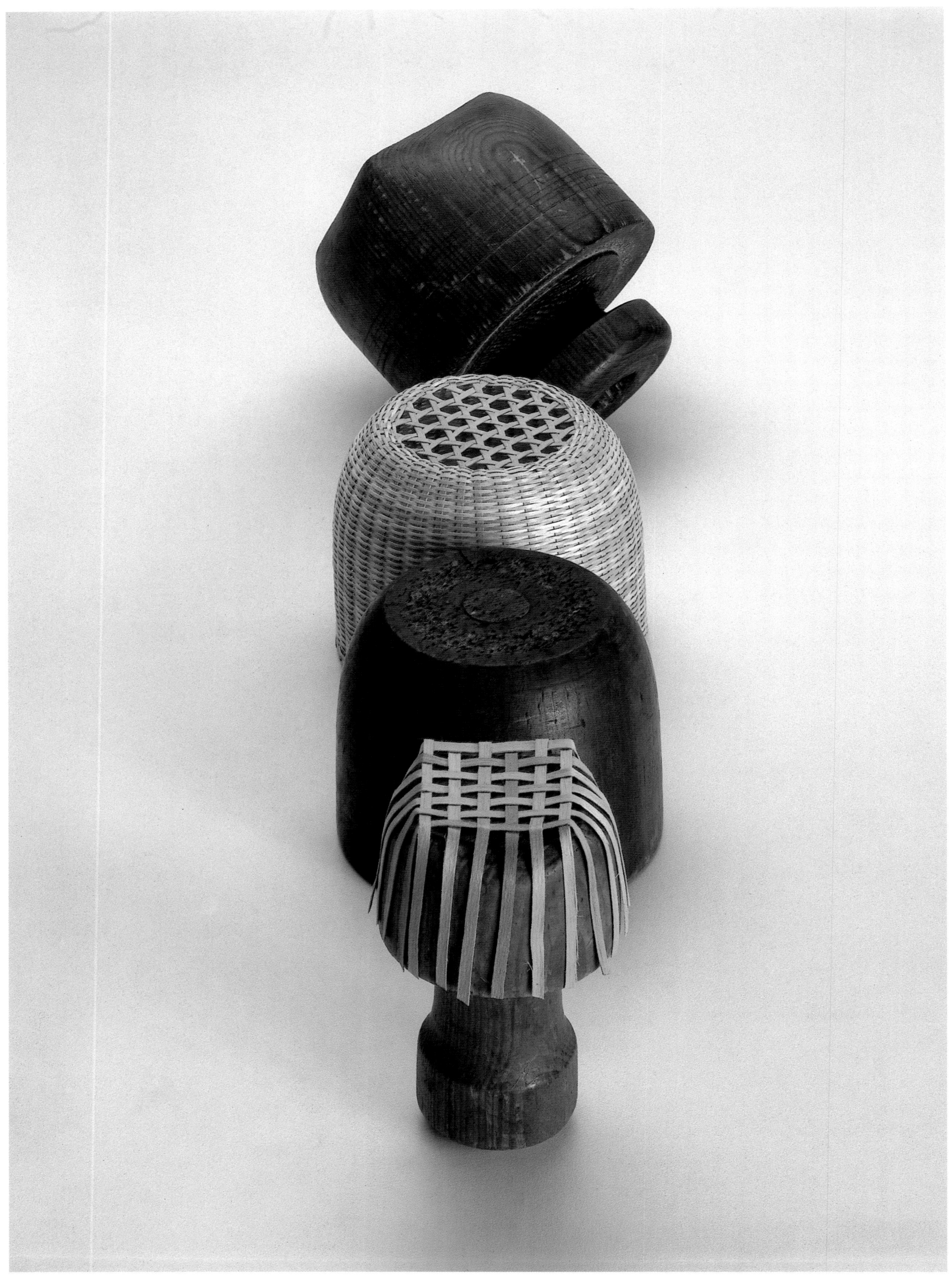

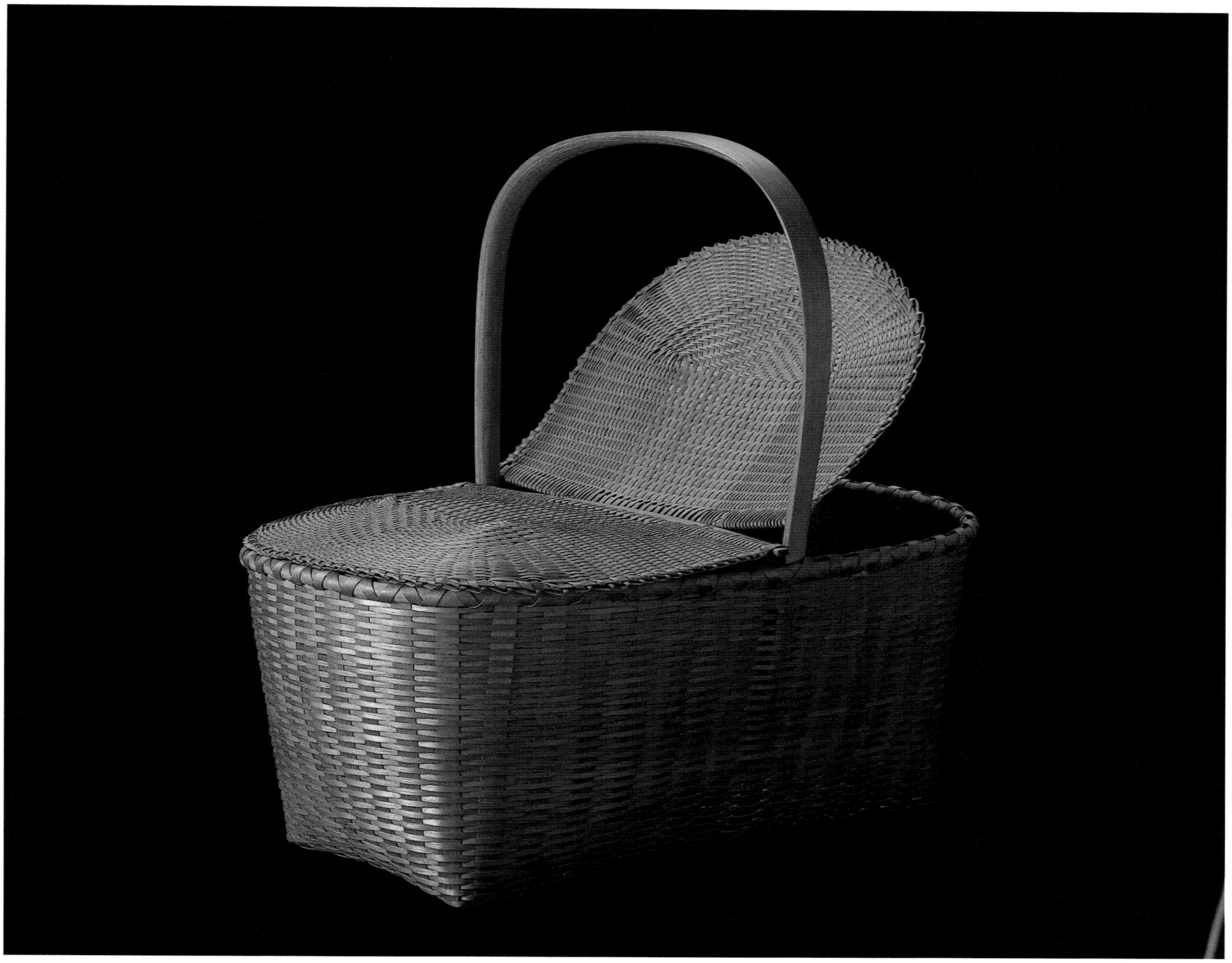

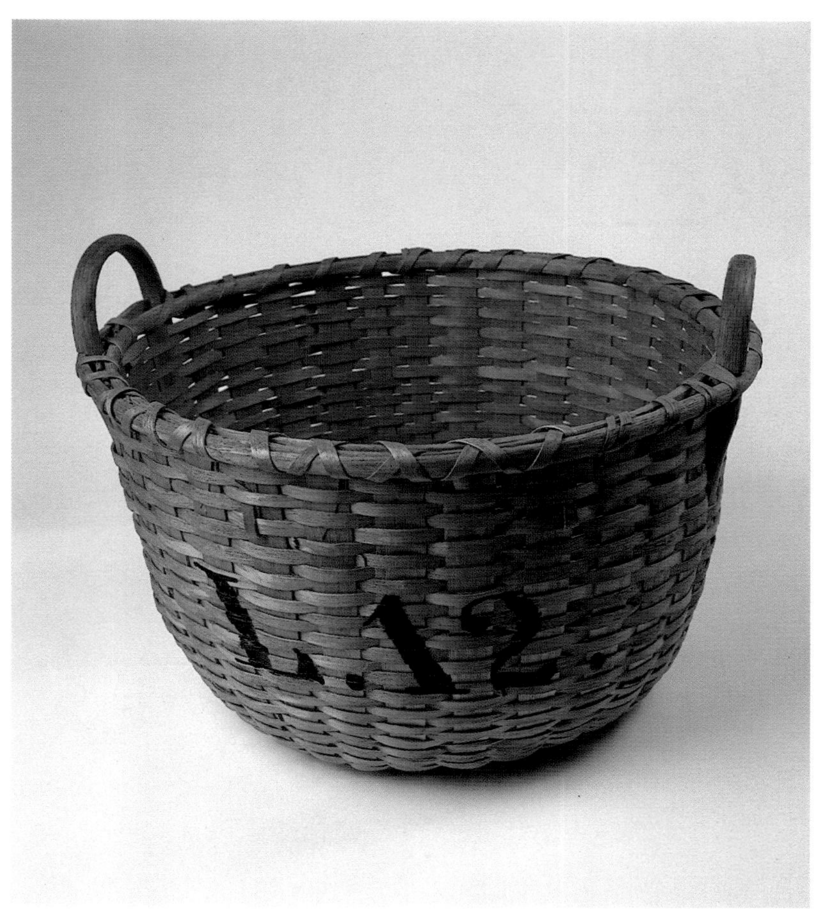

LEFT:
Basket molds
Hancock Shaker Village, Pittsfield, MA
Photo by Paul Rocheleau

ABOVE:
Covered knife basket
Hancock Shaker Village, Pittsfield, MA
Photo by Paul Rocheleau

RIGHT:
Woven laundry basket
Canterbury Shaker Village, Canterbury, NH
Photo by Todd Buchanan

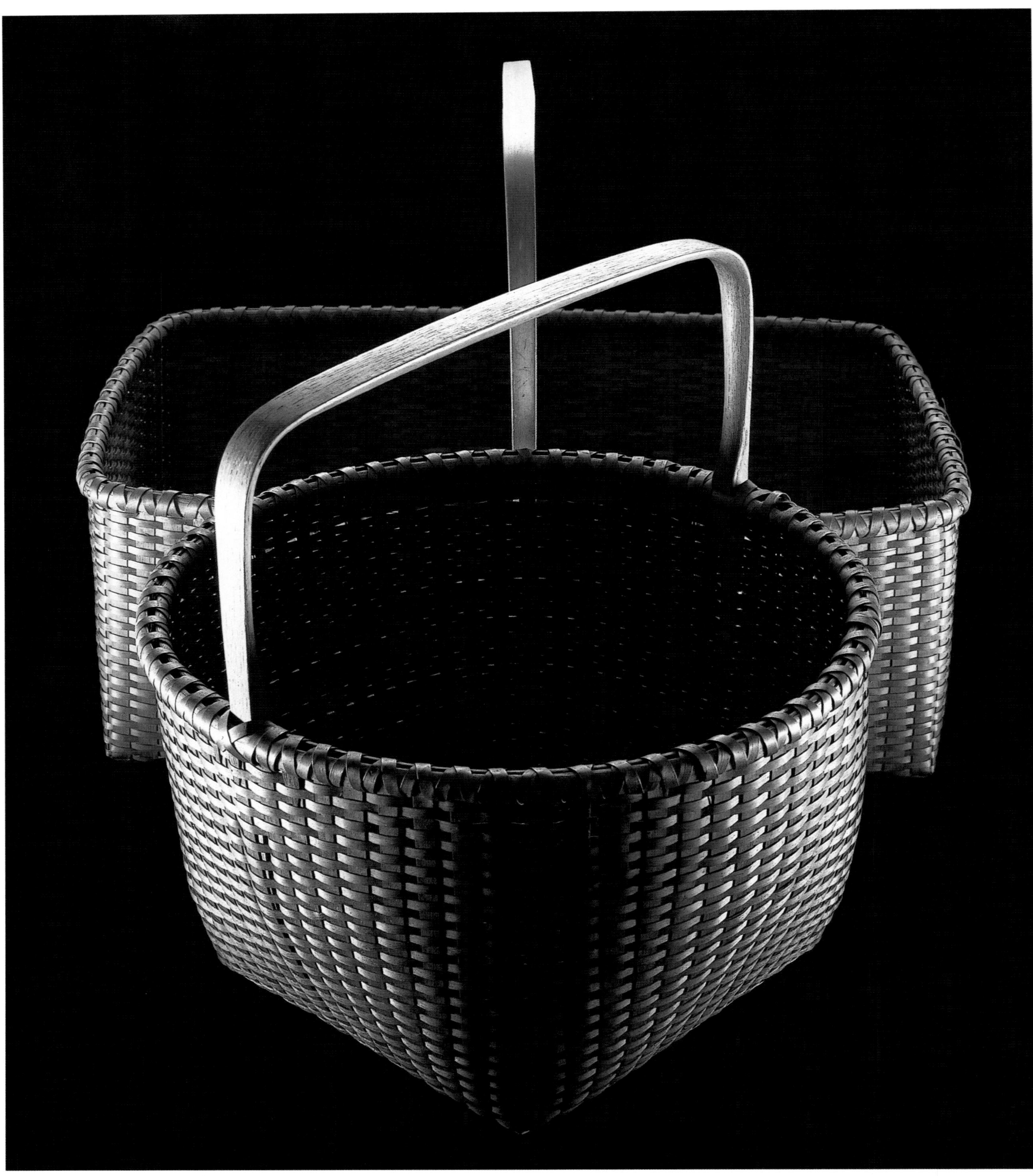

Baskets, c. 1835-70, New Lebanon, NY
The Shaker Museum and Library, Old Chatham, NY
Photo by Paul Rocheleau

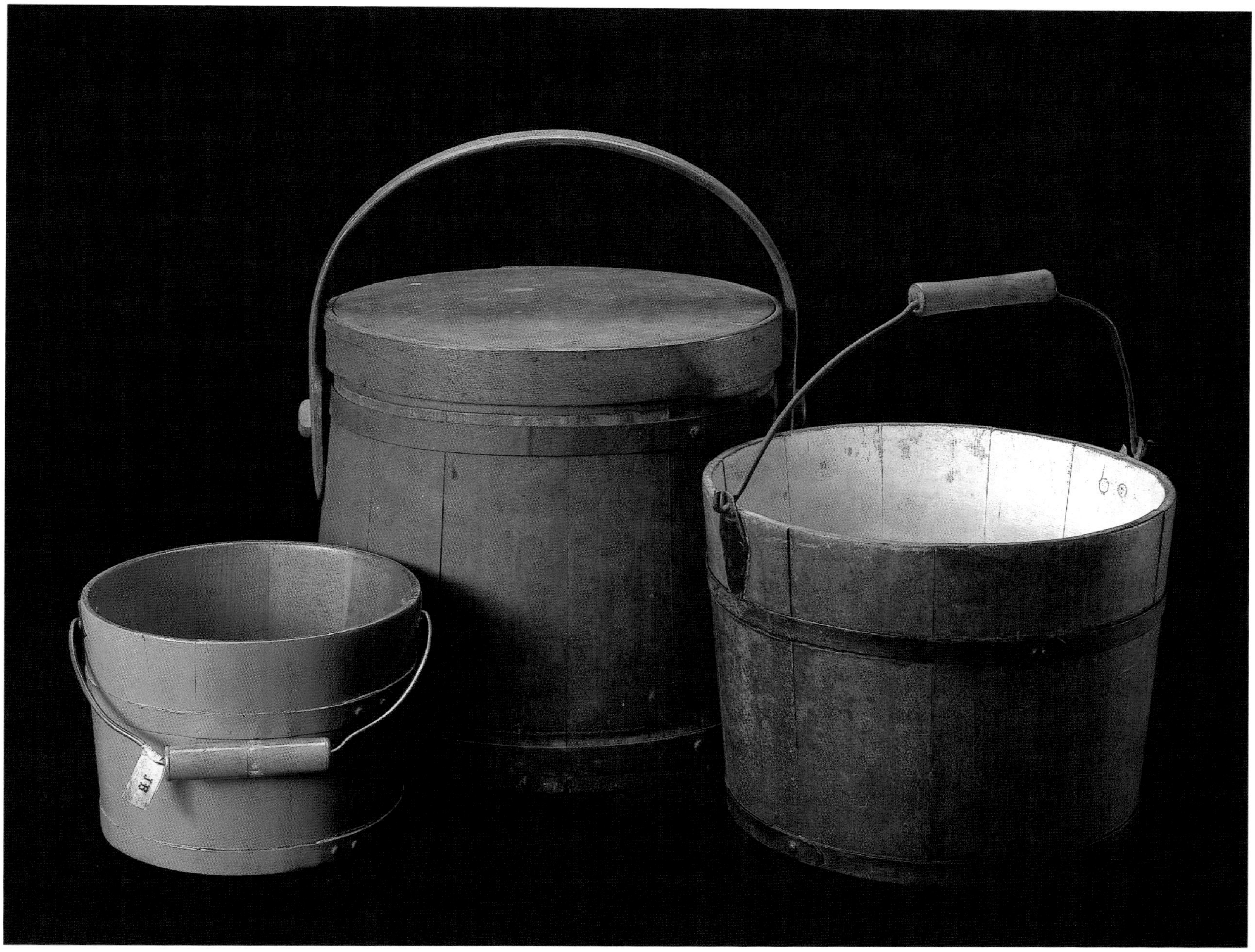

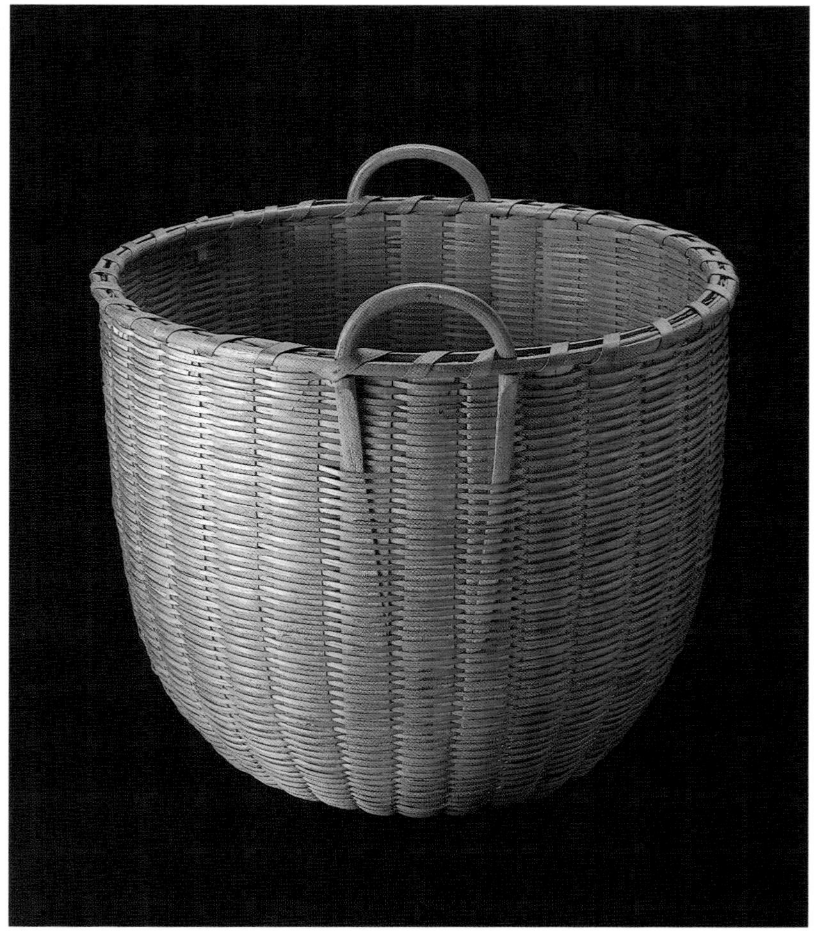

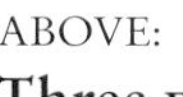

ABOVE:
Three wooden pails
Hancock Shaker Village, Pittsfield, MA
Photo by Paul Rocheleau

RIGHT:
Circular basket with two handles, c. 1840-60
Hancock Shaker Village, Pittsfield, MA
Photo by Paul Rocheleau

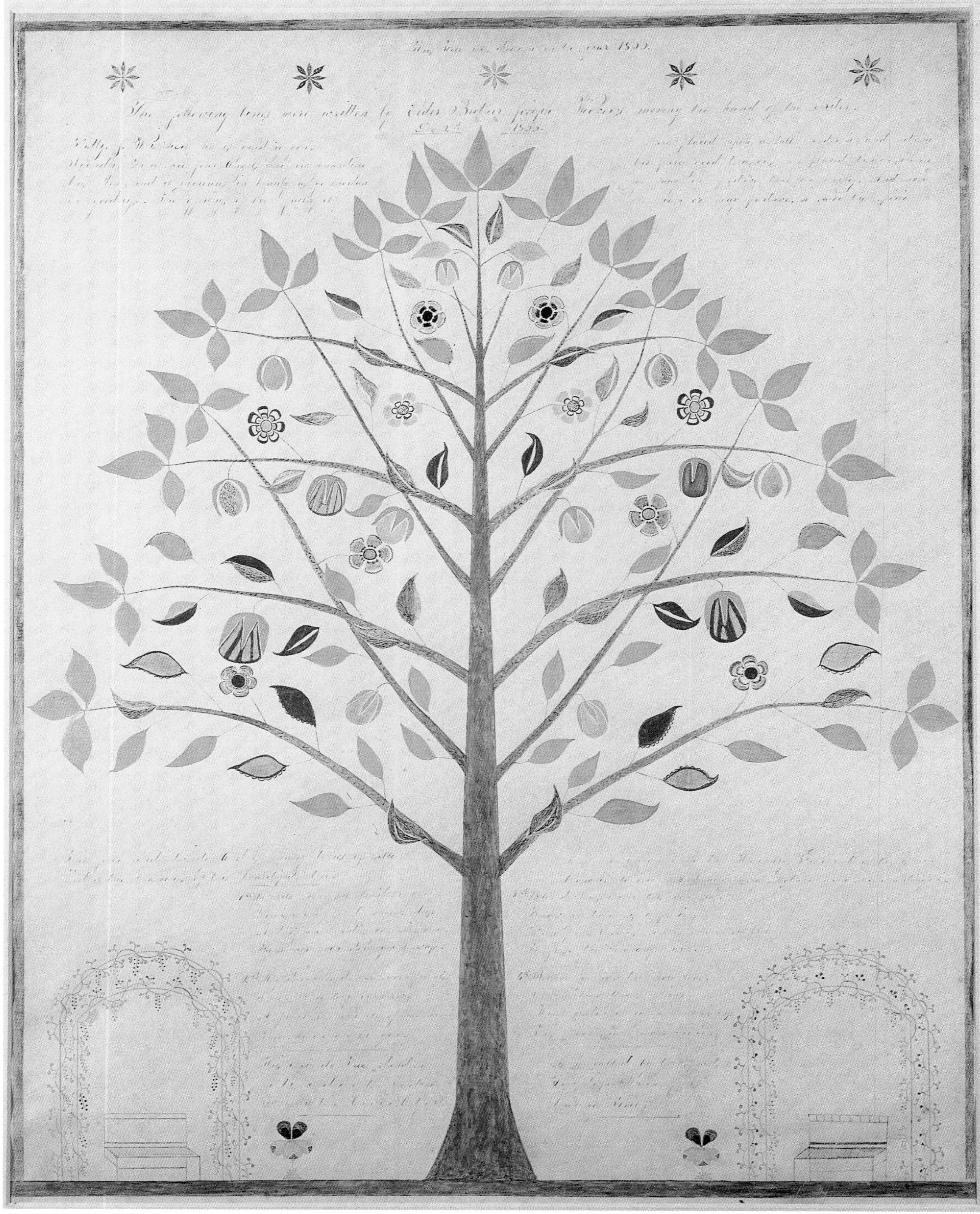

CHAPTER IV

MANIFESTATIONS OF SPIRIT

One of the most remarked-upon attributes of the Shakers' faith was its rejection of the arts, not only as individual expression but even as part of the community's ideals. This might be partially explained by the fact that most Shakers came from backgrounds with no particular artistic traditions. Yet many of them had grown up in Christian communities where at least their own churches took pride in artistic creations – paintings and engravings, carvings and sculptures, stained glass and fine tapestries. The early Shakers would have none of this: They absolutely banned works of art, decorations of all kinds, anything that smacked of the frivolities and vanities of the world. This ban was not limited to the places of worship. One of the Millennial Laws warned that "no pictures or paintings shall ever be hung up in your dwelling rooms, shops or office." Mirrors were allowed, but only small ones for making sure that one was neat and clean.

There was a notable exception to this banishment of the arts: music and dancing. Songs, usually accompanied by shuffling or jumping movements, were an integral part of the Shakers' worship services; indeed, they were the focus, the very essence of the Shakers' ritual life. In the earliest years, as they were seized by the spirit of God, Shakers went into all sorts of gyrations, jerkings, and other movements. These were accompanied by various forms of chanting or droning, shouts and singing in unknown "tongues" or nonsense syllables – not necessarily sung to the same music by all present and not using meaningful words.

By 1805 Shakers were composing their own songs and hymns, some based on traditional tunes but most with original (if derivative) melodies. They wrote these down, using a simple notation system of their own that assigned the letter names of the notes to words, with dots and dashes to indicate the lengths. Their hymns, eventually numbering at least 9,000, were occasionally printed in collections; when sung, they were sometimes accompanied by stylized hand motioning. (It was 1871, however, before the first musical instrument, a small pump organ, was introduced into a Shaker service, at Canterbury, New Hampshire.) Their dancing also became more organized, as the participants arranged themselves in rows or lines – the two sexes always separate – and to the accompaniment of chanting or singing moved through various "marches" (processions) or "wheels." These formal patterns were often broken up by more spontaneous movements – the "dancing" that attracted many outsiders to visit and exclaim over the Shakers' exotic ways (and sometimes accuse them of immorality because of their uninhibited dancing).

The most extraordinary exception to the Shakers' banning of artistic expression, however, came during the period known as the Era of Manifestations, which extended from 1837 into the early 1850s. Visions, dreams, voices, prophecies, clairvoyance, healings, miracles of tongue-speaking – spiritual, ecstatic and mystical phenomena of many kinds had been a part of the Shaker faith from its inception. Shakers called them "gifts," as in the Biblical sense of manifestations of God. As the communities grew and prospered in the first decades of the 19th century, that aspect of Shakerism tended to get brushed aside by the more practical activities and concerns of turning the villages into self-sustaining enterprises. Then in 1837 – according to tradition, beginning with some girls at the original settlement of Watervliet (formerly Niskeyuna) – Shakers began to experience a new intensity of "gifts," mystic exaltation that took the form of dreams, visions and revelations. As this phenomenon swept through the Shaker communities, it produced a marvelous revival of the spiritual life as manifested in new rituals, dances, hymns and songs. This was an especially fertile period for Shaker hymns: the best known of these, "Simple Gifts," was said to have been set down by Joseph Brackett at Alfred, Maine.

The most extraordinary of the "gifts," however, were the many drawings and watercolors set down after their makers had experienced some voice. Many Shakers reported hearing directly from everyone from Jesus Christ and the Holy Mother of Wisdom to historical personages such as Mother Ann Lee and George Washington. Virtually all of the 190 or so surviving spirit, or inspirational, drawings come from either the New Lebanon, New York, or Hancock, Massachusetts, communities; although they were evidently also made at most of the other Shaker communities, they have been lost or destroyed. Most of these are on sheets of paper, often squares (about one foot on each side) or rectangular (usually about 18 iches by 24 inches); some are in the shape of circles, leaves or hearts, a few were made into fans, several were part of a longer roll; most were done in plain ink or in ink with delicate watercolors. The most entrancing ones combined texts with a variety of fanciful, decorative elements, each of which had some symbolic or emblematic significance: apples represented love, chains represented unity or strength, a clock meant mortality, and so on. Everything about these drawings was said to have been dictated or passed down from the spirits that visited the person who subsequently did the drawing: even when being creative, the Shakers had to deny any personal expression. In fact, several look like the work of deliberate (if frustrated) artists - in particular, the drawings of Eldress Polly Reed, Sister Mary Hazard, and Sister Hannah Cohoon. What this list of names brings to the fore is the other distinguishing aspect of the spirit drawings: all the surviving ones are by women, and indeed it is believed that this particular aspect of the Era of Manifestations was probably limited to women.

Although scholars do not agree about the extent to which these drawings may have been influenced by other examples of art, the closest source they have come up with are the so-called Fraktur drawings of Pennsylvania Germans. Whatever the source of their inspiration, these Shaker women left one of the loveliest treasures of American folk art and a distinctive legacy of the Shaker style.

"The Gospel Union, Fruit Bearing Tree," 1855
attributed to Polly Collins, Hancock, MA
Hancock Shaker Village, Pittsfield, MA

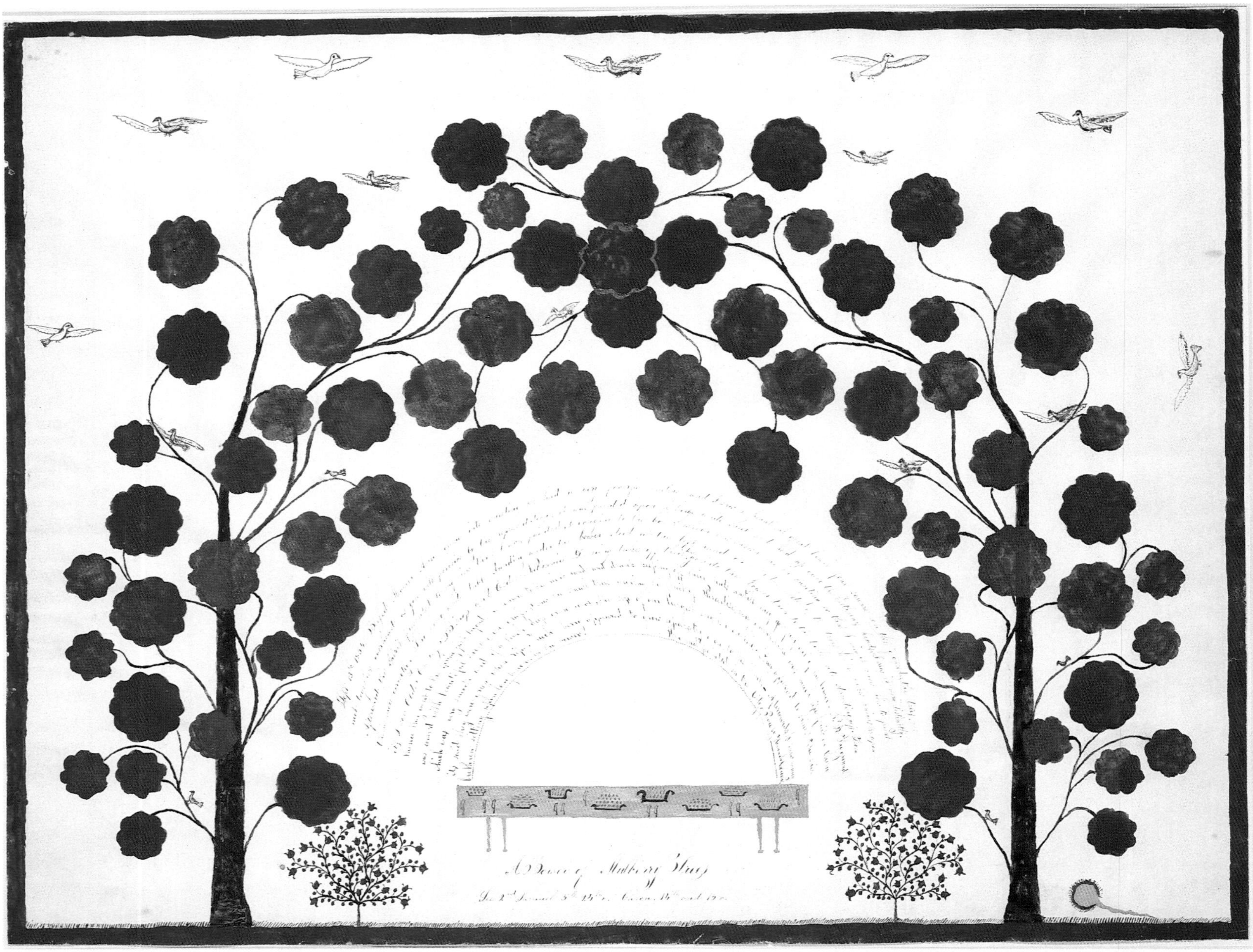

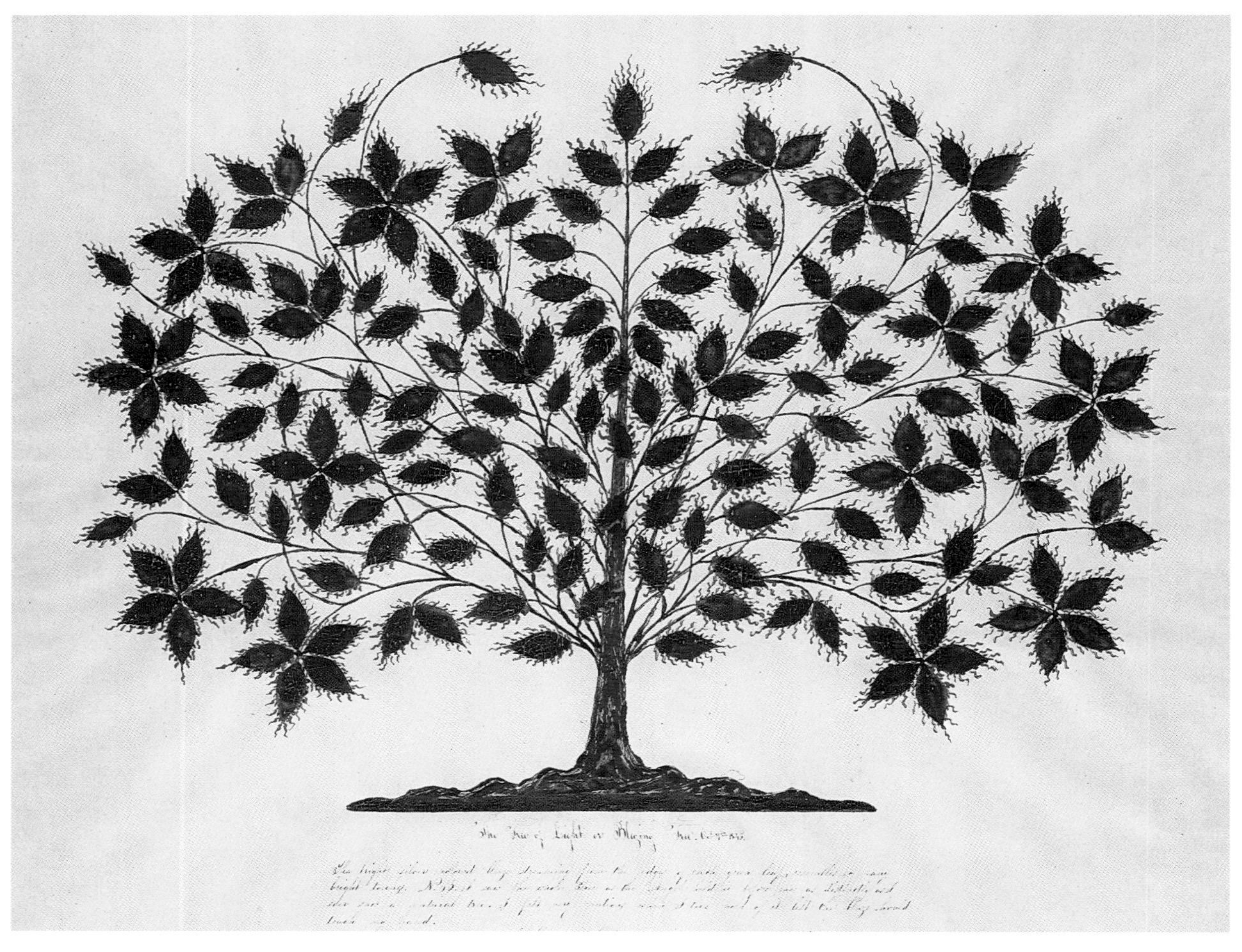

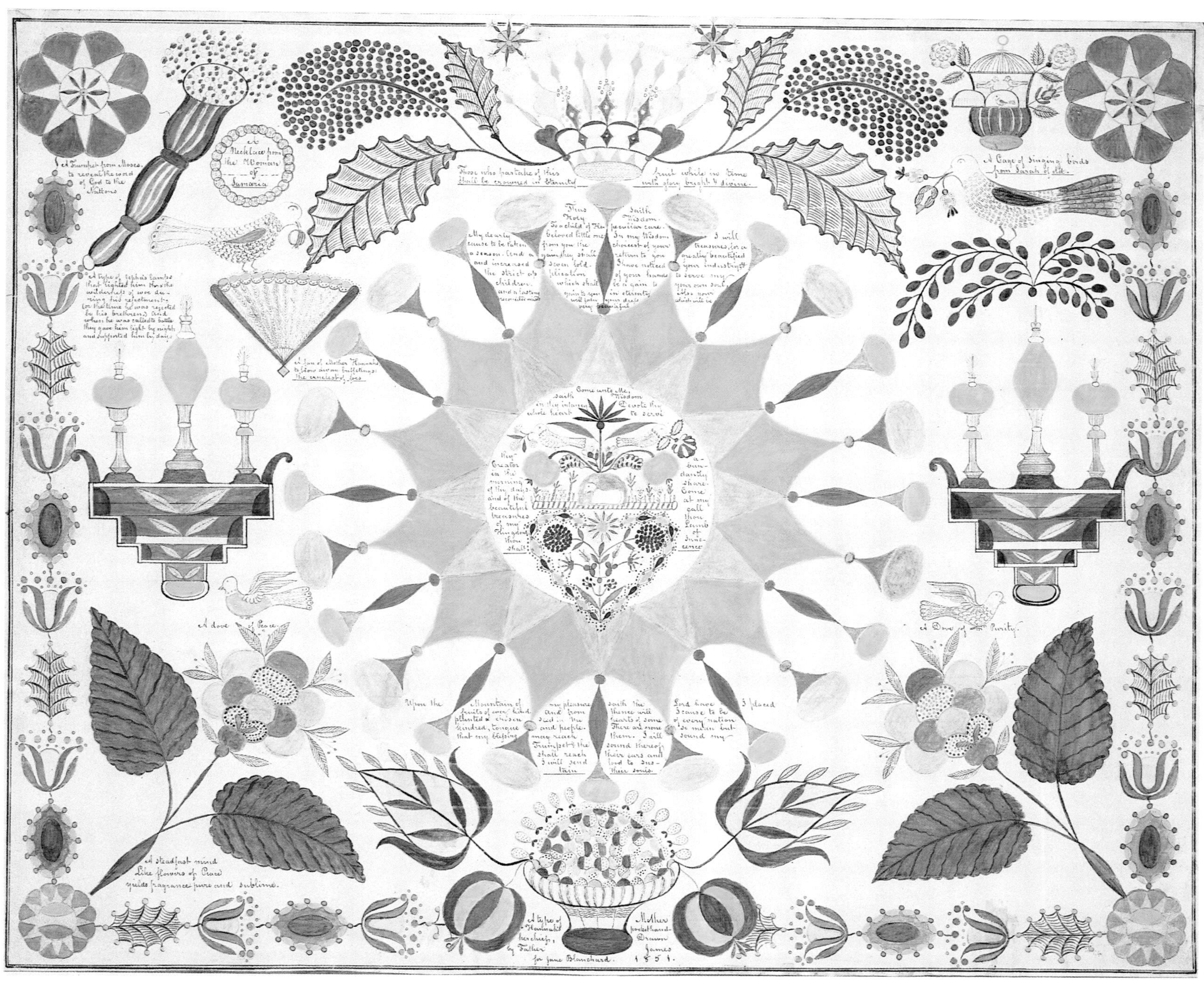

ABOVE LEFT:

"A Bower of Mulberry Trees," September 13, 1854
by Hannah Harrison Cohoon, Hancock, MA
Hancock Shaker Village, Pittsfield, MA

LEFT:

"The Tree of Light or Blazing Tree," October 9, 1845
by Hannah Harrison Cohoon, Hancock, MA
Hancock Shaker Village, Pittsfield, MA

ABOVE:

"A Type of Mother Hannah's Pocket-Handkerchief," 1851
attributed to Polly Jane Reed, New Lebanon, NY
Hancock Shaker Village, Pittsfield, MA

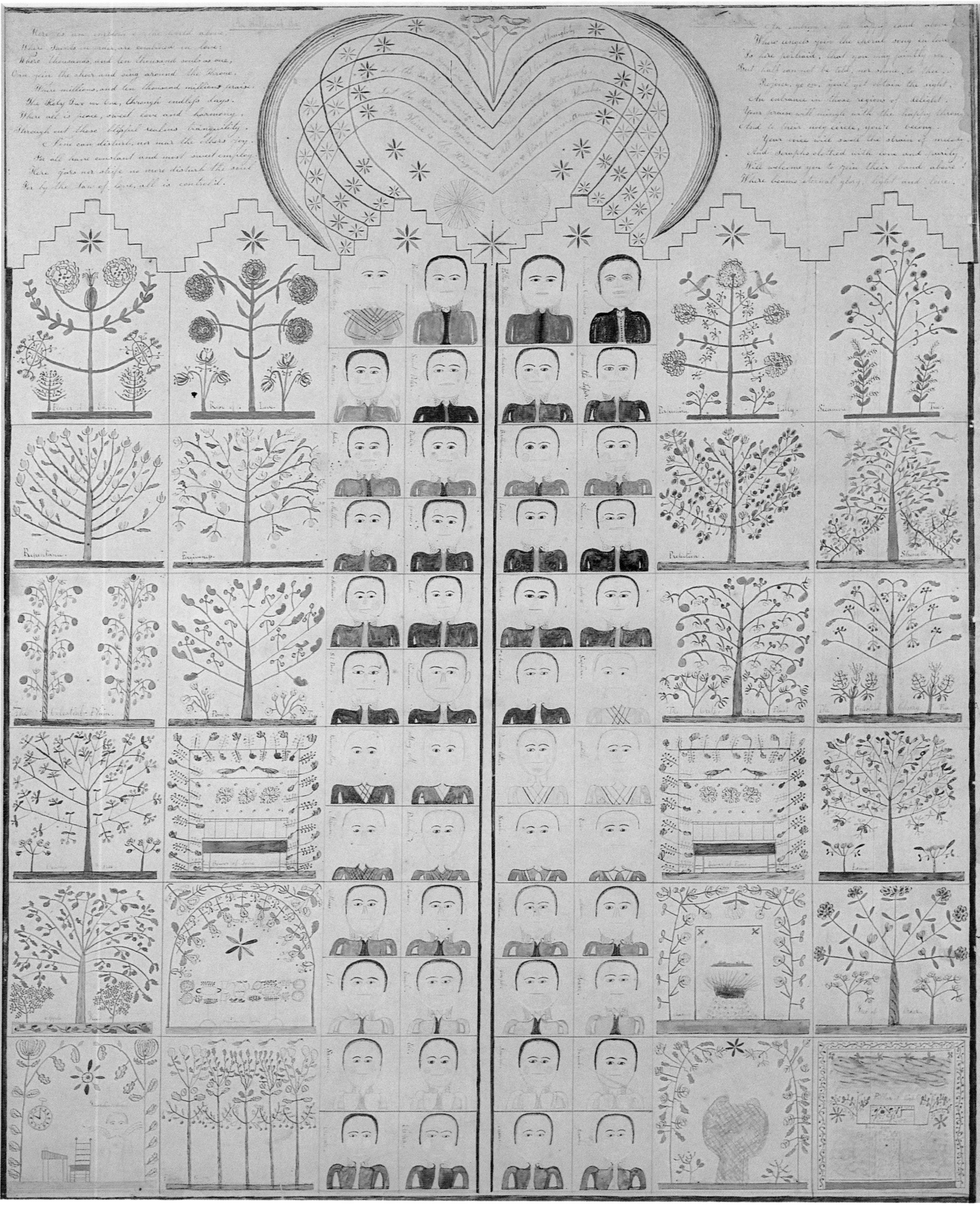
Where thousands, and ten thousand souls as one,
Can join the choir and sing around the throne.
Where millions, and ten thousand millions raise
Where all is peace, sweet love and harmony.
Throughout these blissful realms tranquility.
None can disturb, nor mar the others joy.
For all have constant and most sweet employ.
For by the law of love, all is controll'd.
But half can not be told, nor shown, to thee.
An entrance in those regions of delight.
Your praise will mingle with the happy throng
And Seraphs clothed with love and purity
Will welcome you to join their band above!
Where beams eternal glory, light and love.

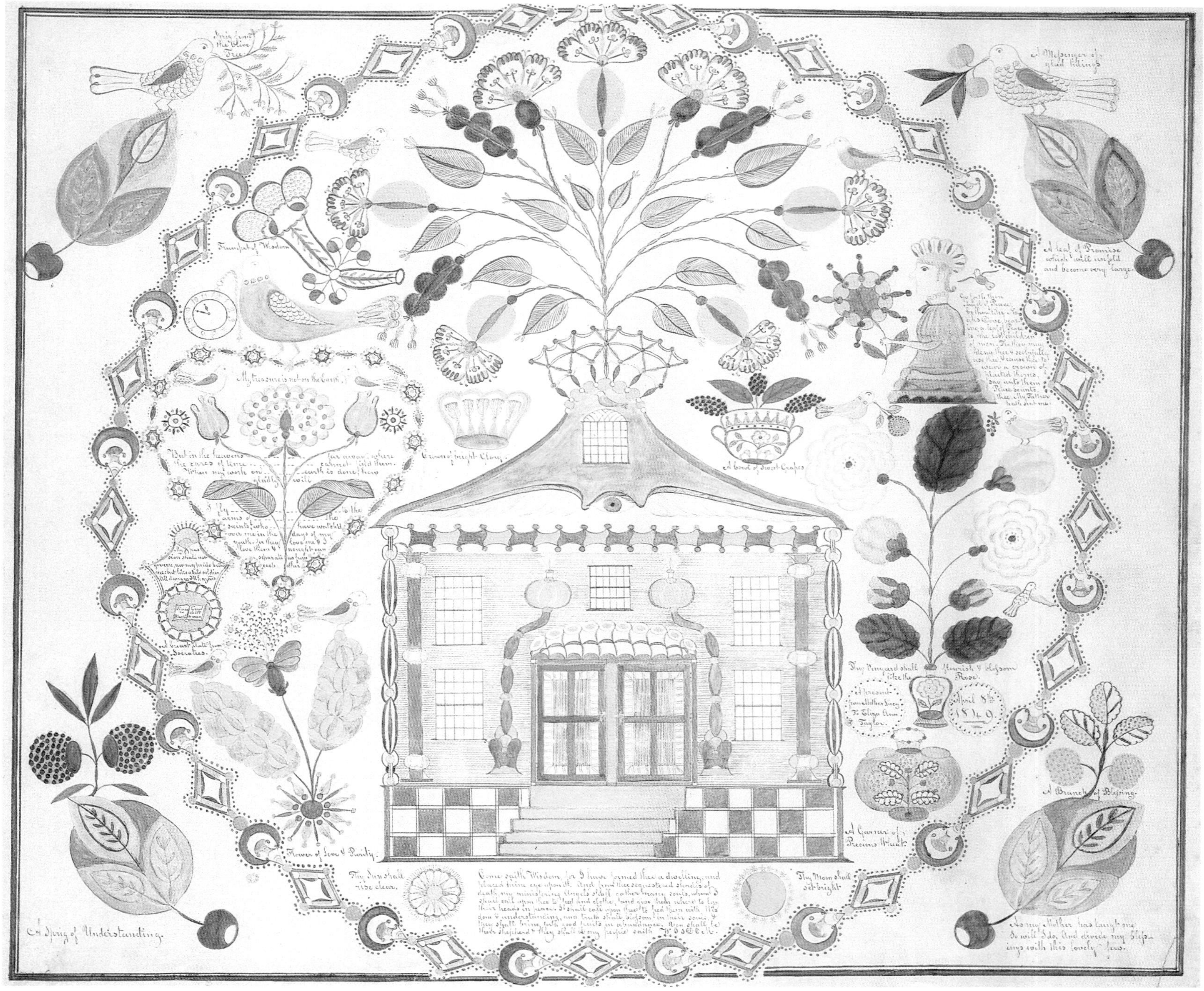

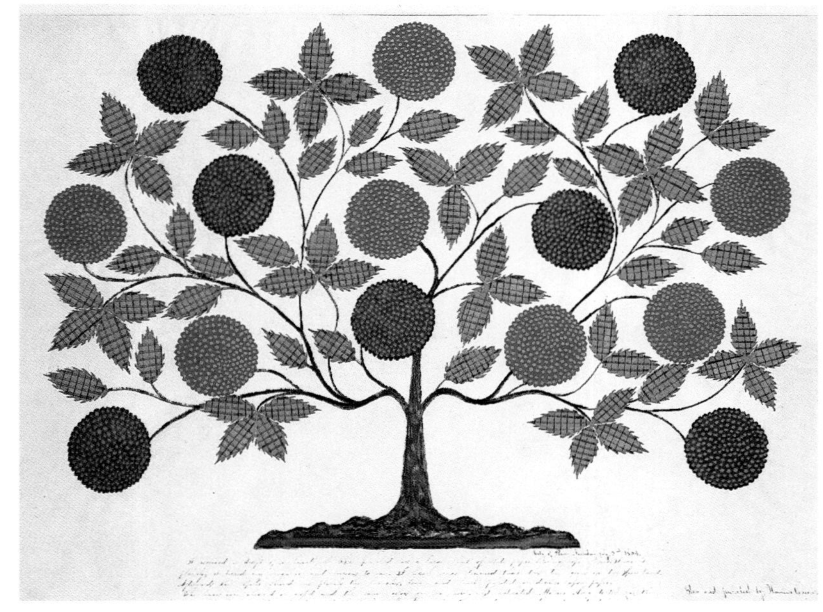

LEFT:
"An Emblem of the Heavenly Sphere," January, 1854
attributed to Polly Collins, Hancock, MA
Hancock Shaker Village, Pittsfield, MA

ABOVE:
"A Present from Mother Lucy to Eliza Ann Taylor," April 8, 1849
attributed to Polly Jane Reed, New Lebanon, NY
Hancock Shaker Village, Pittsfield, MA

RIGHT:
"Tree of Life," July 3, 1854
by Hannah Harrison Cohoon, Hancock, MA
Hancock Shaker Village, Pittsfield, MA

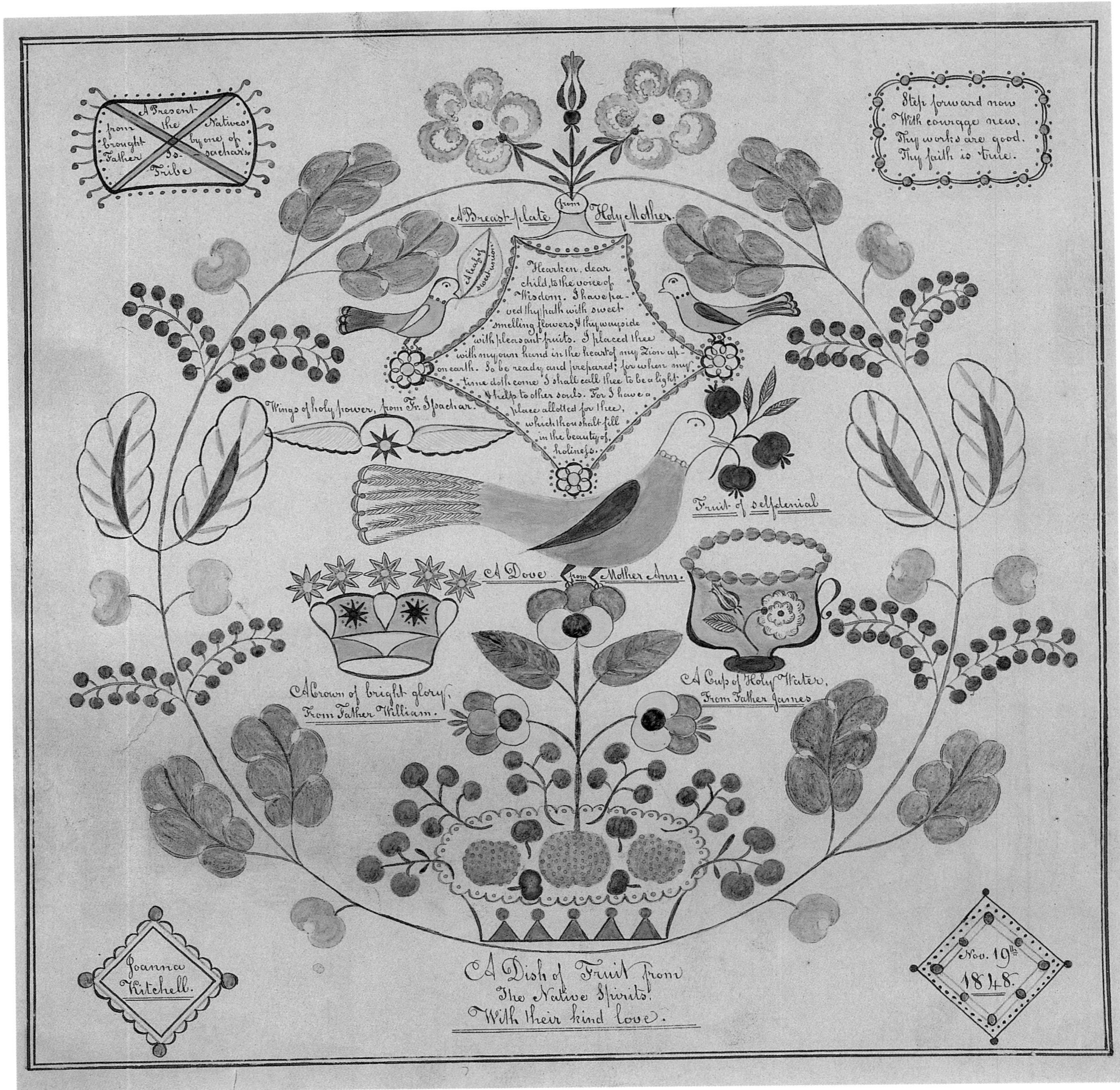

"Gift for Joanna Kitchell (Polly Reed's Gift Drawing)", November 19, 1848
The Western Reserve Historical Society, Cleveland, OH
(MS 3944)

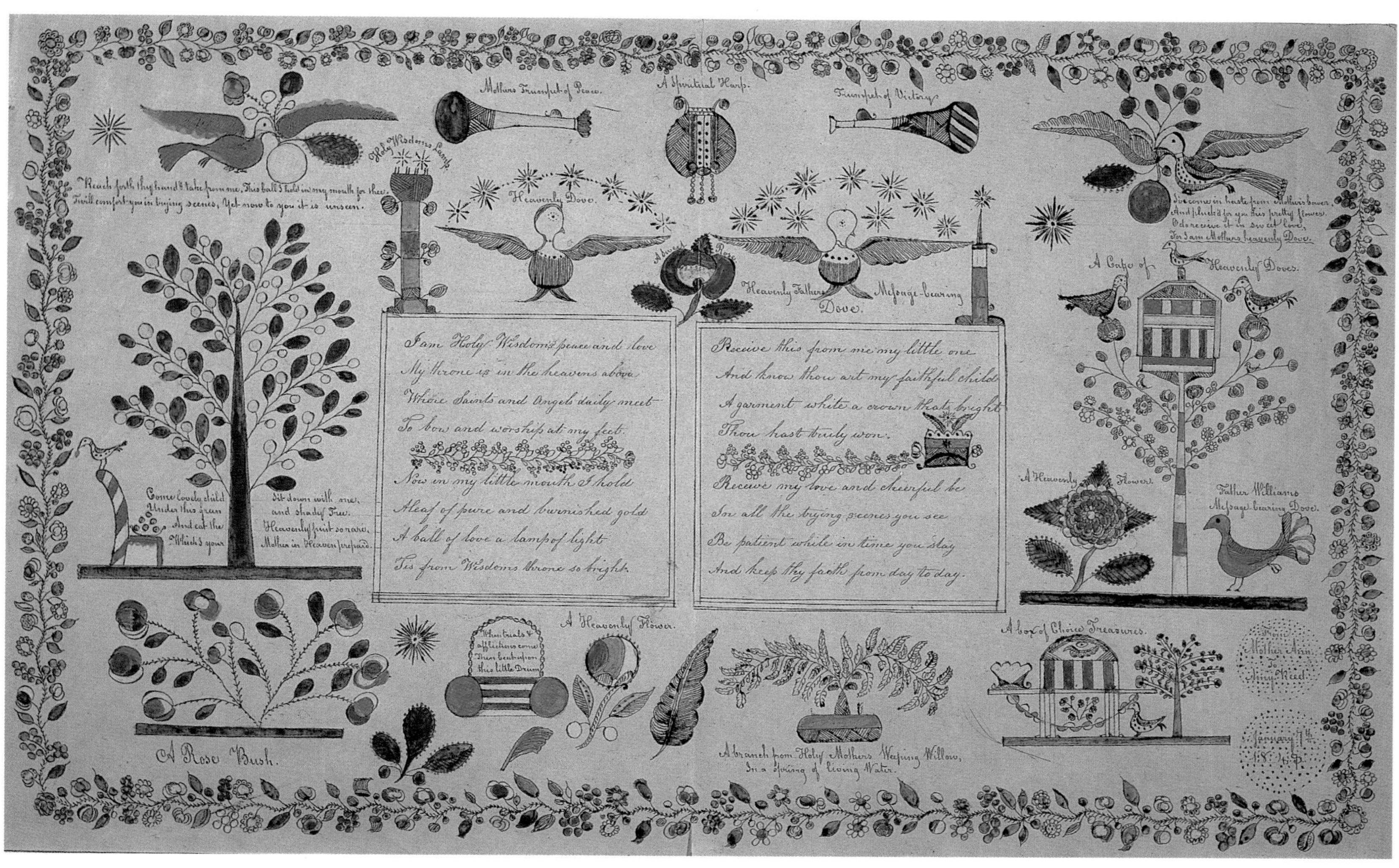

"From Mother Ann to Amy Reed," January 7, 1848
The Shaker Museum and Library, Old Chatham, NY
(11520)

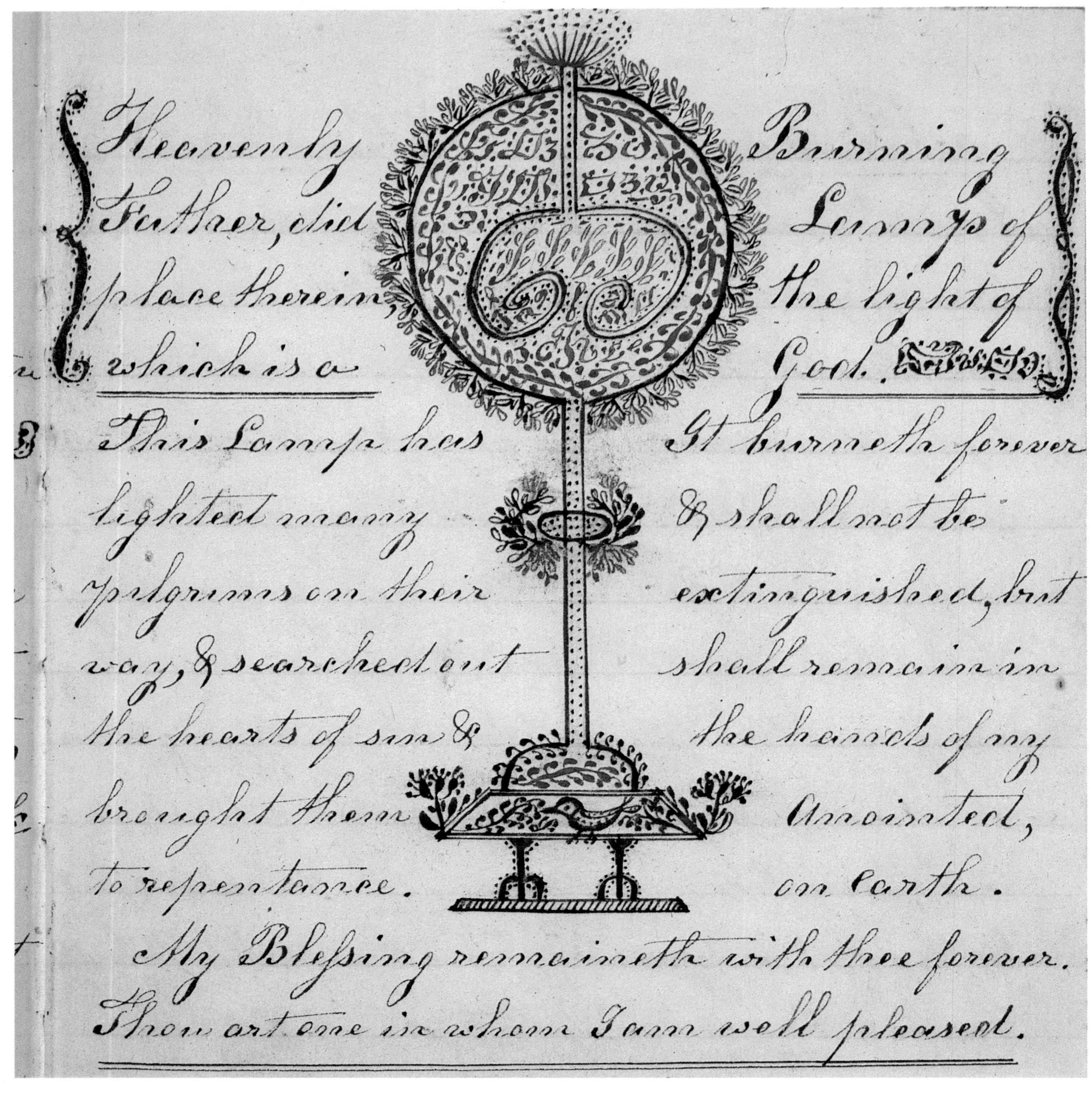

Heavenly Father, did place therein, which is a Burning Lamps of the light of God.

This Lamp has lighted many pilgrims on their way, & searched out the hearts of sin & brought them to repentance.

It burneth forever & shall not be extinguished, but shall remain in the hands of my Anointed, on Earth.

My Blessing remaineth with thee forever. Thou art one in whom I am well pleased.

"A Short Notice from the Heavenly Father, From Holy Mother Wisdom...their Seals of Approbation and Blessing," April, 1845 copied by Eleanor Potter
The Shaker Museum and Library, Old Chatham, NY (13496)

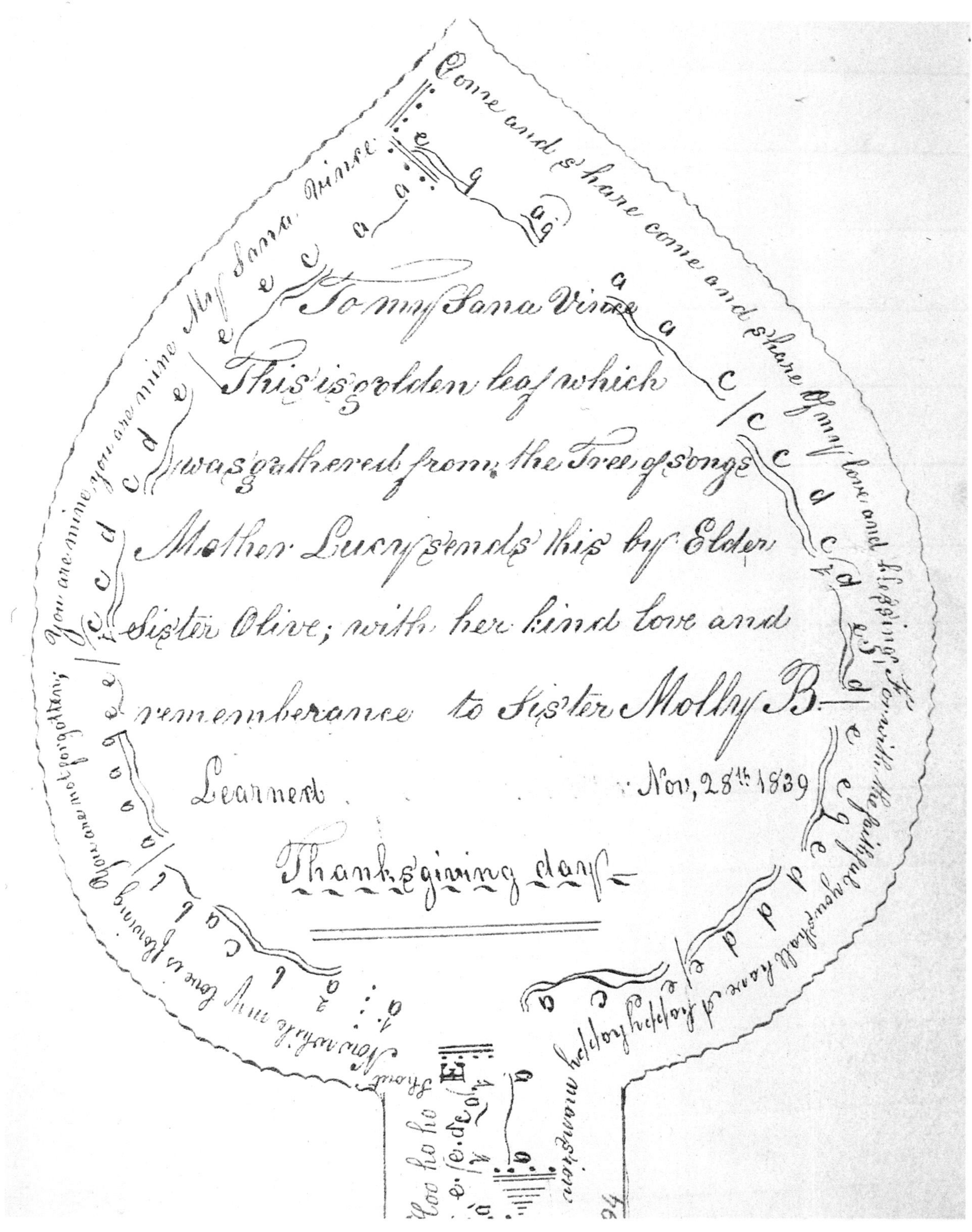

Leaf Sketch, page in a song book,
by Mary Hazzard, New Lebanon, NY, 1839
The Edward Deming Andrews Memorial Shaker Collection
Courtesy, The Winterthur Library, Winterthur, DE

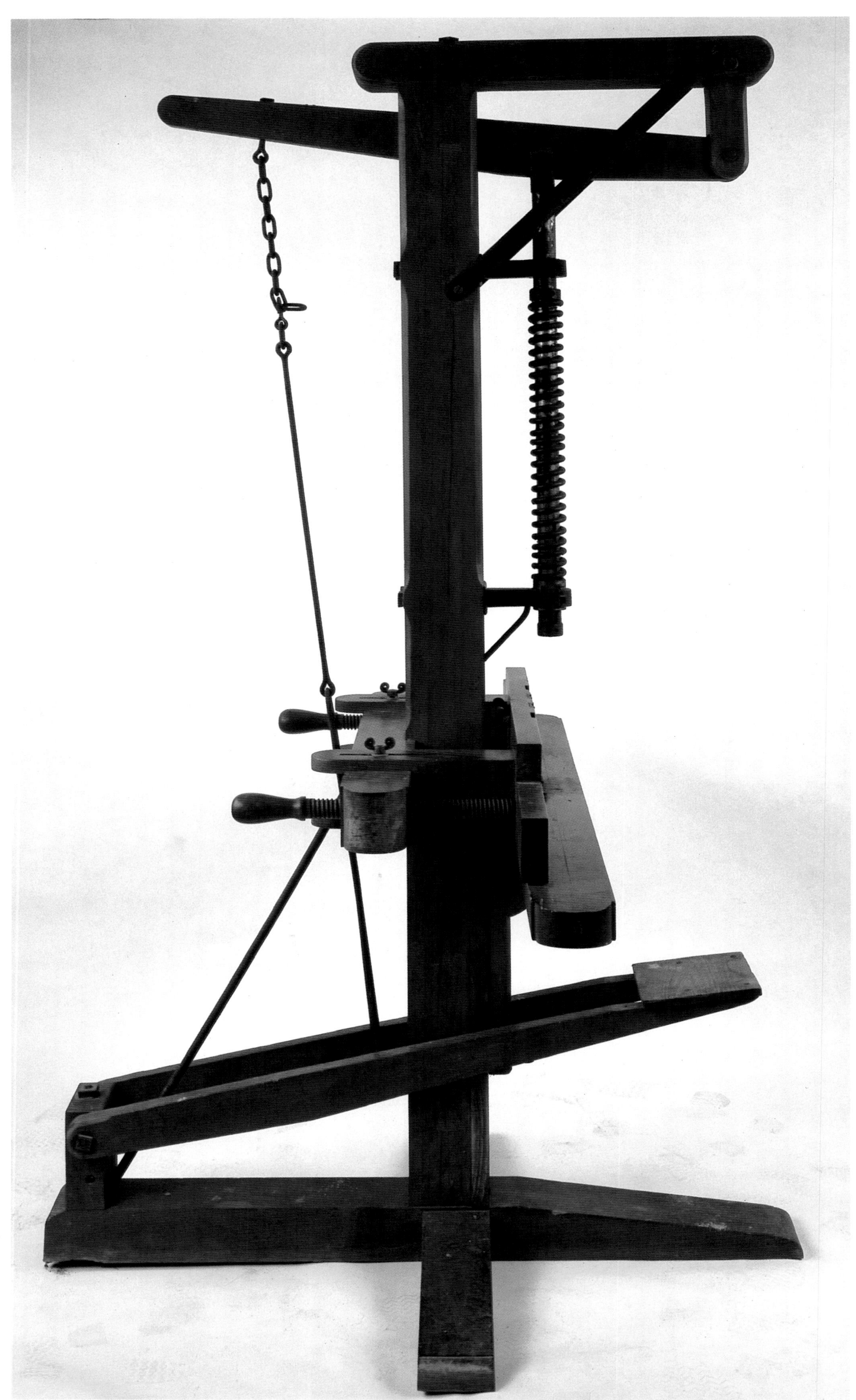

CHAPTER V

INGENIOUS DEVICES

The Shakers were clearly rooted in rural America. Most were lacking in formal higher education. They deliberately isolated themselves from contemporary mainstream society. They might even be characterized as essentially a pre-industrial sect. Yet somehow these people have come to be associated with numerous technical inventions and ingenious mechanical devices. How did this apparent contradiction come about?

Most Shaker inventions were in fact modifications or improvements of existing designs. In the early decades Shakers did not try to patent any of their devices. They did not want to participate in the secular society, its commercial practices and the government bureaucracy that controlled patents. Beyond that, they felt that everything good should be for the benefit of all and that the world at large would appreciate their well-made products. Not until the 1850s did some Shakers begin to patent certain devices – about two dozen altogether in the ensuing decades. Even these patents, however, tended to be for modifications of long-existent devices. None of this detracts from or diminishes the Shakers' accomplishments. It certainly does not change the fact that the Shakers displayed an attraction to labor-saving devices, mechanical devices, and all kinds of helpful gadgets. These devices may be grouped under several categories based on where they were used.

Since agriculture remained at the base of their survival and economy, it is no wonder that the Shakers devised many mechanical aids for farming such as mowing and threshing machines, a rotary, or revolving harrow, a wooden seeder and a fertilizing machine. Then there were the various devices used by the specialized worksites, craftspeople and artisans. The Shakers devised many variations on basic tools and machinery that in some cases had been around for hundreds of years: a governor for an overshot waterwheel; a turbine waterwheel; machinery for splintmaking, basket working, box-cutting, and for making oak shooks for barrels; a circular saw for a powered mill saw – its invention is credited to a Shaker woman; a machine for twisting whips; machines for filling seed bags and herb packets; a loom for weaving palm-leaf bonnets. In addition to improving such relatively large and complicated machinery, individual Shaker craftspeople were often making small improvements to their hand tools. Also in this category is clockmaking which, even for Shakers who were accustomed to doing things on their own, was a specialized skill. Most Shaker clocks were made at the original community at Niskeyuna, by then renamed Watervliet.

Another category of devices the Shakers modified and improved were those used in domestic chores – a cheese press, a clothes rack, a "swift" (a reel used for winding yarn), a carding machine (for combing wool), an apple-parer, a stove for heating several clothes irons at the same time, a stove-cover lifter. Two of the best-known and most important of the Shakers' inventions fall under this category. One was the famous washing mill, or washing machine, in which water was forced through a wooden trough divided into six tubs and "dashers" powered by the forced water shook the clothes back and forth in the tubs. This device was patented in 1858 but seems to have been developed by Shakers over many years. It won a gold medal at the United States Centennial Exposition at Philadelphia in 1876 and was sold to numerous purchasers outside the Shaker communities. The other was a revolving oven, attributed to Eldress Emiline Hart at Canterbury, New Hampshire. This was a large brick oven in which four circular iron shelves holding the items being baked revolved in order to distribute the heat evenly. This, like the washing machine, was sold to purchasers outside the Shaker communities.

The final category of Shaker inventions comprises those miscellaneous objects that were used in the more ordinary activities of many Shakers in their daily lives. These would include two of the best-known Shaker inventions – the basic wooden two-pronged clothespin and the flat broom (most brooms were round). The Shakers made various mops and brushes – the Shakers believed that cleanliness brought them closer to Godliness. They modified the basic iron box stoves used to heat rooms. They made a yardstick that had one side curved to measure circular material. They are credited by some with inventing metal pen points; they did not, but one of them did make a special five-pointed pen to draw musical staves. To improve ventilation, they developed an adjustable transom for interior doorways and a sash balance for exterior windows. They made some ingenious footscrapers (to remove mud and dirt before entering a building) and at least one set of stone steps to assist in climbing in and out of horse-drawn carriages.

The Shakers chose to make these devices because they wanted to make the best use of their time. For them, time was not money – it was God's work. The easier a task could be performed with an improved tool or machine, the more attention and time could be given to the quality of its product.

As to how these mostly rural people with little or no technical training could make so many ingenious devices – that, too, is no mystery. They were living in a part of the world and at a time when there was great interest in inventing new machines and technologies. This was the era when Eli Whitney, Samuel Colt, Linus Yale, Elias Howe, Cyrus McCormick and countless other American inventors were at work. The Shakers had withdrawn from the society that rewarded such inventors but they could not entirely suppress its aspirations. They simply applied their intelligence and ambitions to improving their own realm of work and living. That was their reward.

Mortising Machine, c. 1830-40, New Lebanon, NY
The Shaker Museum and Library, Old Chatham, NY
Photo by Paul Rocheleau

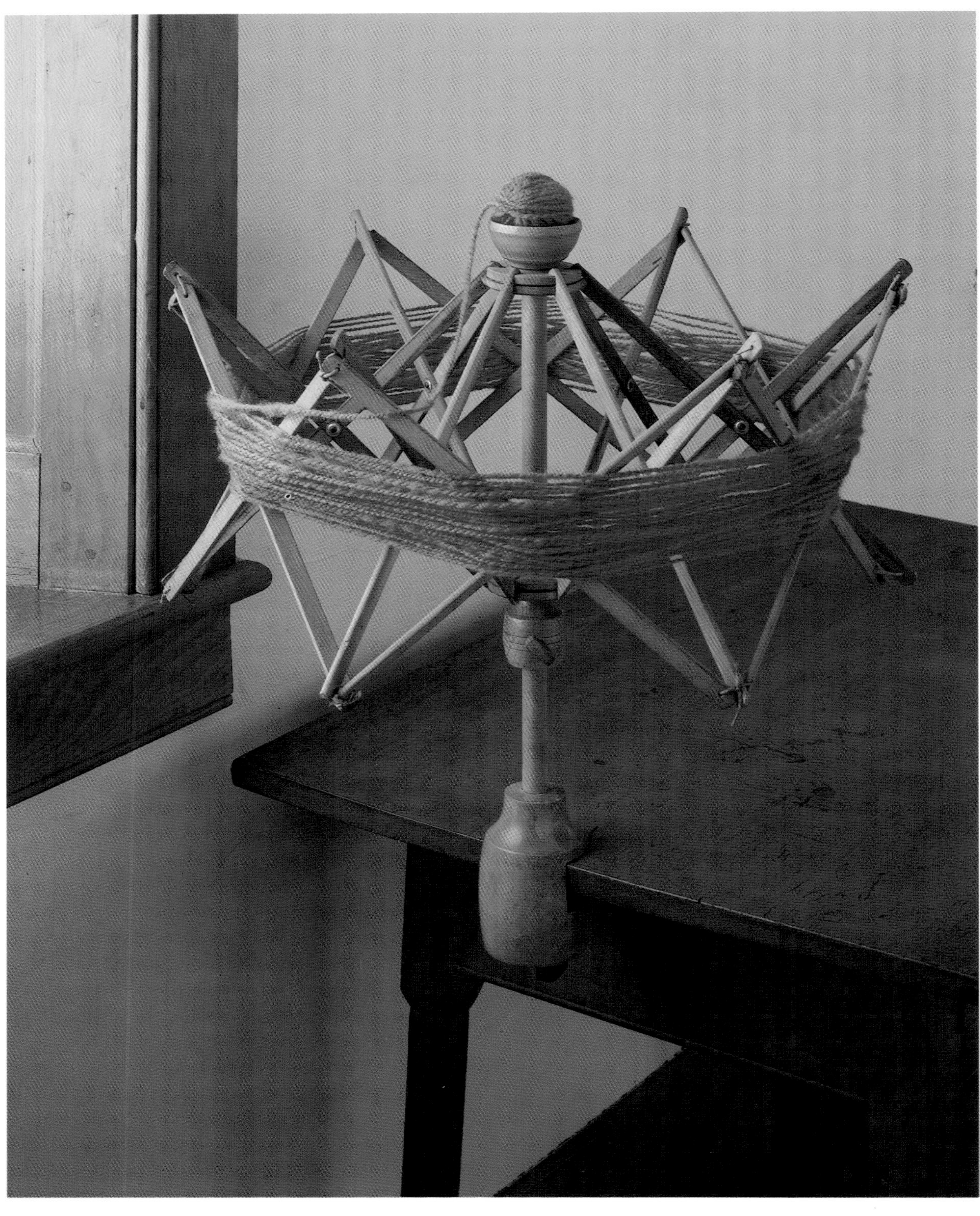

ABOVE:
Table Swift, c. 1850-60
Hancock Shaker Village, Pittsfield, MA
Photo by Paul Rocheleau

RIGHT:
Tape Loom
Hancock Shaker Village, Pittsfield, MA
Photo by Paul Rocheleau

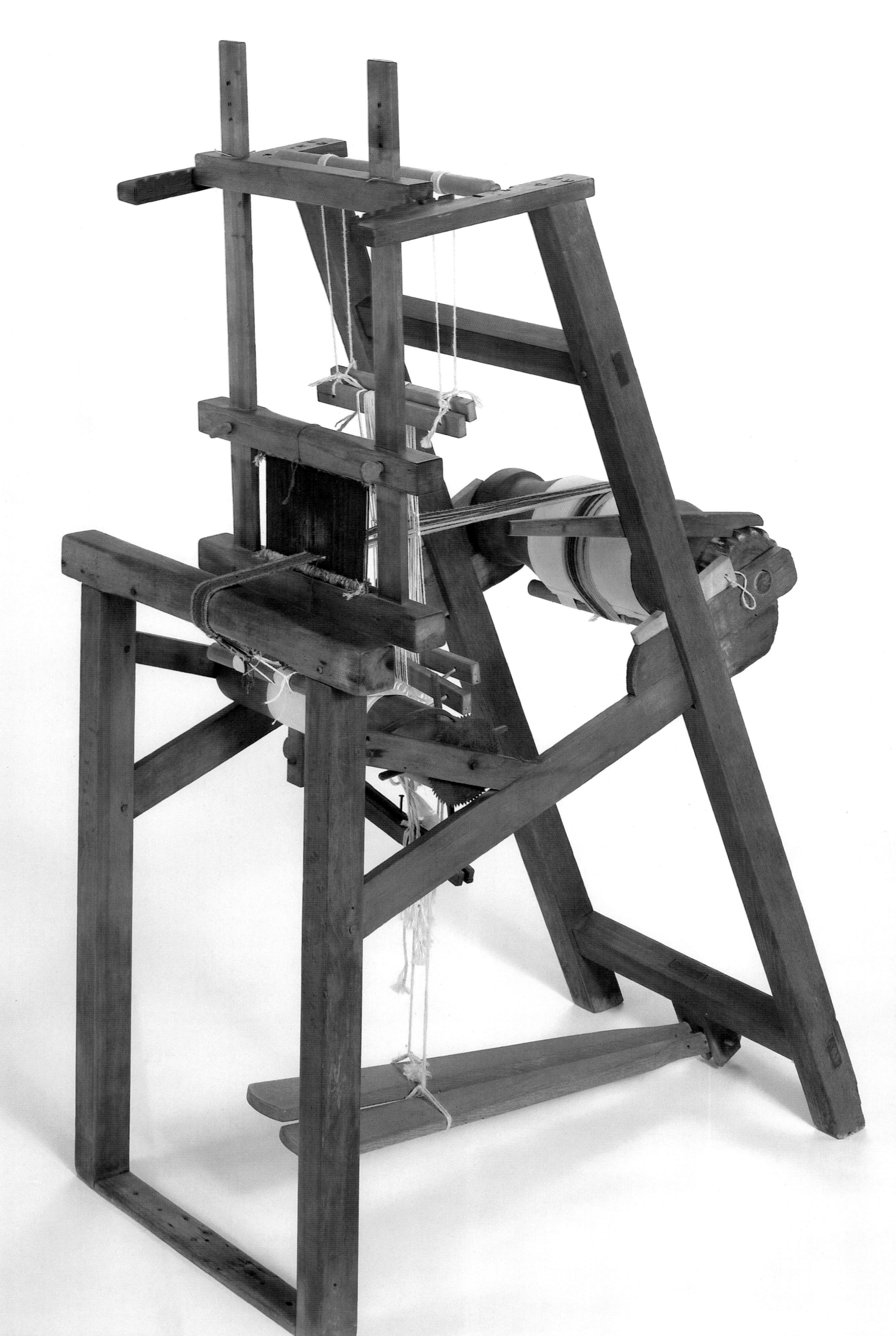

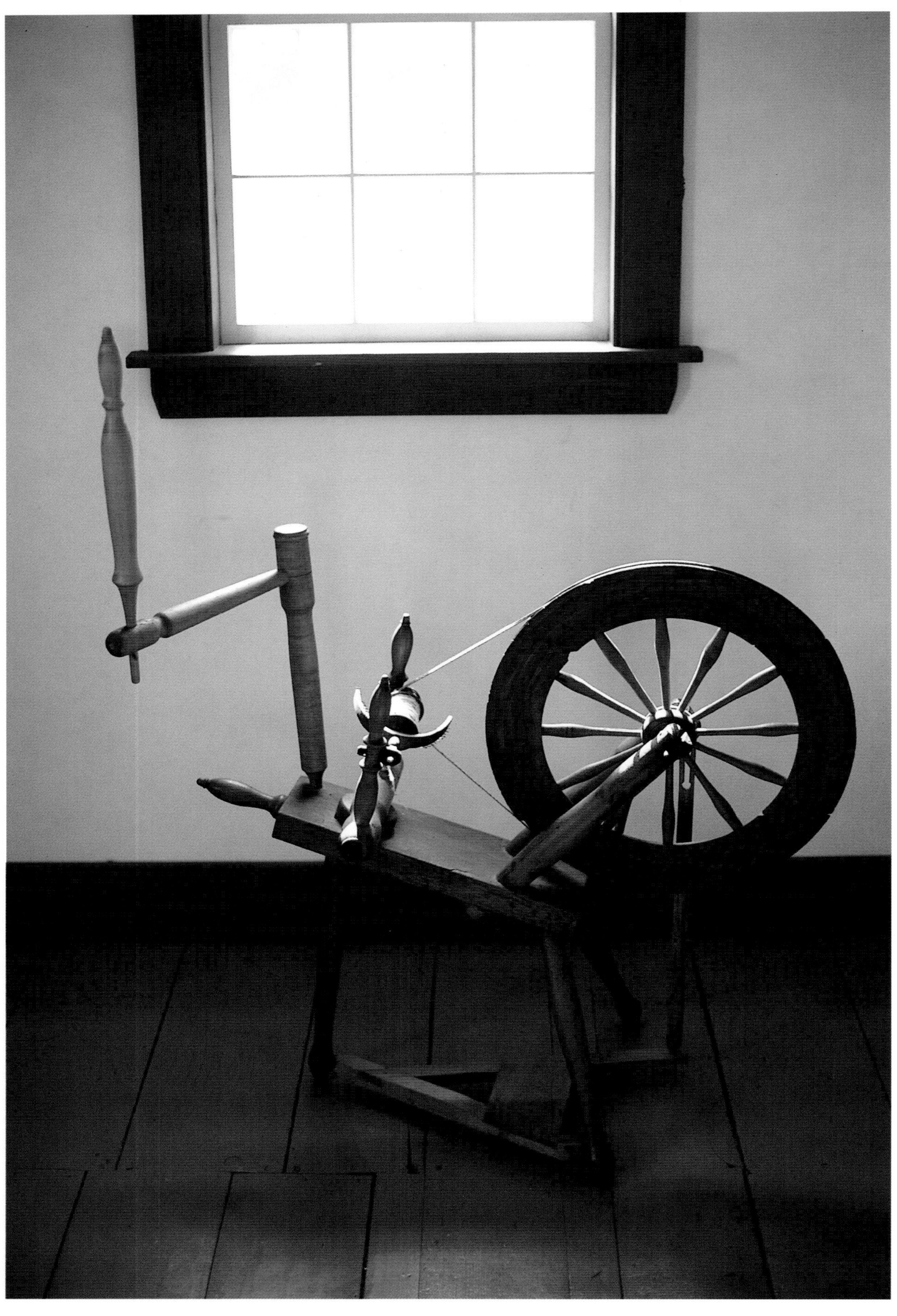

Spinning Wheel, Sabbathday Lake, ME
Photo by Brian Vanden Brink

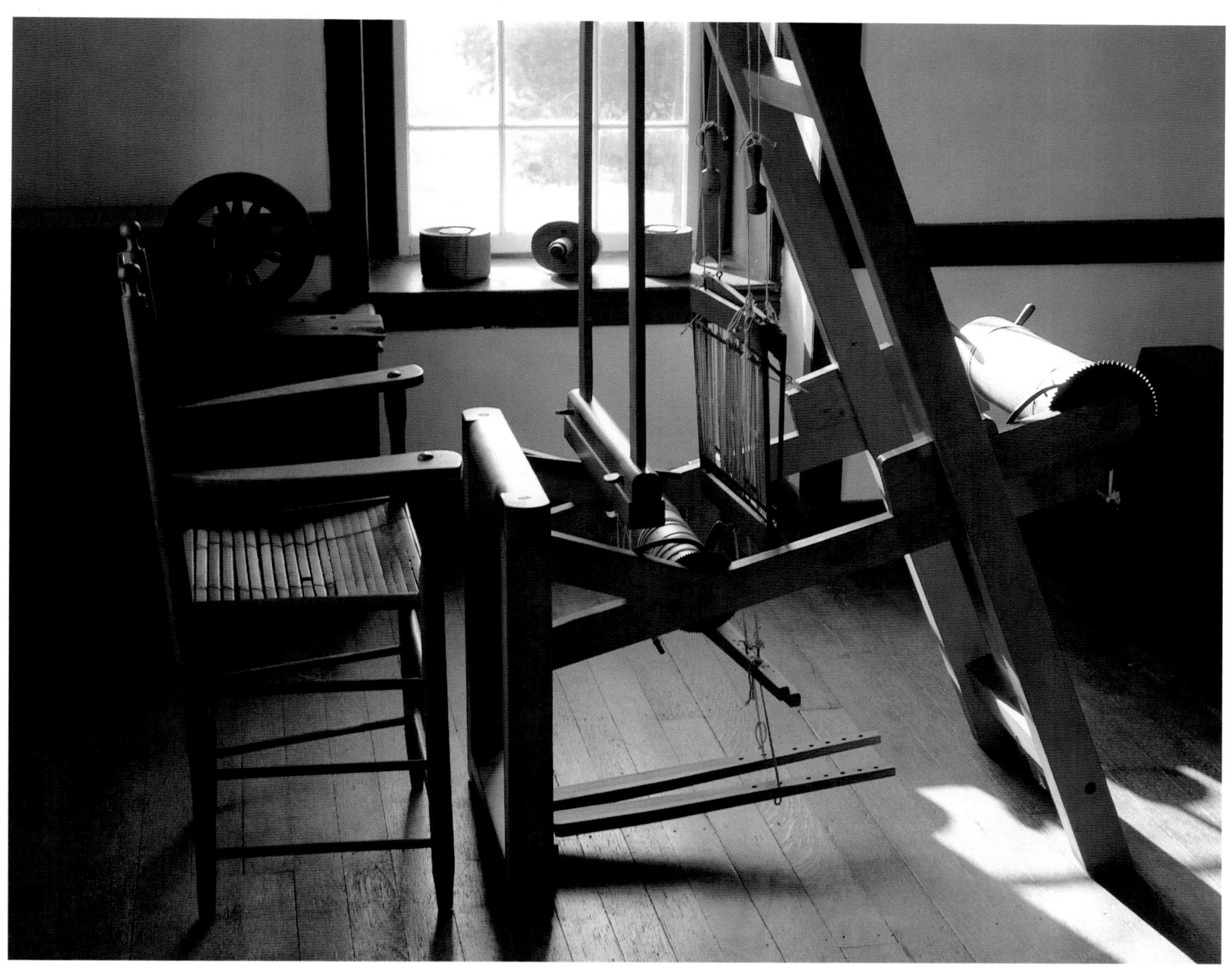

Two-Harness Textile Loom, Pleasant Hill, KY
Photo by James Archambeault

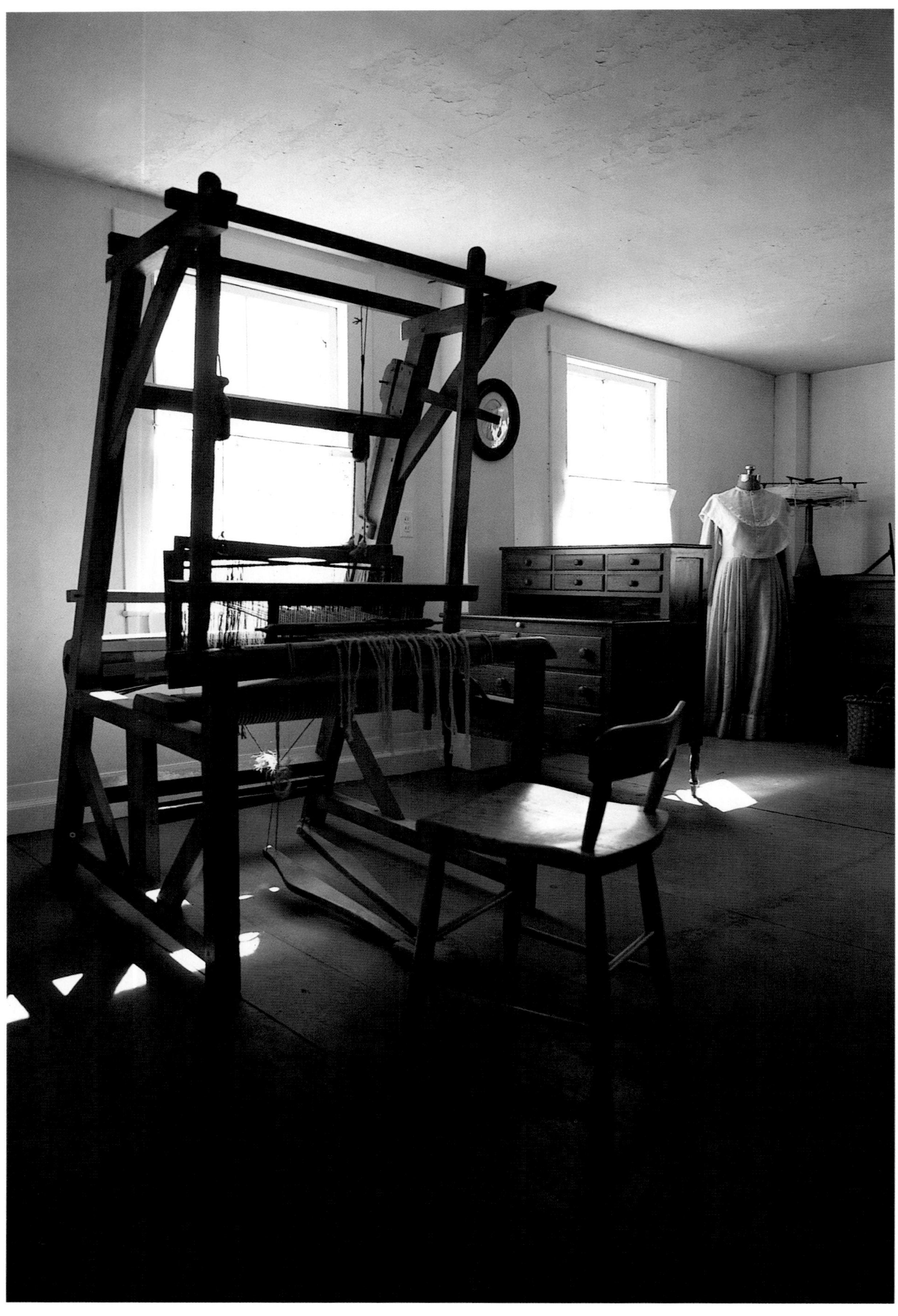

Loom, Sabbathday Lake, ME
Photo by Brian Vanden Brink

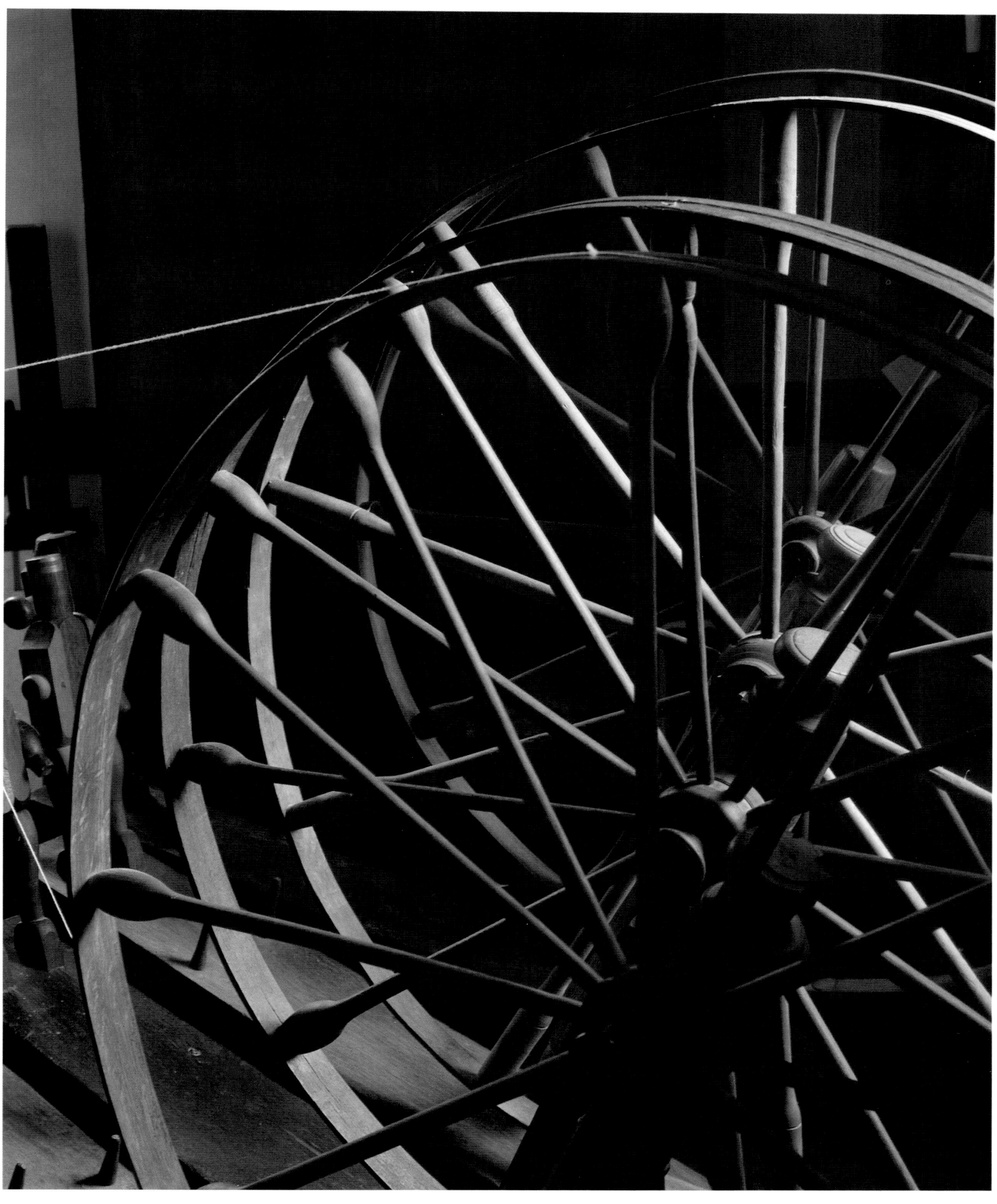

Spinning Wheel, Pleasant Hill, KY
Photo by James Archambeault

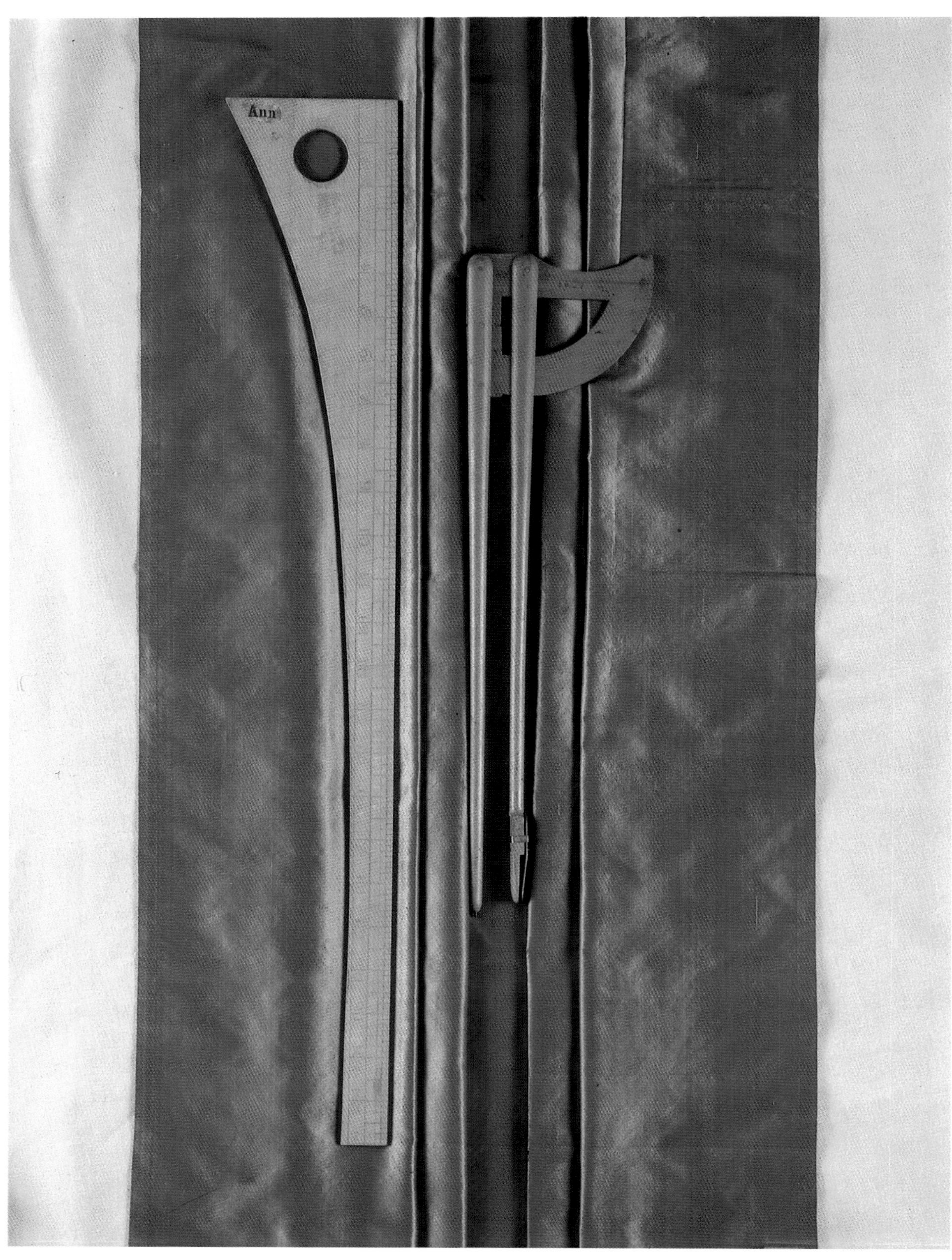

Tailors' Ruler, c. 1850, New Lebanon, NY, and Compass, 1827, Hancock, MA
Hancock Shaker Village, Pittsfield, MA
Photo by Paul Rocheleau

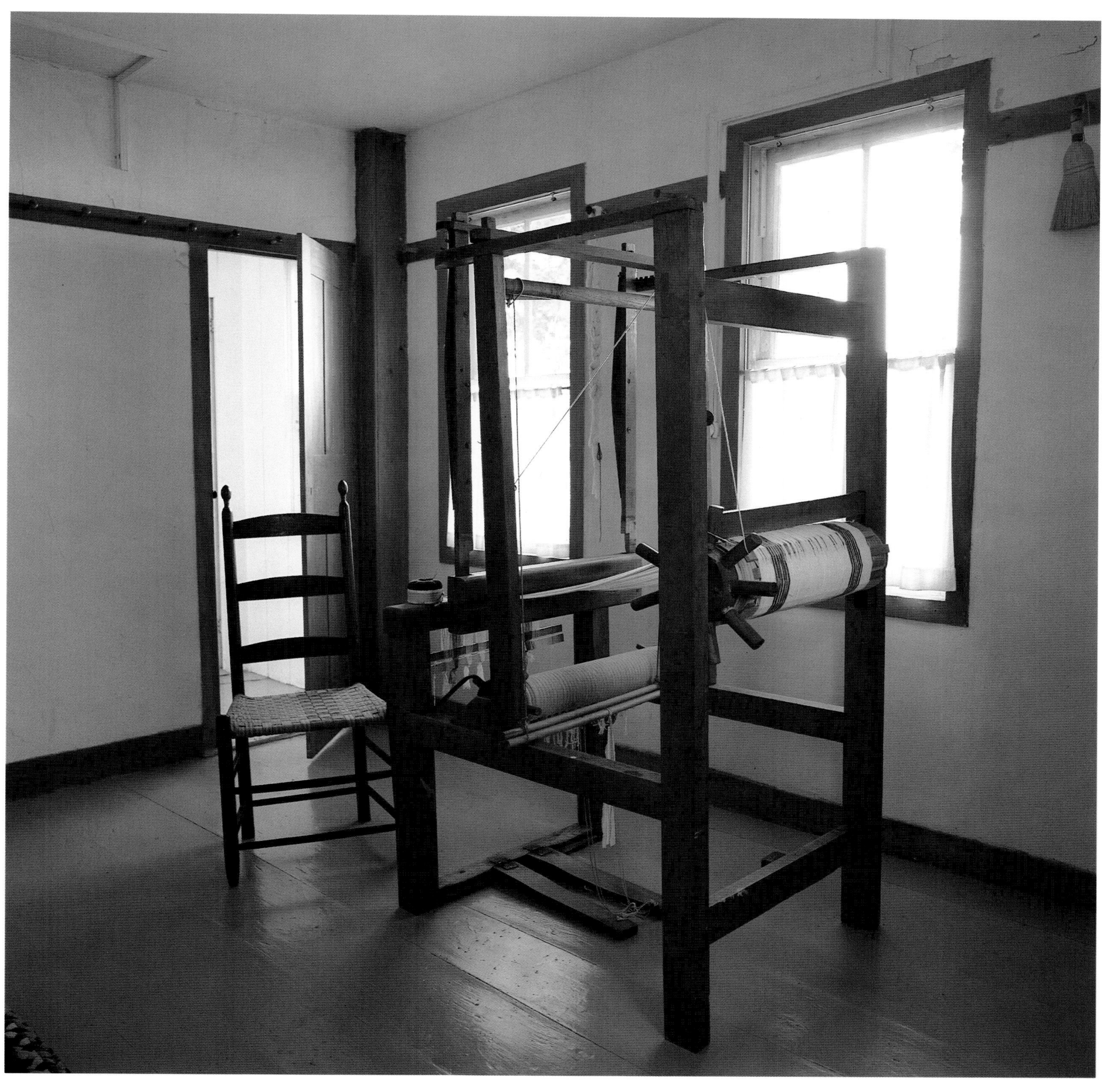

Loom, Sisters' Shop, Canterbury Shaker Village, Canterbury, NH
Photo by Todd Buchanan

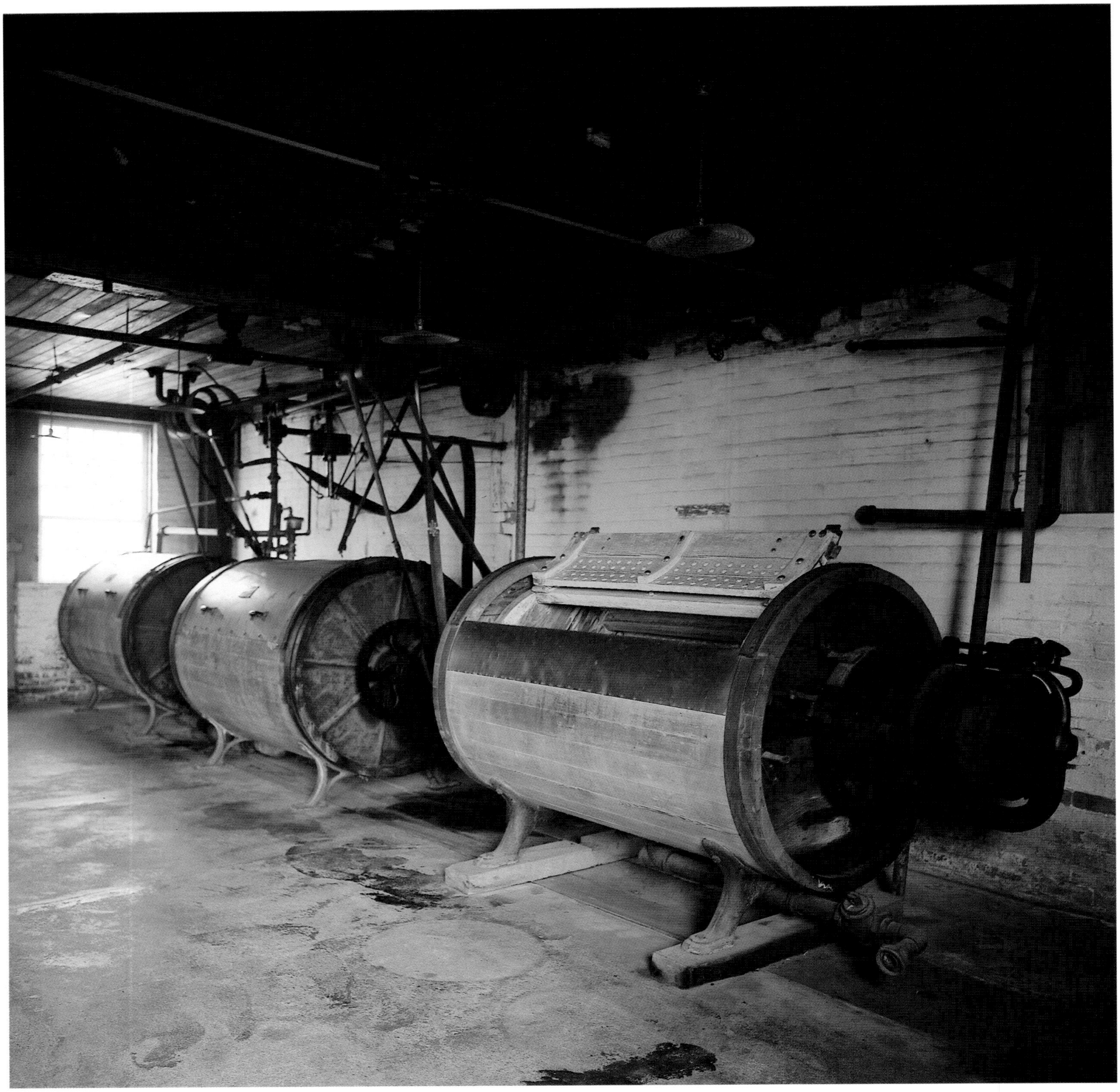

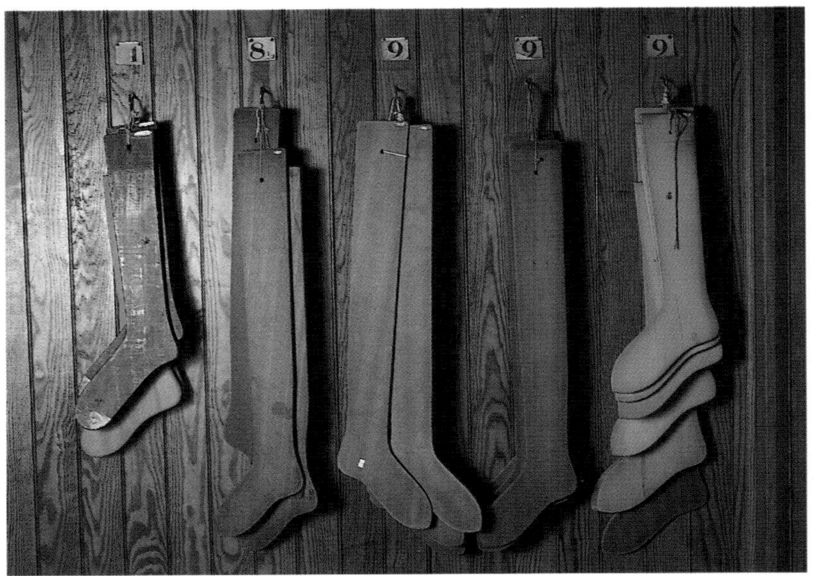

ABOVE:
Wash basement, with wash tubs and wash machines, Canterbury Shaker Village, Canterbury, NH
Photo by Todd Buchanan

LEFT:
Sock sizes and shapes, drying forms hanging from wall Laundry, Canterbury Shaker Village, Canterbury, NH
Photo by Todd Buchanan

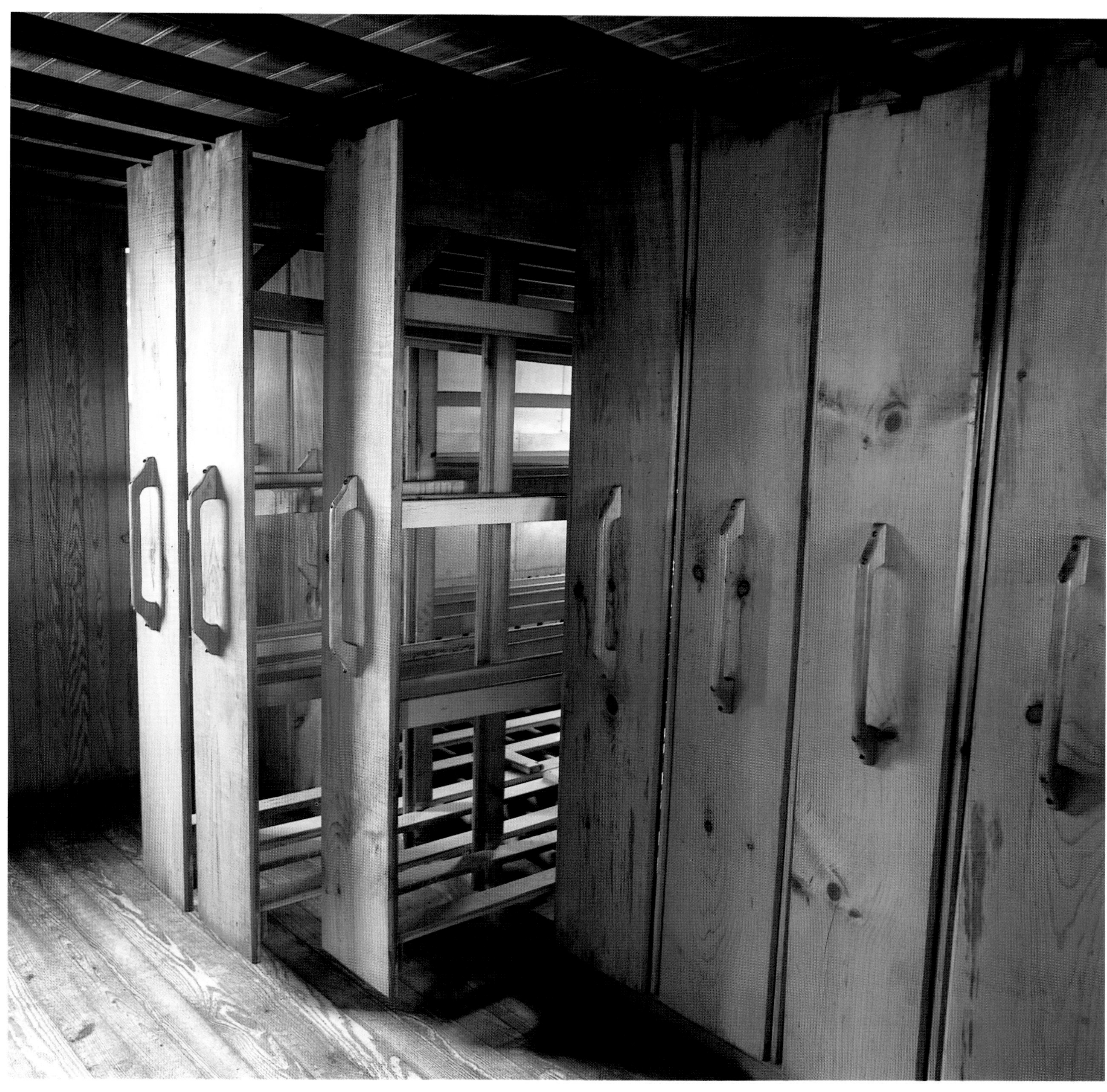

Drying racks on rollers
Laundry, Canterbury Shaker Village, Canterbury, NH
Photo by Todd Buchanan

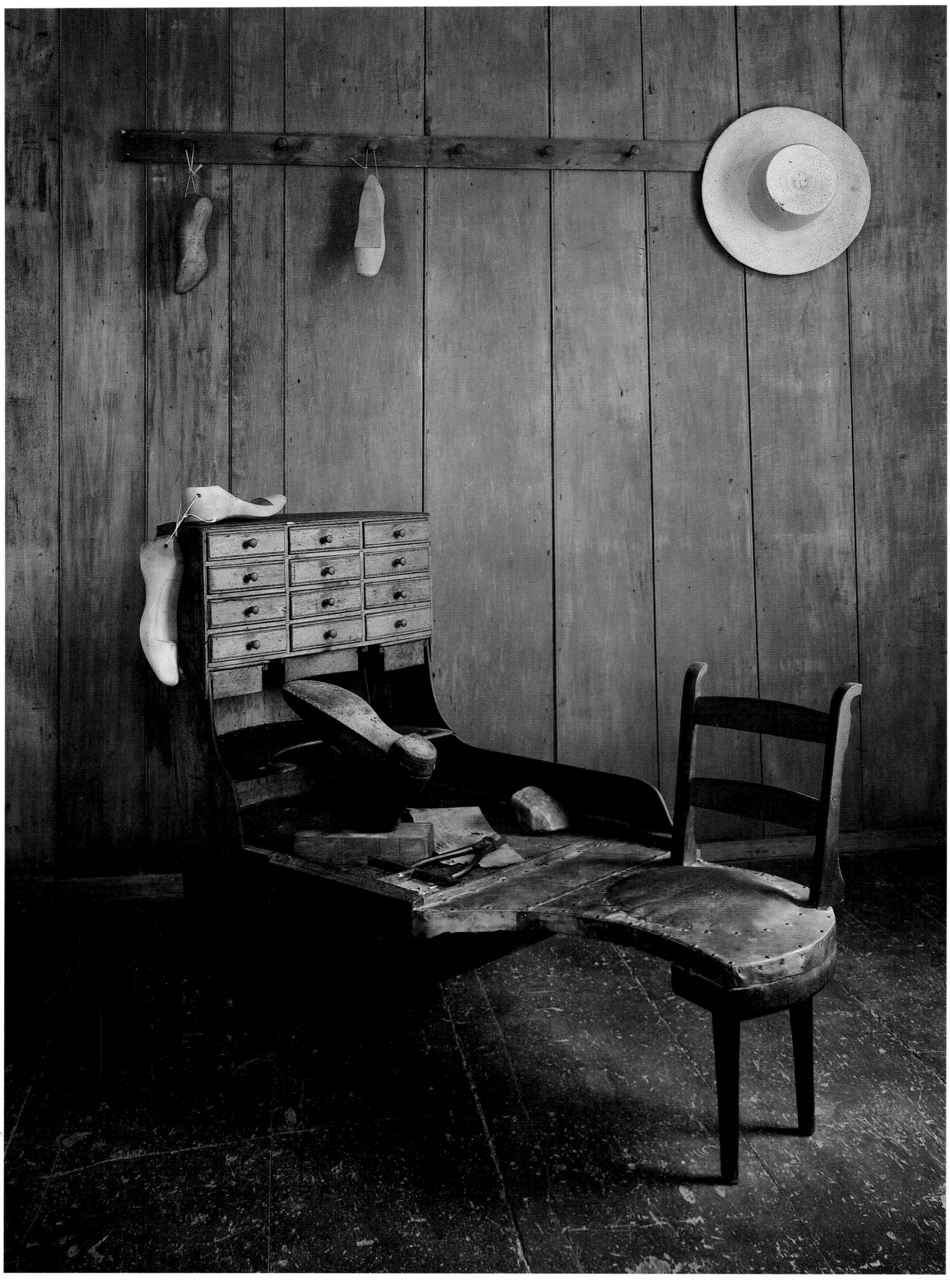

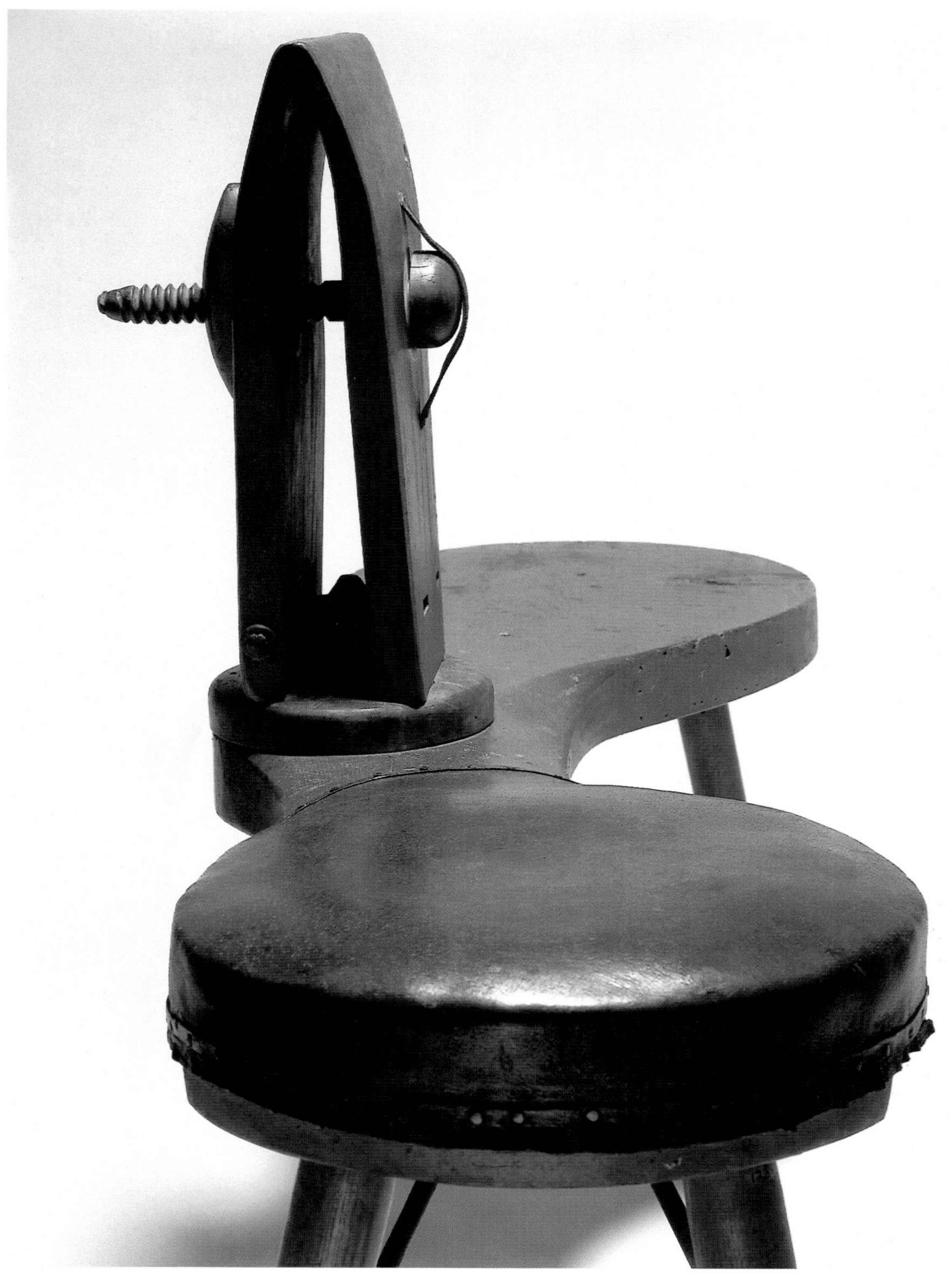

LEFT:
Cobbler's Bench
Hancock Shaker Village, Pittsfield, MA
Photo by Paul Rocheleau

ABOVE:
Harness Vise, New Lebanon, NY, 1835
The Shaker Museum and Library, Old Chatham, NY
Photo by Paul Rocheleau

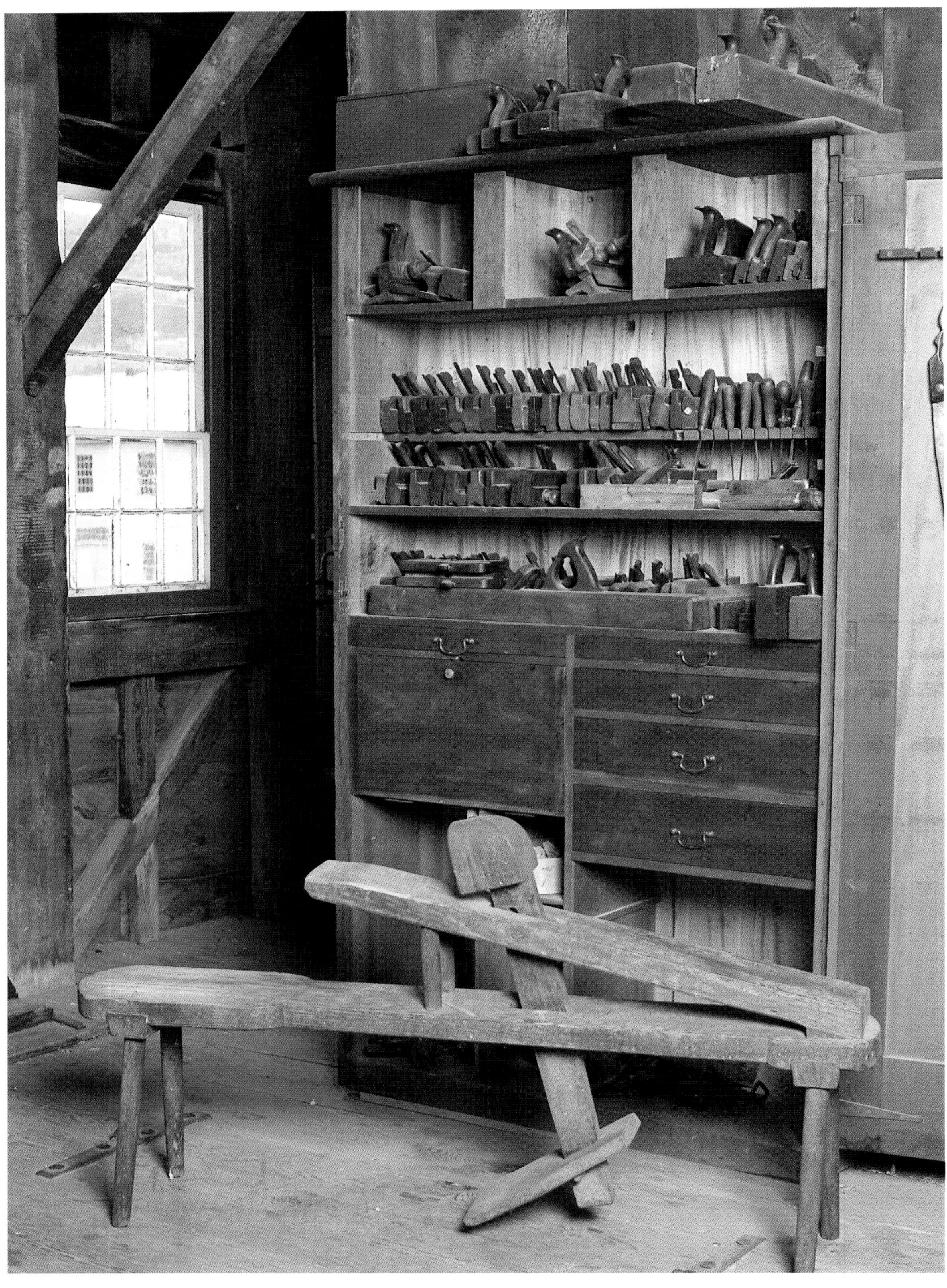

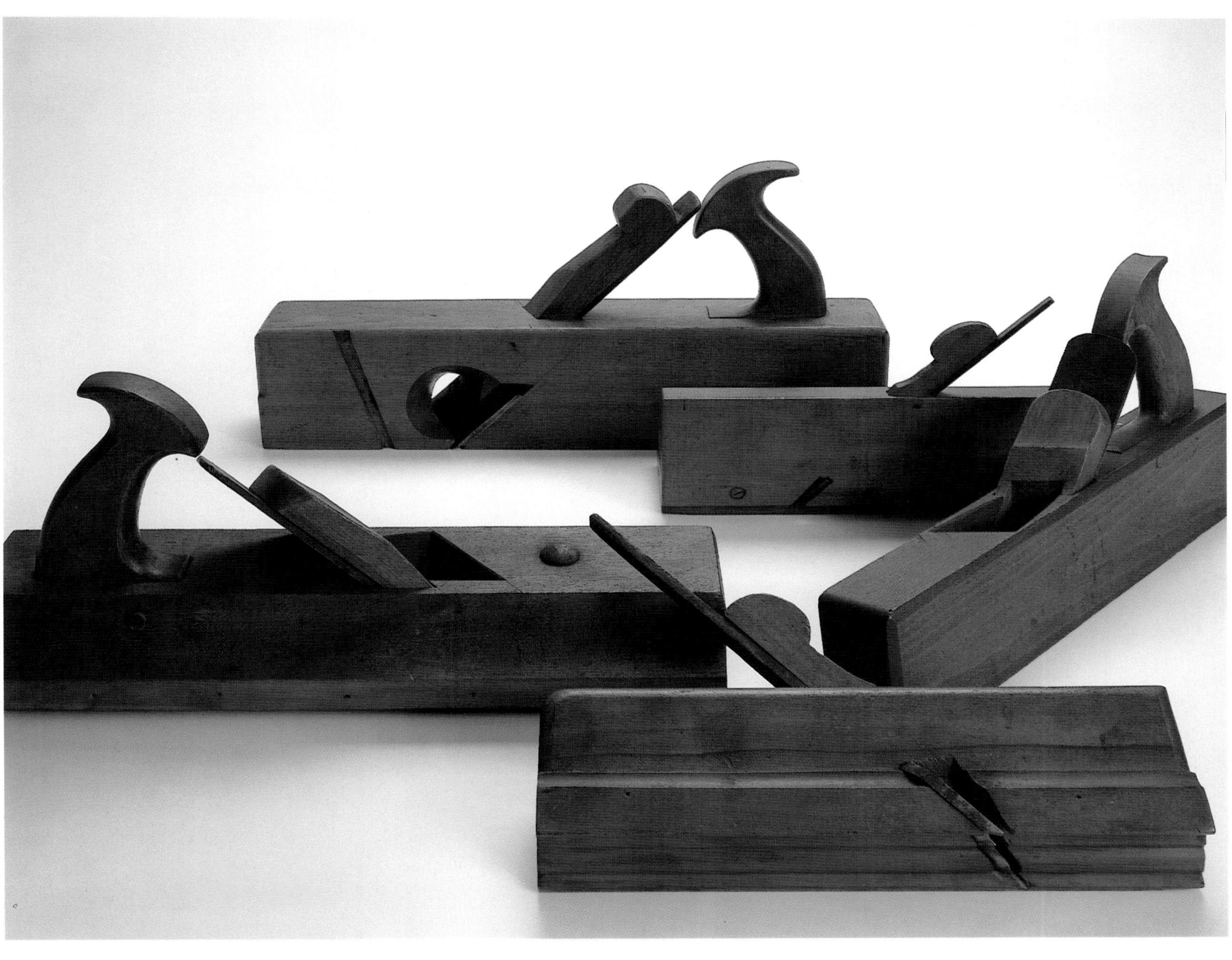

LEFT:
Tool chest with planes and cooper's bench
Hancock Shaker Village, Pittsfield, MA
Photo by Michael Fredericks

ABOVE:
Shaker planes
Hancock Shaker Village, Pittsfield, MA
Photo by Paul Rocheleau

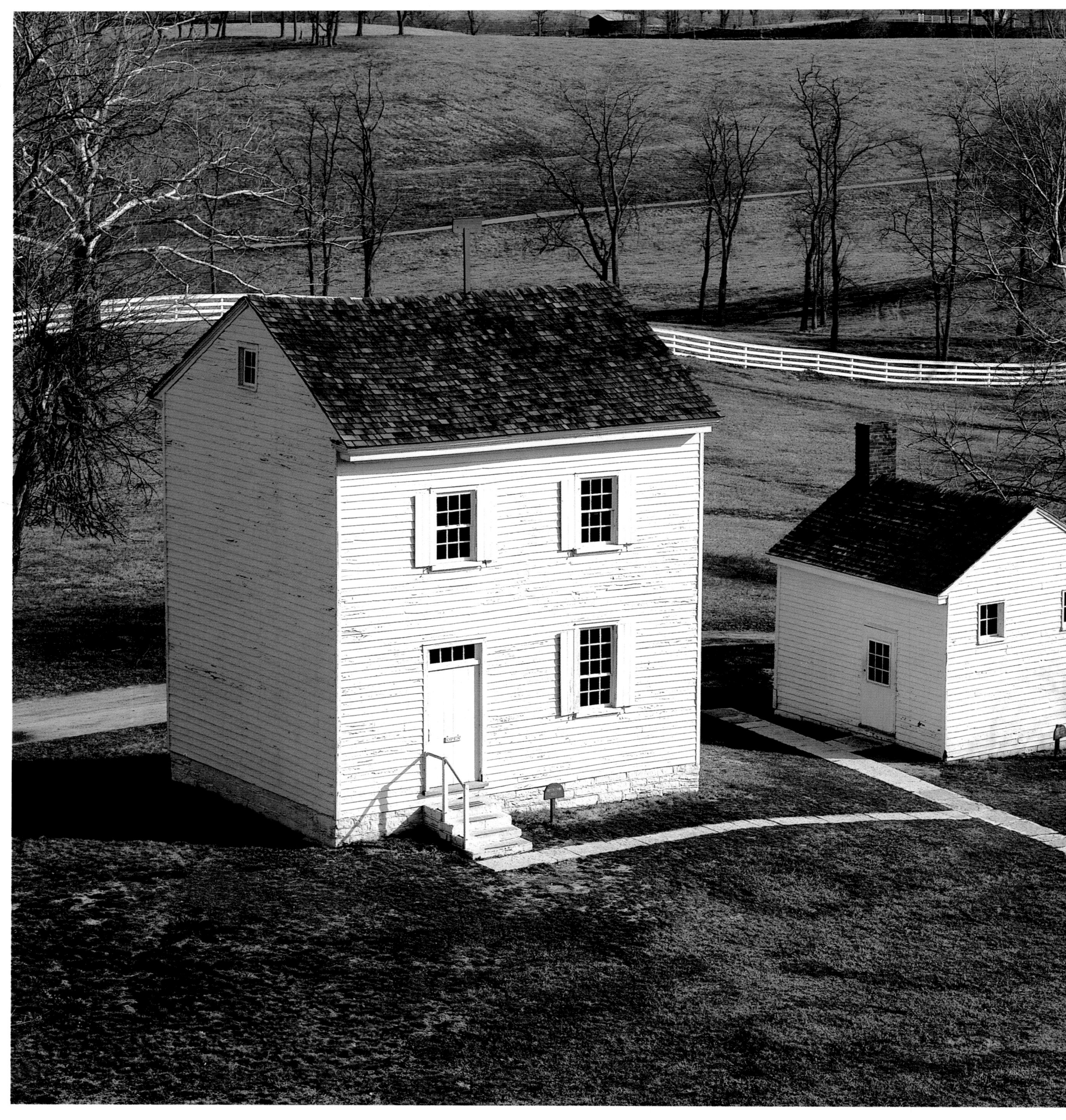

At Pleasant Hill, KY, water was pumped by horsepower to a reservoir within the Water House, 1833, and a raised cypress tank fed water to community dwellings (Brethren's Bath House, 1860, on right)
Photo by James Archambeault

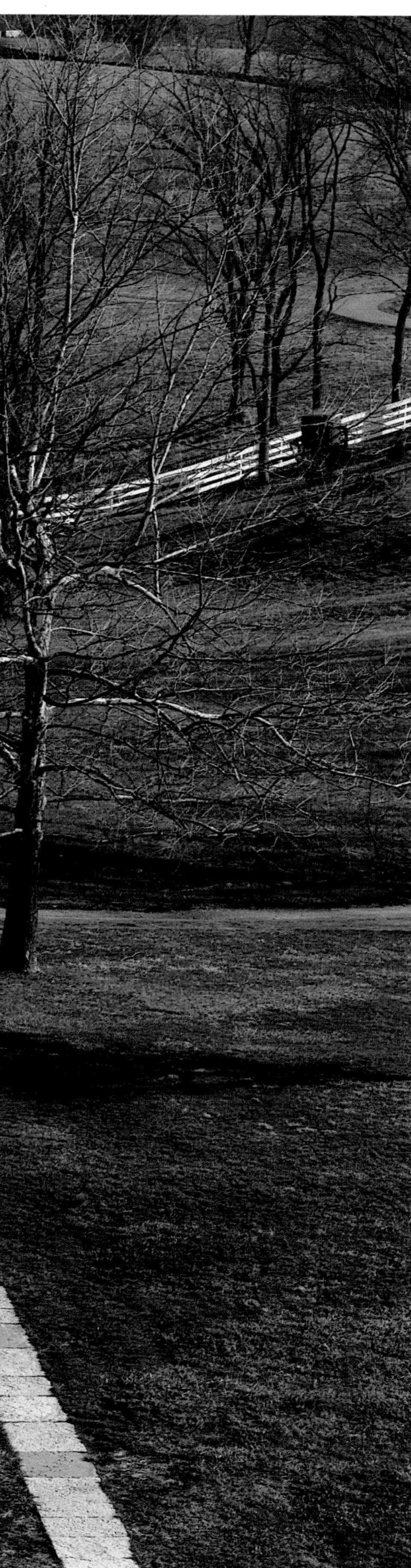

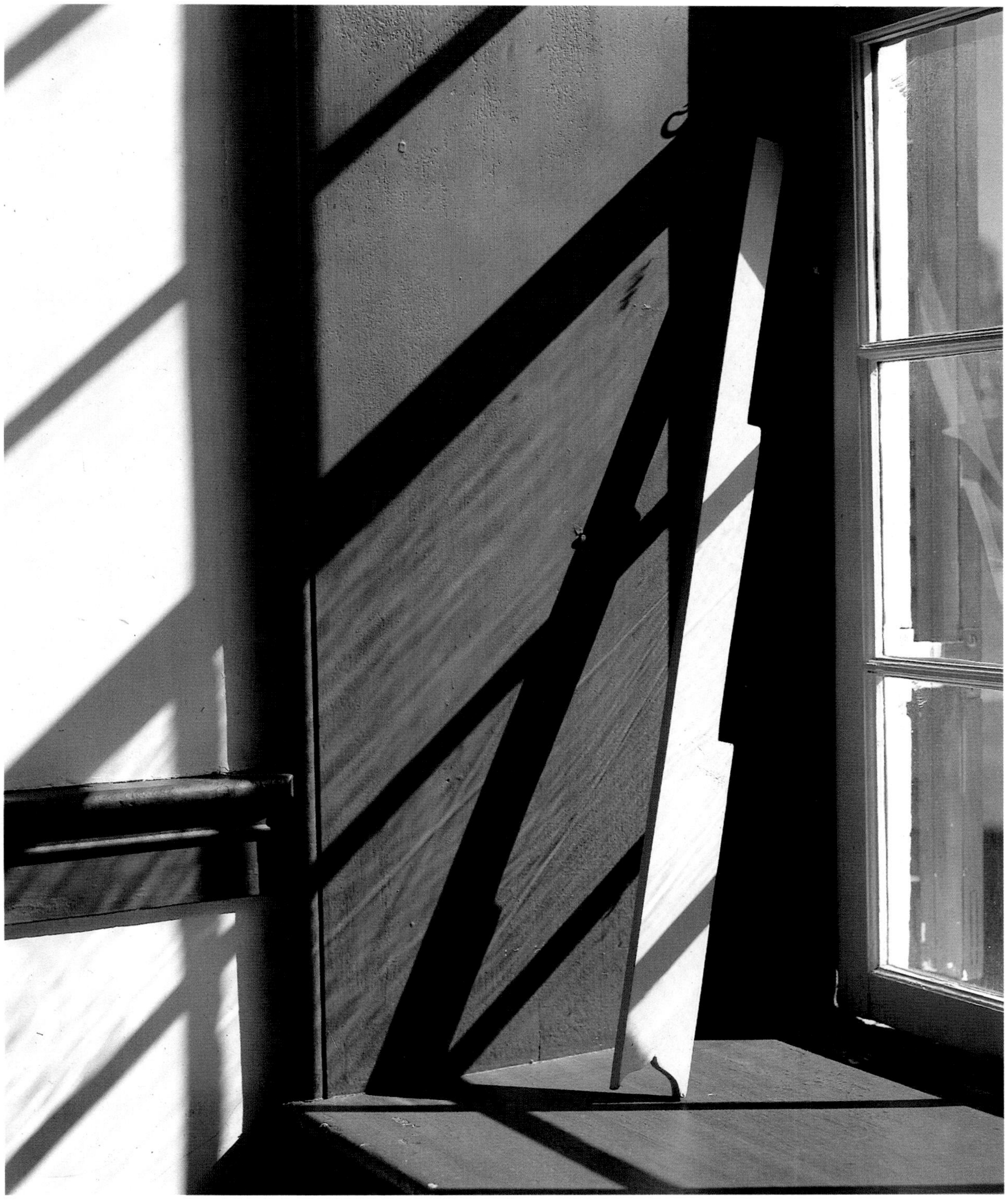

ABOVE:
Window prop, Centre Family Dwelling, Pleasant Hill, KY
Photo by James Archambeault

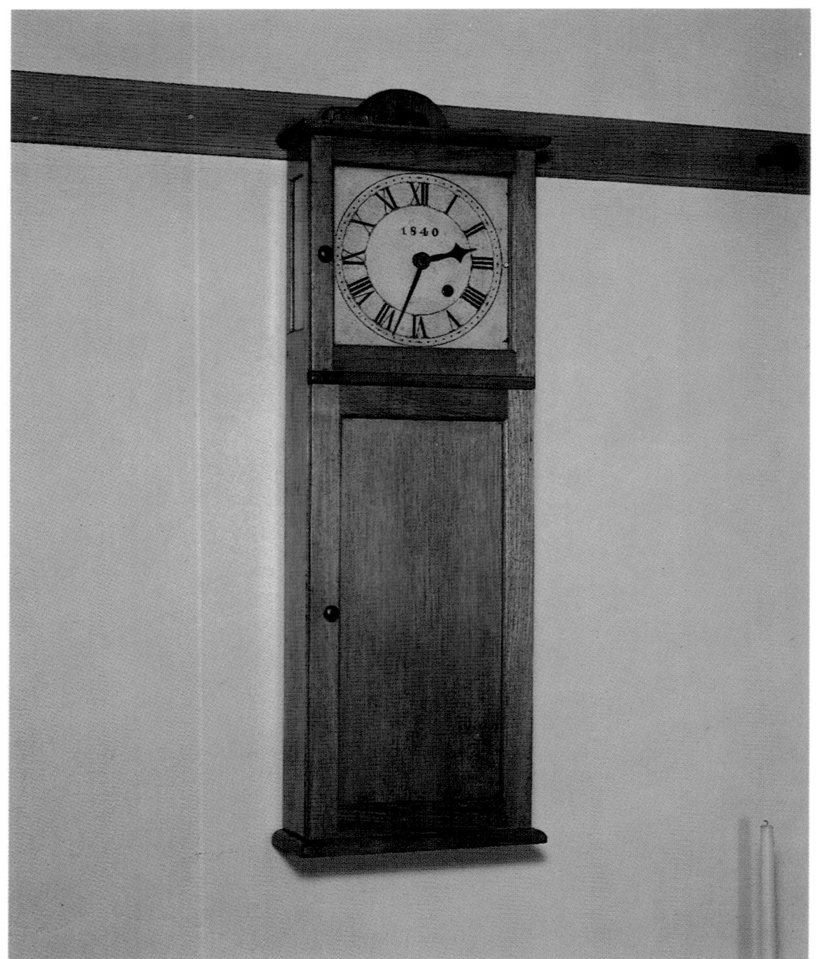

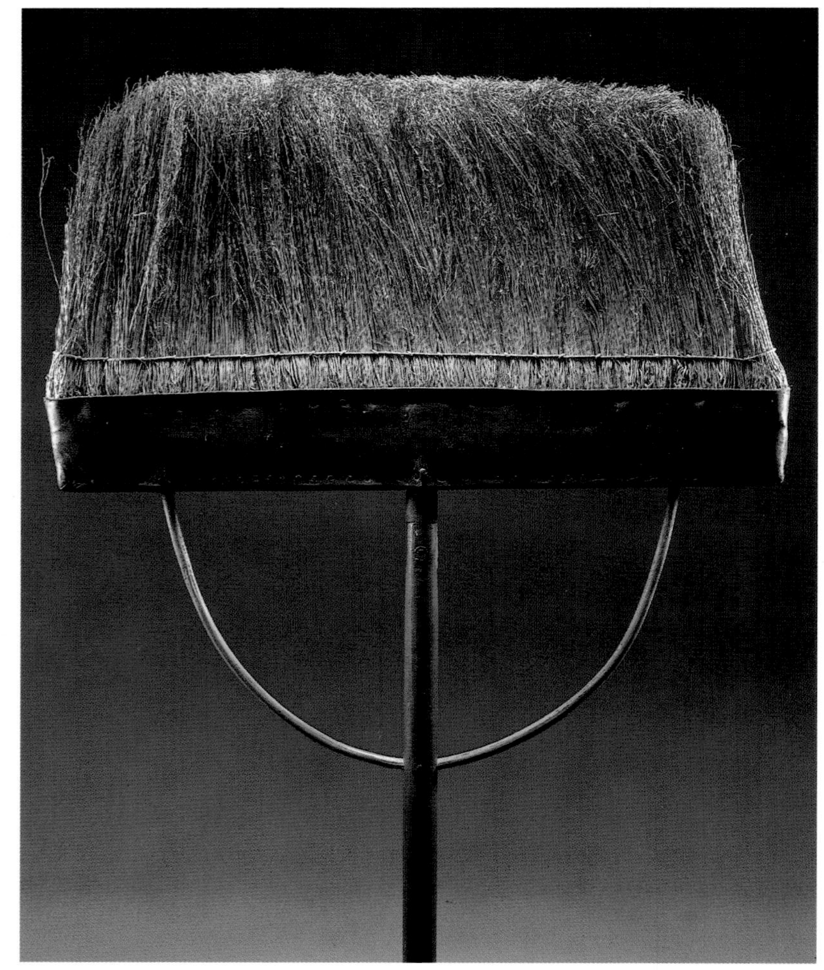

ABOVE:
Isaac Youngs Hanging Clock
Hancock Shaker Village, Pittsfield, MA

ABOVE RIGHT:
Broom, 19th century
The Shaker Museum and Library, Old Chatham, NY
Photo by Paul Rocheleau

RIGHT:
Wall clock, brooms and chair
Meetinghouse, Canterbury Shaker Village, Canterbury, NH
Photo by Todd Buchanan

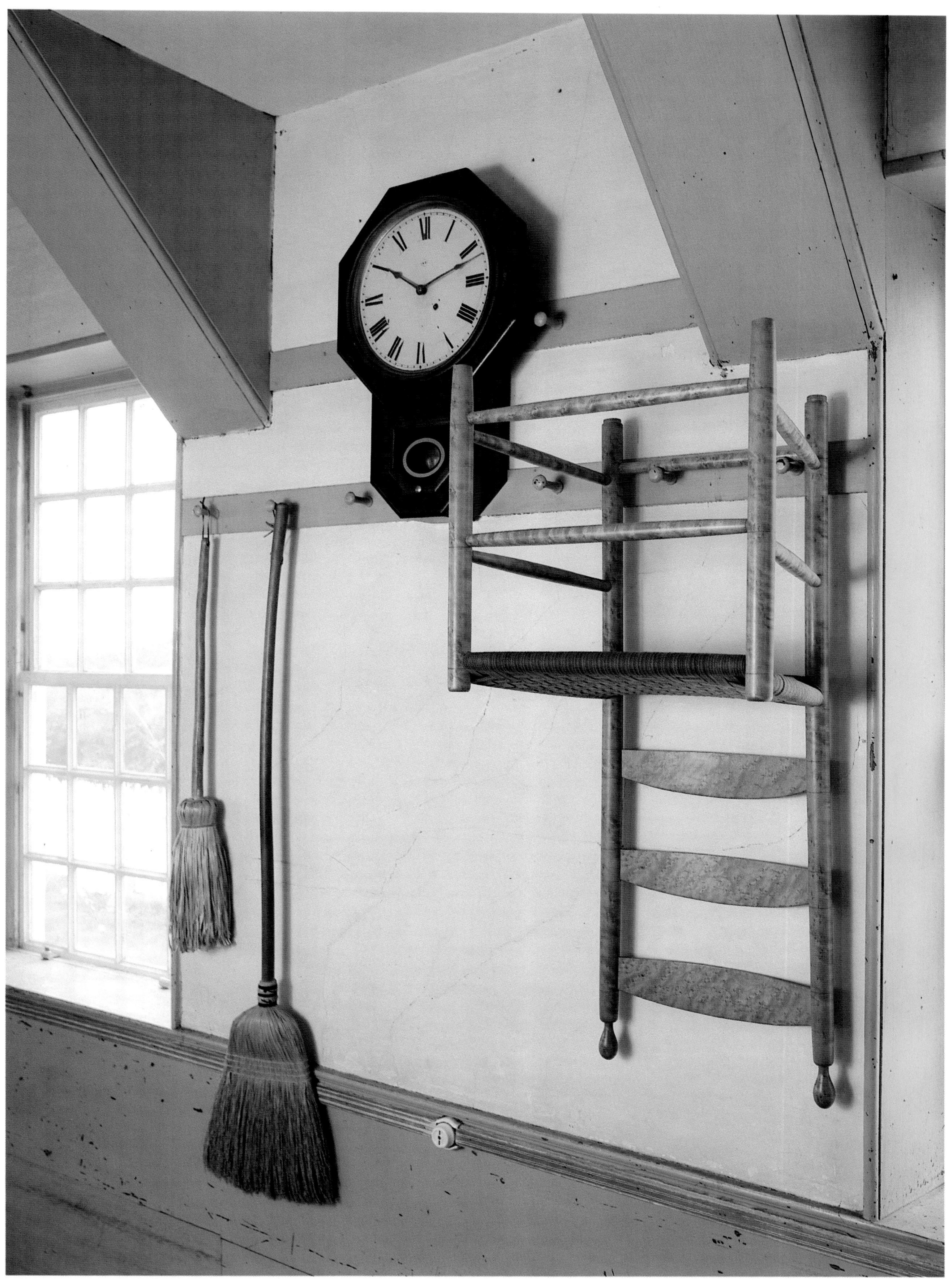

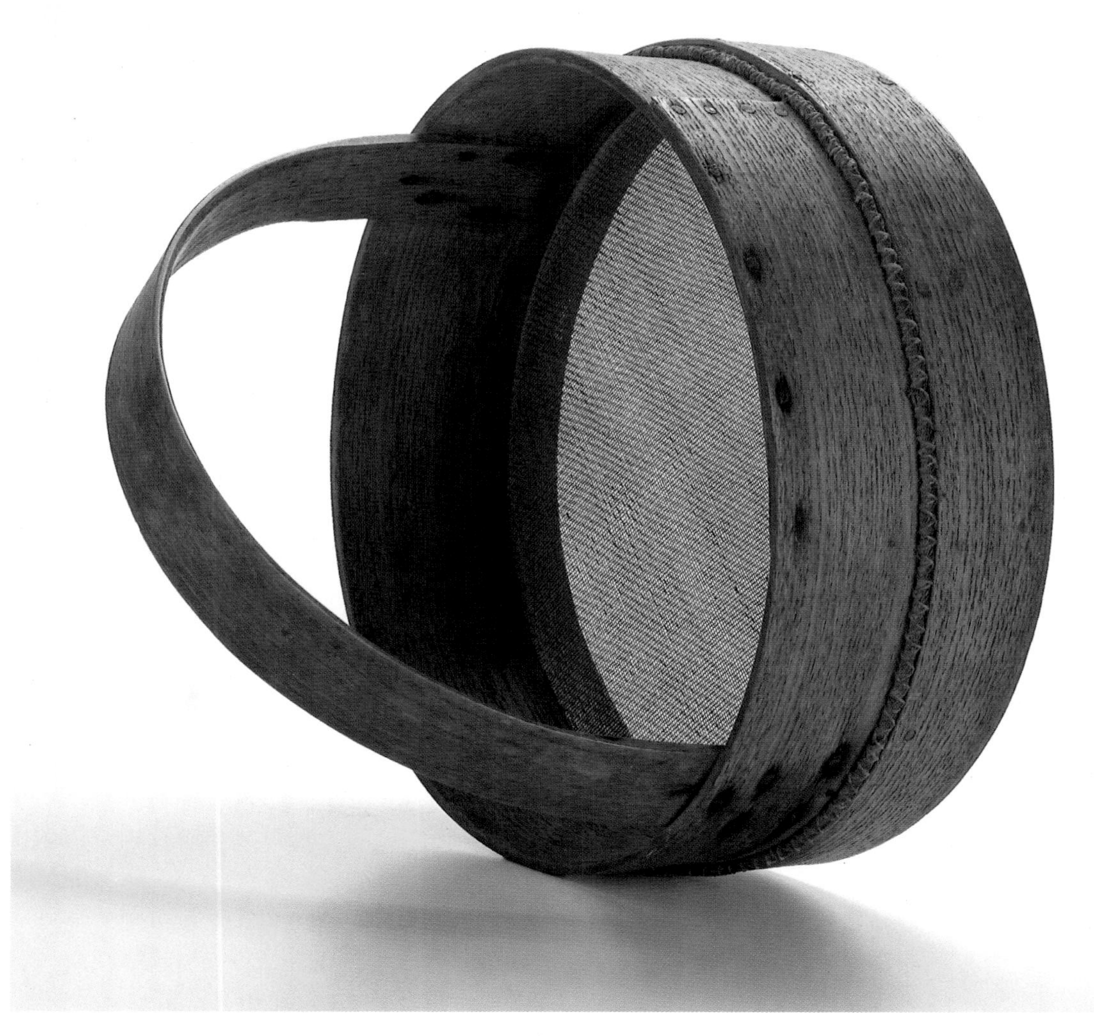

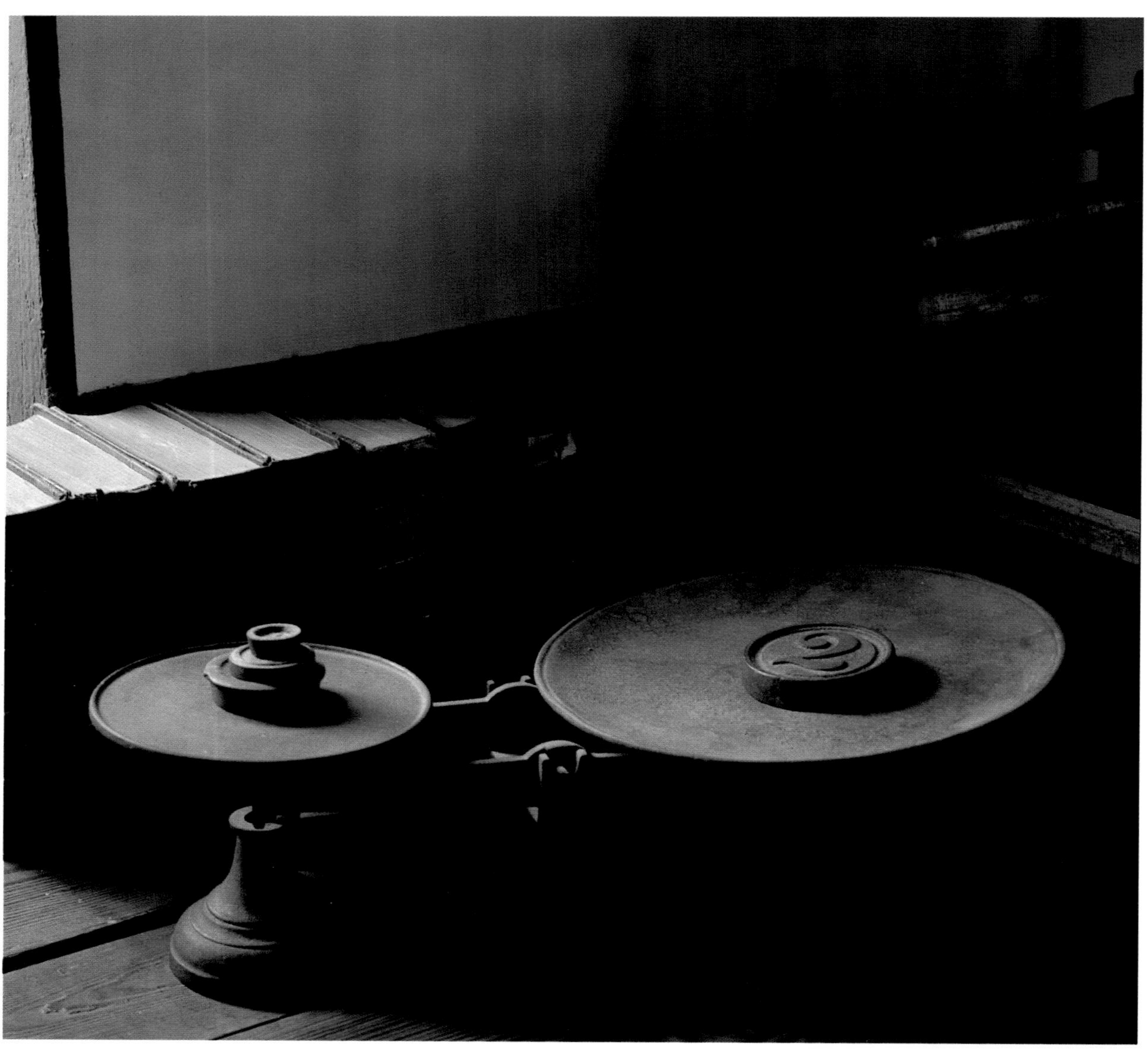

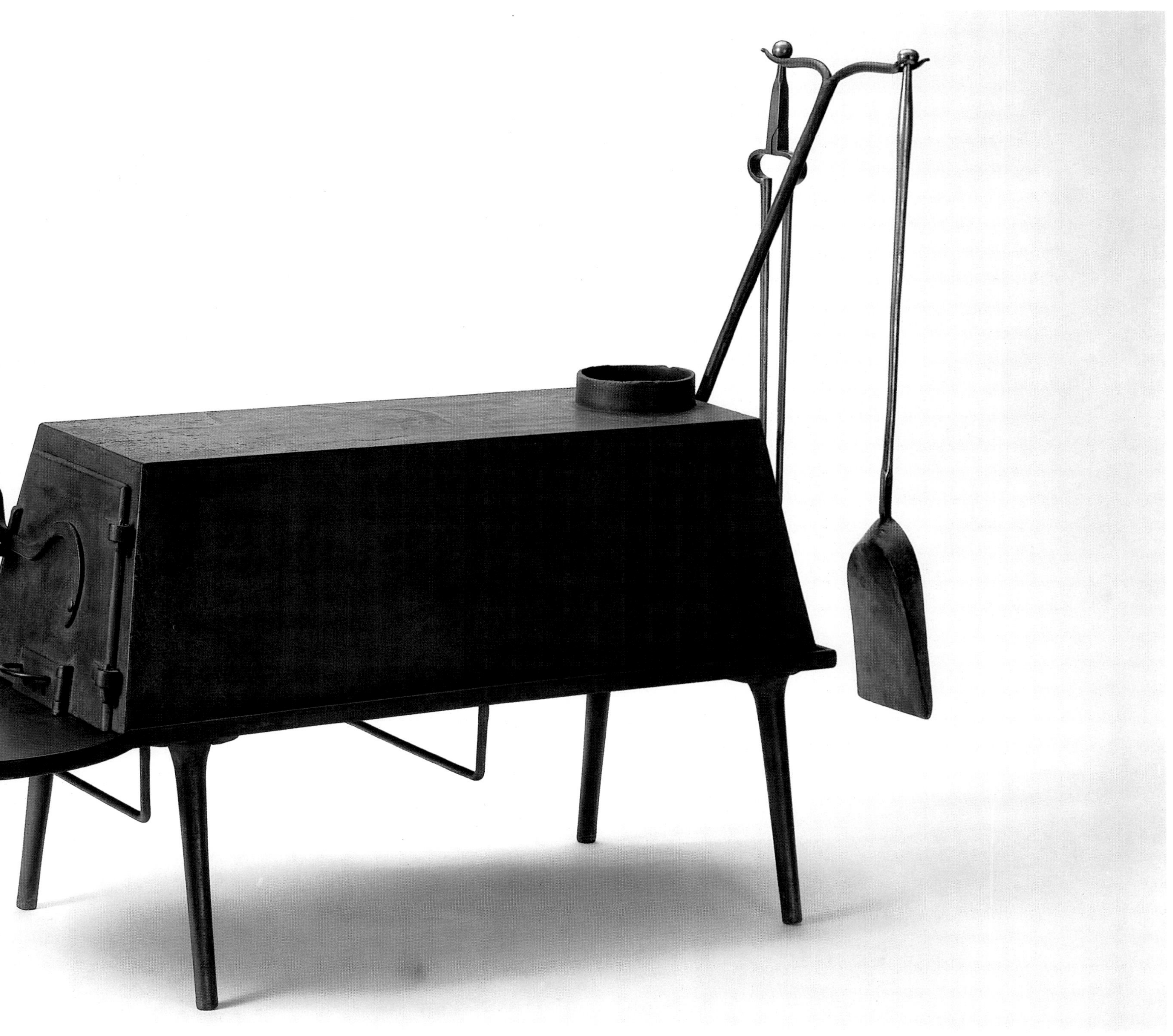

ABOVE LEFT:
Sieve with handle
Hancock Shaker Village, Pittsfield, MA
Photo by Paul Rocheleau

LEFT:
Weights and scale, Pleasant Hill, KY
Photo by James Archambeault

ABOVE:
Shaker stove with tools
Hancock Shaker Village, Pittsfield, MA
Photo by Paul Rocheleau

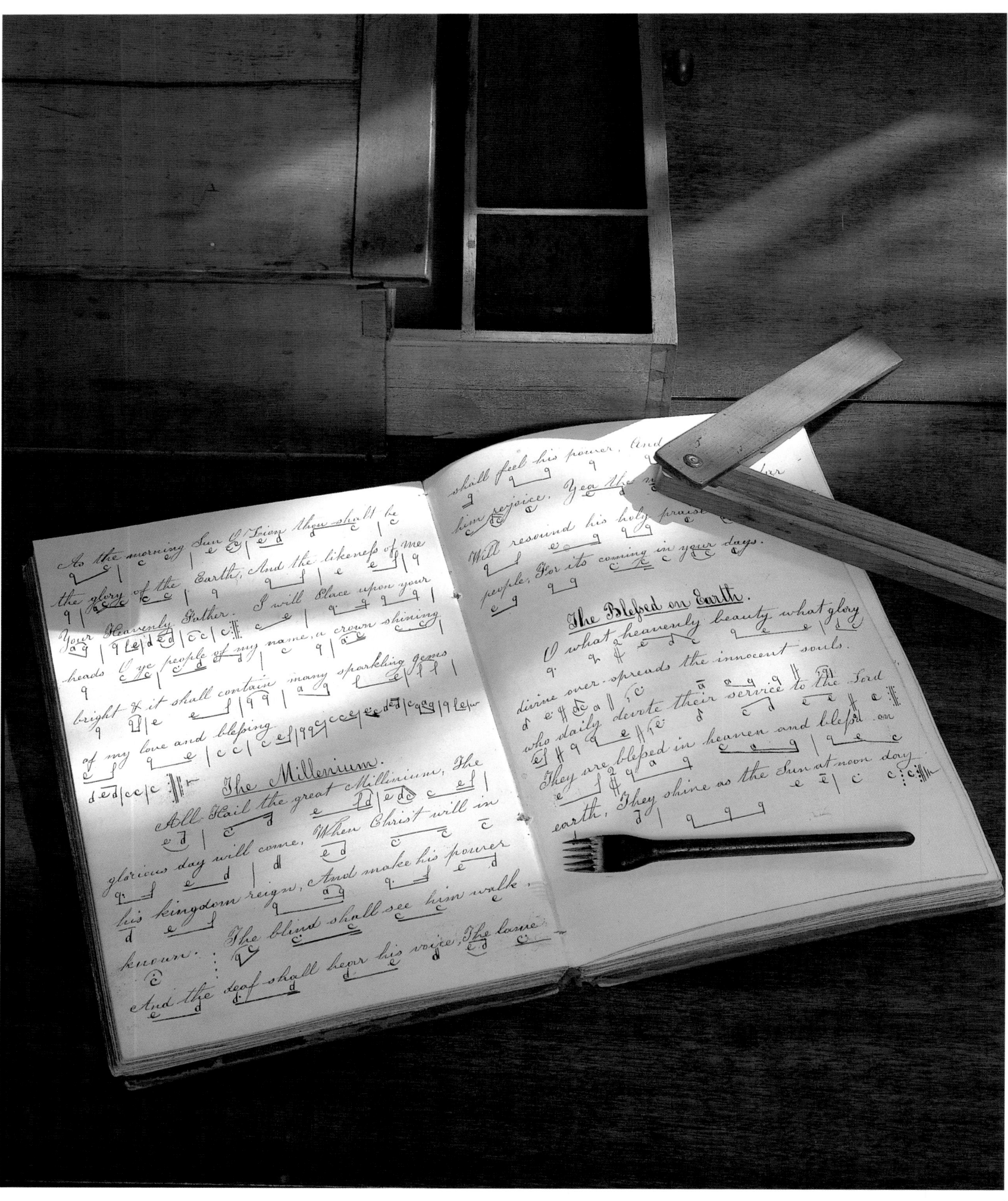

Music with pen for drawing musical staff
Hancock Shaker Village, Pittsfield, MA
Photo by Paul Rocheleau

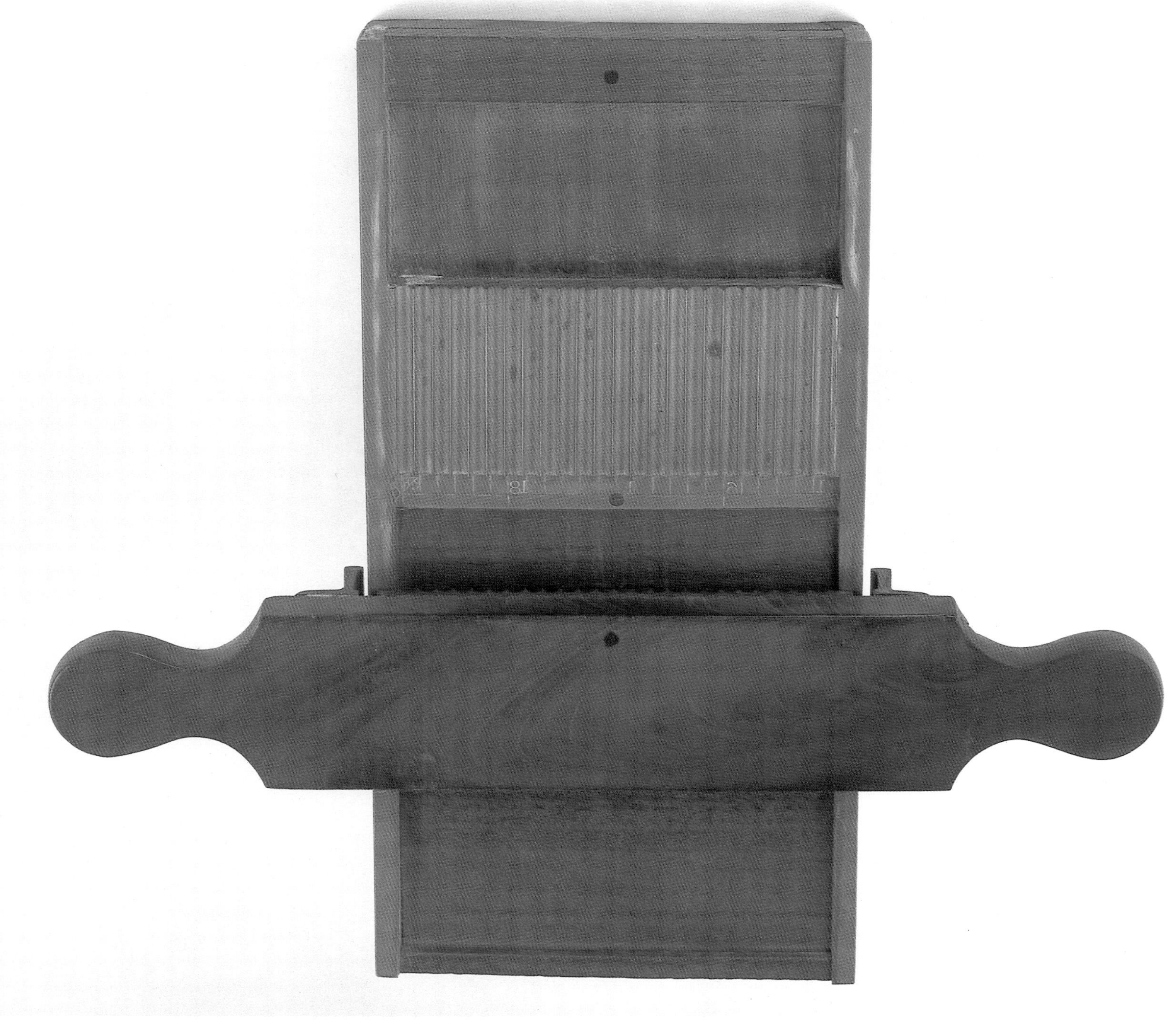

Pill-making device, c. 1850
Walnut, brass
Fruitlands Museum, Harvard, MA
Photo by Paul Rocheleau

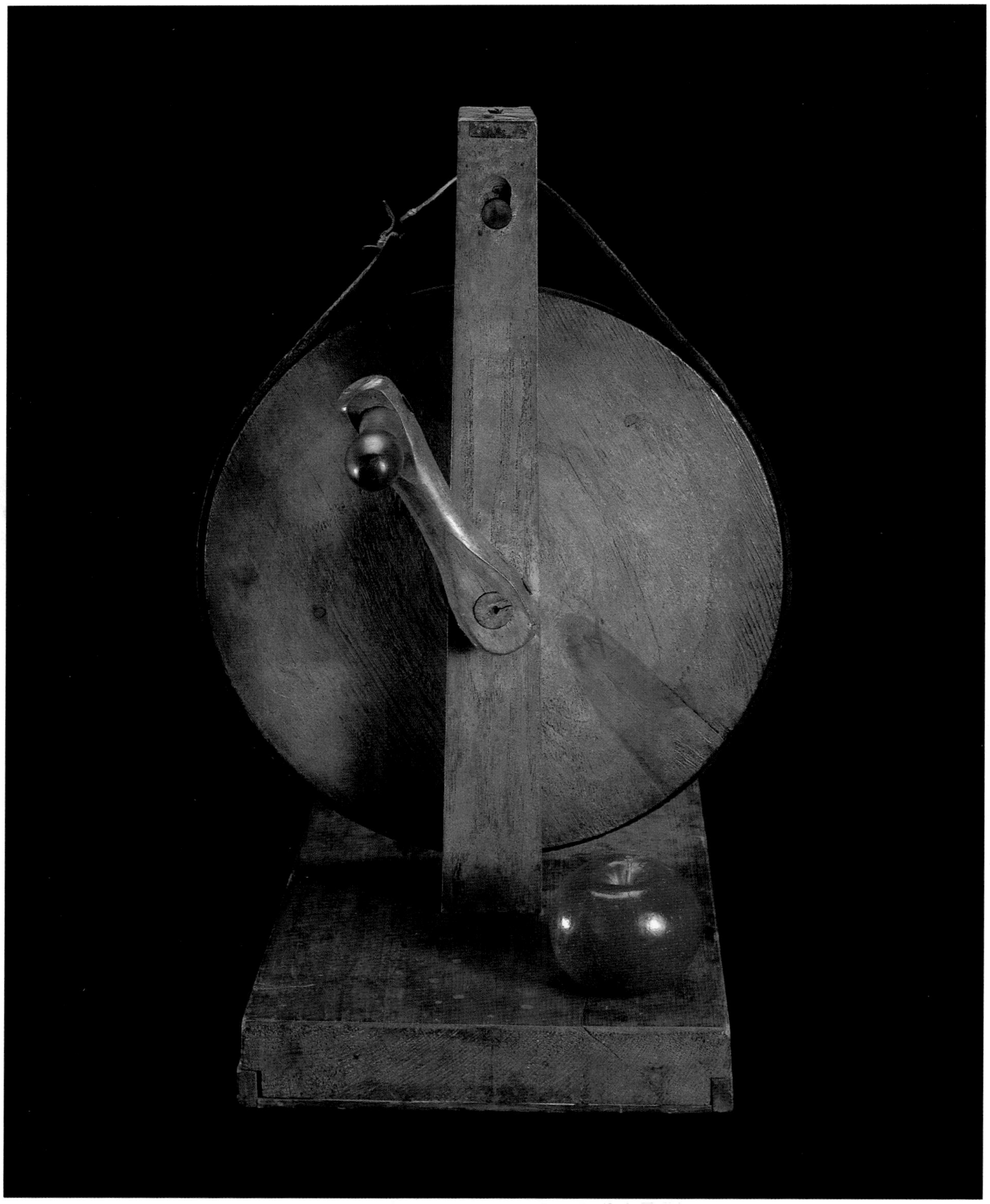

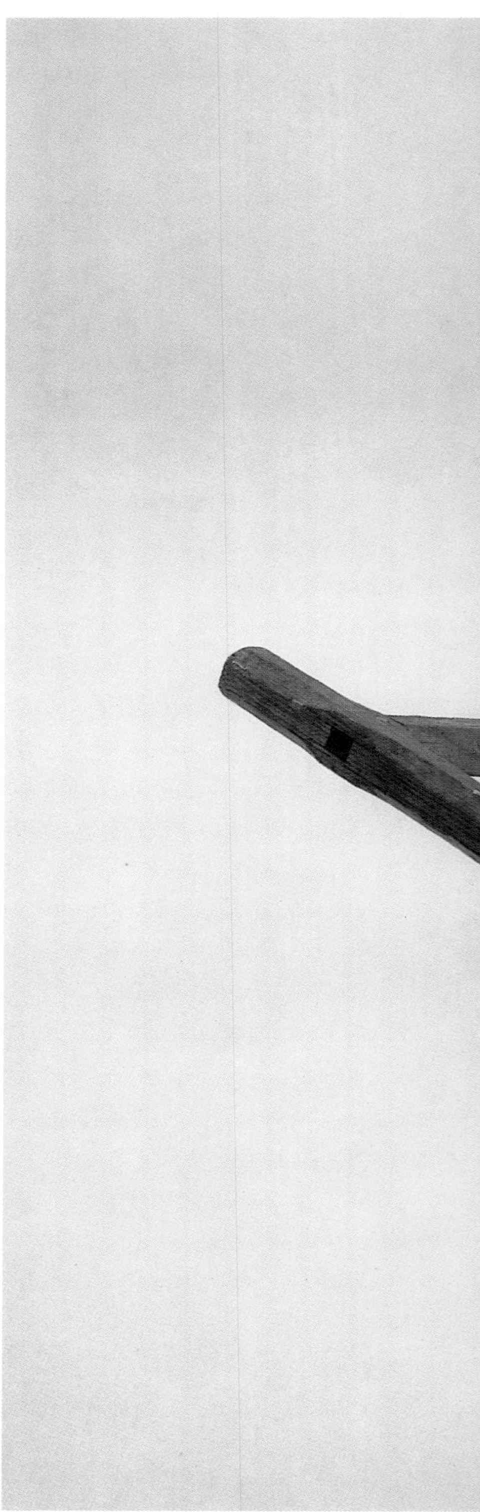

Apple Peeler
Hancock Shaker Village, Pittsfield, MA
Photo by Paul Rocheleau

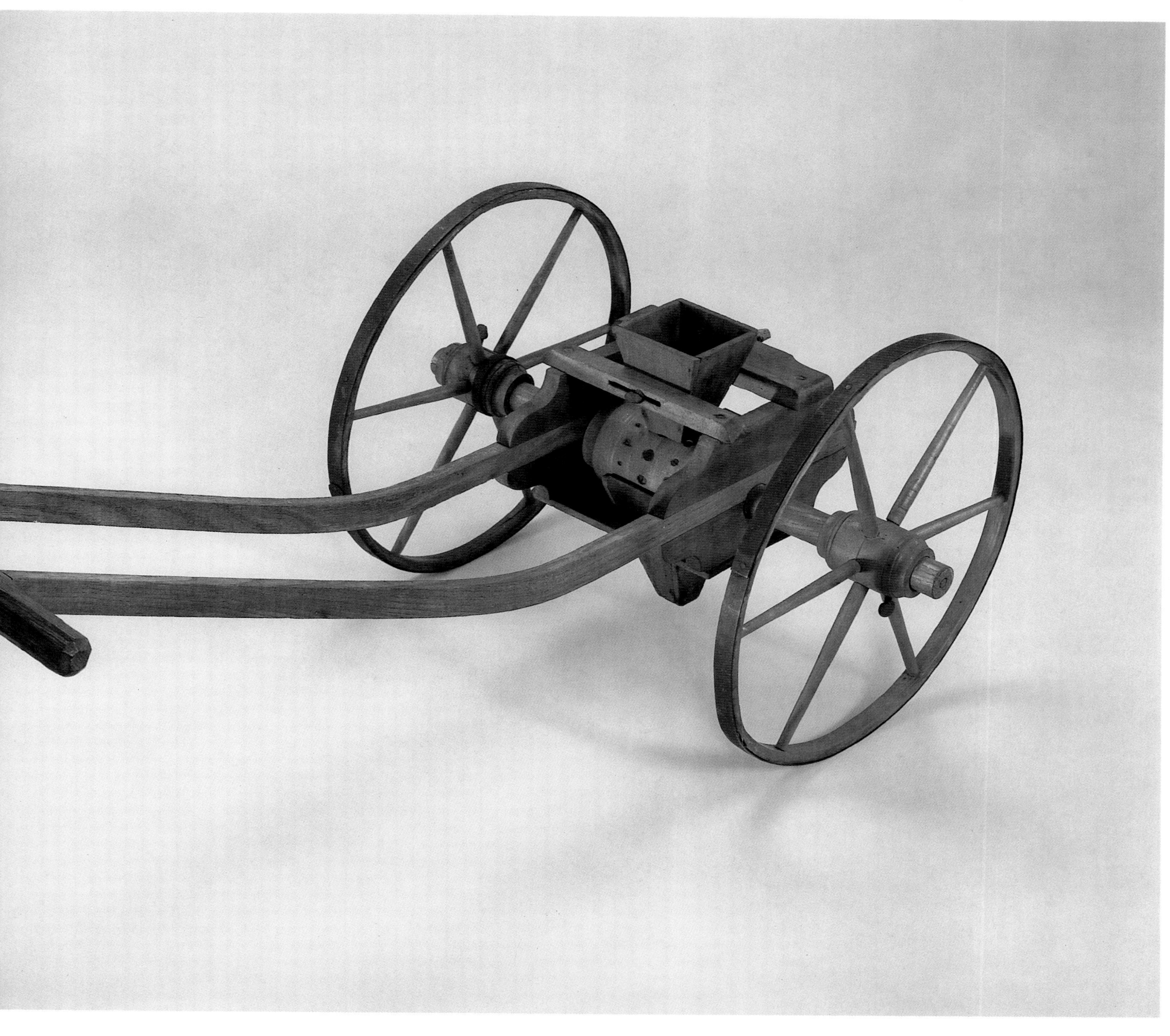

Seeder, c. 1840-70
Hancock Shaker Village, Pittsfield, MA
Photo by Paul Rocheleau

APPENDIX

Although there is only one active Shaker community – Sabbathday Lake in Maine – there are several former Shaker settlements that are now open to the public as historical sites and museums. There are also several major collections of Shaker artifacts and documents at museums in the Northeast.

SHAKER COMMUNITIES AND MUSEUMS

KENTUCKY
Shaker Village of Pleasant Hill
Harrodsburg, KY
606-734-5411

Shakertown at South Union
South Union, KY
502-542-4167

MAINE
United Society of Shakers
Sabbathday Lake
Poland Spring, ME
207-926-4597

MASSACHUSETTS
Hancock Shaker Village
Pittsfield, MA
413-443-0188

NEW HAMPSHIRE
Canterbury Shaker Village
Canterbury, NH
603-783-9511

NEW YORK
Darrow School
New Lebanon, NY
518-794-6000

Shaker Heritage Society
Albany, NY
518-456-7890

OTHER COLLECTIONS

DELAWARE
Henry Francis DuPont Winterthur Museum
Winterthur, DE
302-888-4600

KENTUCKY
Filson Club Historical Society
Louisville, KY
502-635-5083

The Kentucky Museum
Bowling Green, KY
502-745-2592

MASSACHUSETTS
Fruitlands Museum
Prospect Hill Road
Harvard, MA
508-456-3924

NEW HAMPSHIRE
The Museum at Lower Shaker Village
Enfield, NH
603-632-4346

NEW YORK
Metropolitan Museum of Art
New York, NY
212-879-5500

New York State Museum
Albany, NY
518-474-5877

The Shaker Museum and Library
Old Chatham, NY
518-794-9100

OHIO
Dunham Tavern Museum
Cleveland, OH
216-431-1060

Shaker Historical Society Museum
Shaker Heights, OH
216-921-1201

Warren County Historical Society Museum
Lebanon, OH
513-932-1817

Western Reserve Historical Society Museum
Cleveland, OH
216-721-5727

PENNSYLVANIA
Philadelphia Museum of Art
Philadelphia, PA
215-763-8100

VERMONT
Shelburne Museum
Shelburne, VT
802-985-3344

WASHINGTON, DC
The Library of Congress
(Manuscripts on microfilm)
202-707-5000

And in GREAT BRITAIN
The American Museum in Britain
Claverton Manor
Bath, England
011-441-225-46-0503